**HARDPRESS**.NET
HOME OF HARD-TO-FIND BOOKS

A Journal During a Residence in France, from the Beginning of August, to the Middle of December, 1792
by John Moore

Address:
HardPress
8345 NW 66TH ST #2561
MIAMI FL 33166-2626
USA
Email: info@hardpress.net

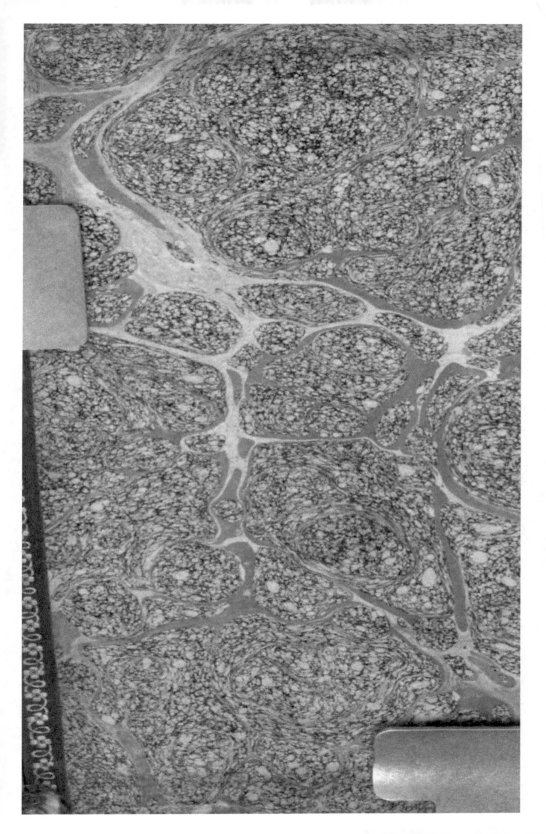

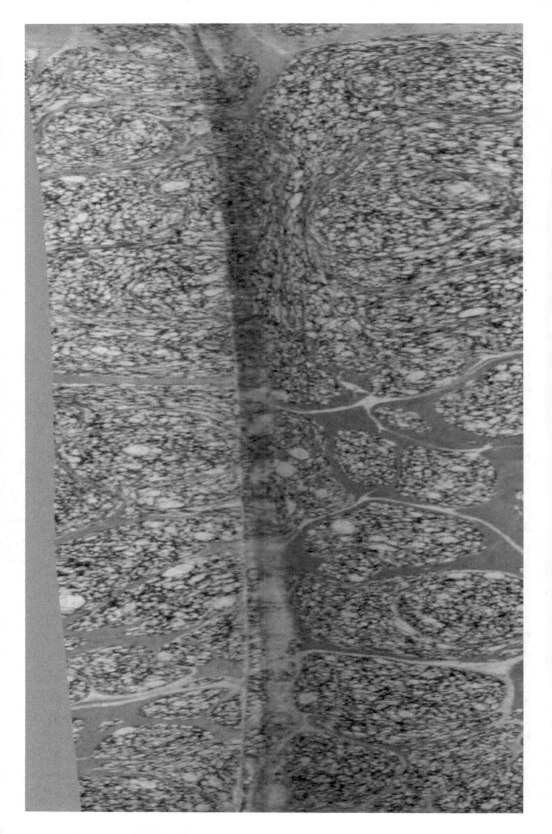

# A JOURNAL

## DURING A RESIDENCE IN FRANCE,

FROM THE

### BEGINNING OF AUGUST,

TO THE

## MIDDLE OF DECEMBER, 1792.

but we had very great difficulty in finding lodgings: all the inns being full of people, particularly of women and children from Lille, we were obliged to drive about in the dark from inn to inn for a confiderable time before we could find one to receive us; and at laft were glad to be allowed to take fhelter in a miferable nafty houfe, with the fign of the Three Kings over the door. Nothing can be a ftronger proof of the neglected and defpifed ftate of this inn, than that a fign fo obnoxious is tolerated, or rather overlooked.

We were much difappointed on our arrival at Aire, to find the accounts of the retreat of the Auftrians from before Lille as uncertain and contradictory as thofe of Calais. Not trufting to the information I received at our own wretched inn, I went to a coffee-houfe in fearch of fome more to be depended on: I addreffed myfelf to a grave looking man who fmoked his pipe at the door; I

foon

foon found that he knew nothing of the matter, and was more difpofed to afk queftions
than to anfwer them.   He faid he perceived
I was a ftranger, and afked where I lodged ;
I anfwered, *Aux Trois Rois.* " Aux Trois
Rois !" repeated he with a grimace, " ma
foi, Monfieur, vous avez choifi là des hôtes
qui ne font plus à la mode\*."

Although none of the inhabitants of Aire,
with whom I converfed, could inform me
whether the Auftrians had left Lille or
not, they were all able and moft willing to
tell many ftories of their cruelties.  Whether
they added *aught in malice* I know not, but
I am perfuaded they did *nothing extenuate.*
The maid of the inn, after giving a terrible
account of the devaftation and deftruction
occafioned by the pillaging in the villages,

---

\* At the three Kings !—Truly, Sir, you have chofen
your lodgings with people who are not much in fafhion
at prefent.

faid

said it was not easy to tell whether the Hulans or the red-hot bullets were the most mischievous; but, continued she, " Ce qui est certain, Monsieur, est, que le sang coule dans ce pauvre Lille depuis huit jours comme l'eau coule dans les rues d'Aire—ah ! Monsieur, cela déchire le cœur !*"

Having pronounced this with a sympathising accent, she went out of the room, and I heard her singing a very gay tune as she went down stairs.

The road to Paris this way is much more agreeable than that by Boulogne, the land being more fertile, the fields better cultivated, the country better inhabited, and the peasantry richer. A great deal of tobacco is raised in the country around St. Omers, and between that town and Aire : the leaves are hung up to dry on the walls of the cot-

* What is quite certain, is, that blood flows in that poor town of Lille, in as great abundance as water in the streets of Aire. It is enough to break one's heart.

tages,

tages, and on the fides of the ftacks of corn and of beans in the farm-yards.

We paffed long trains of waggons with grain for the army now affembling near Lille.

Arras, October 8.

Aire has the appearance of a very poor town, and it might be imagined that the number of women and children who have fled to it from Lille would render it alfo a very melancholy place : I could not help remarking, however, that the firft thing we heard laft night when we entered the town, was the tune of *ça ira;* and on quitting it this morning the fame tune was refounding through the ftreets, the paffengers, whether going to their work or to matins, moving their heads and fteps in cadence all the way.

As a great many poft-horfes are employed in the public fervice, it was with great difficulty that we got to Bethune. When we arrived at the poft-houfe, which is on the outfide of the fortifications, we were in-

B 3 formed,

formed, that we could not get horfes for the chaife in lefs than three or four hours, and none for the fervants even then.

We walked into the town, which is beautifully fituated on a rifing ground, with a delightful profpect of a rich country all around. It was market day, and the town was crowded with well dreffed cheerful looking peafants.

We entered into converfation with an officer of cavalry on the public fquare : he had left Lille three days before. He faid that the firing was violent when he came away, but there had been none heard fince Saturday night:—this is Monday. He had fince heard that the enemy had retired to the diftance of a league from the town; whether they meant to renew the bombardment or not, he did not know, but at any rate he was perfuaded they would not be able to take the town, as the inhabitants were refolved to be buried in the ruins rather than furrender.

Another perfon accofted me foon after, as

as I was looking at the tree of Liberty which
is planted in the market place; it was hung
round with garlands of flowers, with emblems of freedom, and various inſcriptions.
He informed me that it was not yet certainly
known whether the Auſtrians had entirely
relinquiſhed their attack on Lille; that at the
worſt they could only deſtroy the houſes,
but would never be able to take the town.
On my aſking if he thought we ſhould be
allowed to enter the town, in caſe we were
to proceed by that route, he anſwered, that
the town had never been entirely blockaded,
and that even during the bombardment,
which was made on the oppoſite ſide, the
gate towards Bethune had been kept open
for ſeveral hours every day; that as we were
provided with paſſports we would be admitted as ſoon as we arrived, but, he added,
that the roads were very much cut and deſ-
troyed, and he queſtioned whether we ſhould
find horſes at the poſt-houſes between Be-

thune

thune and Lille. On the whole, he faid, we muft expect to meet with many obftacles, and therefore advifed us to go to Paris by Arras.——We determined to follow his advice. He then explained the allegoric figures that had been placed round the tree of Liberty two days before on account of fome public feaft or rejoicing : this led him on to fpeak of the revolution, to which he appeared to be a zealous friend. He profeffed a great efteem for the Englifh, becaufe they are the friends of freedom ; and added, that although fome of his acquaintance had a ftrong perfuafion that the Britifh cabinet was watching for an opportunity of declaring againft France, when fhe was attacked and menaced by fo many other powers, yet he, for his part, could not believe that fo cowardly a policy would be adopted by fo brave a nation. The conduct of the French court towards Great Britain during the conteft with America occurred to me, but

I did

I did not think it expedient to remind him of it. He continued to obferve, that France being now unanimous for a republic, all the efforts of their enemies to conquer the country, or dictate a government to the inhabitants, would prove vain ; they would be exterminated, rather than fubmit to foreign powers, or to their old oppreffors.——" We have been," added he with great warmth, " too long oppreffed by a race of weak luxurious princes, and trode upon by an infolent yet flavifh nobleffe; it is difficult to get rid *de toutes ces vermines,* but as they are now moftly gone, it will be our faults if we ever allow them to return."——Here I could not help reminding him, that many of the nobility had diftinguifhed themfelves as the friends of Liberty, and fome were actually at the head of the armies of the republic at that moment; I mentioned Cuftine, Biron, and Montefquieu. He acknowledged the merit of thofe I had named, and of fome others; " but

as

as for the greater part of the reſt," added he, " the only ſervice they ever rendered their country was by running away from it : if they had all remained, the democrates would not have ſuch an eaſy game, and Heaven knows what might have happened ; but they are gone, and it is our buſineſs to keep them off : let them go and crouch to other kings, and domineer over other ſlaves, none are to be found in France.——This is the land of liberty and equality.——A camp is already formed at Douay, another is forming nearer Lille ; if thirty thouſand more men are required, they will be raiſed in this neighbourhood without difficulty : hardly a peaſant or tradeſman in France, but is zealous in the cauſe of freedom, and ready to ſhed his blood for his country."——The man talked with ſuch animation of voice and geſture as drew a crowd around us, who all ſeemed to ſympathiſe with what he ſaid : this was not unobſerved by the ſpeaker, who

who by the looks he threw on the surrounding circle, and by the elevation of voice, shewed that he was as solicitous to be heard by it as by me.

I was told, after he quitted me, that he was not a citizen of Bethune, as I first imagined, but a Parisian. I understand that there are many spies and emissaries in the various towns of France, hired by the executive power for the express purpose of spreading those sentiments, and also to examine what are the prevailing opinions. Whether this man is one of those I know not, but he could not have shewn himself a more zealous republican had he been ever so well paid for it.

When we returned to the post-house, we were informed that we might have horses for the chaises, but there were no bidets for the servants, all of them being employed by the couriers who were continually passing and repassing on the public service. There was a necessity therefore to take the servants

into

into the chaifes, and in this manner we were dragged through very bad roads to Arras.

We met a battalion of national guards on the way. The citizens of Amiens no fooner heard that Lille was invefted, than they raifed, clothed, and armed this battalion at their own expence. The men feem in high fpirits, and were marching with great ardour to Lille.

Robefpierre is a native of Arras ; this great luminary of the revolution not only renders Arras more confpicuous, but has thrown a ray of light on his brother, who lived here in obfcurity, but is now chofen a deputy to the convention,

Cuvilly, October 9.

We left Arras at fix in the morning, and with much difficulty arrived at this wretched village a little after it was dark : we had been detained feveral hours at Peronne, waiting

for

for the return of poſt-horſes, and afterwards till the poor animals were fed, and had in ſome meaſure recovered their fatigue.

Peronne is ſtrongly fortified, but the only garriſon in it at preſent conſiſts of citizens ; they are however well armed, and moſt of the men, and all the officers, are in the uniform of the national guards.

A battalion of the Gens d'Armes of Paris are expected at Peronne this night. The quarter-maſter with ſome other of the corps are already arrived.

I was witneſs to a ſcene which will give ſome idea of the kind of liberty which exiſts in France at preſent.

I had joined three officers of the city guards, who were walking in the ſquare op-poſite to the poſt-houſe. One of them, a very genteel and obliging man, was giving me what information I aſked, when two men, in the uniform of the expected batta-lion, came up to us, and one of them in a

haughty

haughty and menacing manner, demanded how it happened that the fleurs de lis and other fymbols of royalty, to which he pointed, were not effaced from the fteeple and the front of the town-houfe.

The officer replied, that it was the bufinefs of the mayor, and he knew nothing about it. On which the other burft forth into many abufive expreffions againft the mayor, calling him rafcal and ariftocrate, and fwearing that when he met him, he would cut him in pieces : as he faid this, he drew his fabre and feemed difpofed to quarrel with all around him.

Another officer of the city guards, more advanced in years than the former, addreffed this furious fellow in a foothing manner, affuring him that the municipality had already given orders that the emblems of which he complained fhould all be removed ; that the reafon of its not being already done was becaufe the mayor, who was

a very

a very honeft man, and of courfe no ariftocrate, had been entirely occupied in fending
neceffaries to their diftreffed friends at Lille,
and in providing good quarters for the battalion of Parifians which was expected.

This conciliatory language fmoothed
the threatening brow of the man, who at
laft fheathed his fword, and walked away
with his companion. Each of thefe fellows
had a brace of piftols ftuck in his belt, and
there was fomething in their looks, as well
as their deportment, which gave me a fufpicion that they belonged to the affaffinating
band of September.

For the firft two pofts after leaving Peronne, we were continually meeting fmall
bodies of the Gens d'Armes who were
haftening to the relief of Lille : they march
in a very ftraggling manner. The battalion
confifts of a thoufand men ; I do not fuppofe there was above two hundred in a body,
with the colours. They cried as we paffed,

2                                            Vive

Vive la nation ! vive la république ! and in a manner that sufficiently denoted that it was expected we should do the same, which we did accordingly ; but this ceremony becoming a little fatiguing, one of the servants refrained from joining in the cry when he was invited.——A soldier observing this, seized the bridle of his horse, and ordered him to repeat the words ; with which as the man did not immediately comply, another levelled his piece, and would probably have fired, if Lord Lauderdale had not darted his head out of the window of the carriage, calling out, that the man did not understand their language, that he was un Anglois ; on which the soldier raised his musket, and a young officer waving his hat and calling out Vivent les Anglois ! we passed on. Although there is no danger of a man's losing his money by robbery on the high-way when he travels in France, he is in considerable danger of losing his life, if he happens

not

not to be attentive and obedient to the word of command on occasions like this.

It was fifty to one that this servant was not shot through the head, or thrust through with a bayonet for his tardiness in the present instance; and if he had, some one would have observed, as the man did at Clermont, *C'est un homme de moins*, and no farther notice would have been taken of the incident.

The whole of this battalion consisted of stout men, all well armed and well clothed, but there seemed to be little subordination among them; and I understand that, in general there is less in those regiments which are formed of Parisians than in the other corps.

When we arrived at the post-house, a considerable number were carousing and singing songs in honour of the revolution. They seemed desirous to converse with us, and one who was a good deal elevated with wine, proclaimed aloud the exploits they

C were

were to perform. "After driving *ses Gueux des Autrichiens*," said he, "from Lille, we shall follow them to Bruffels, and there pafs the winter." Another, addreffing Lord Lauderdale, said, " Je vois bien que vous êtes Anglais, Monfieur, mais j'efpere que vous n'êtes pas du chambre des pairs qui font tous de . . ." here he added a very grofs epithet, in too great ufe all over France.

They then proceeded on their march, vociferating certain fongs of the groffeft nature, and fhamefully abufive of the King and Queen. Several were in a fituation which put it out of their power to march to Peronne that day. Their comrades, however, prepared a carriage for them, which at length drove away.

I afked the poft-mafter if thofe men were obedient to their officers: " Comme vous êtes à moi, Monfieur," anfwered he, " et peut-être pas même autant—comme je vais vous le prouver:"—this excited my curiofity—

sity—"For," continued the post-master, as I am persuaded that *Monsieur* is a man who listens to reason, you would par conséquence comply with what I required, provided it were just and reasonable; whereas those men never mind what their officers say, whether it is reasonable or not."

There was something more precise and formal in this man's manner than is usual with Frenchmen, which induced me to enquire a little about him of one of the postillions; who told me he had formerly been a school-master in a neighbouring village.

He gave us another proof of his power of reasoning; on his putting only two horses to a chaise instead of three, which is usual, he advertised us that he expected to be paid for three. I hinted that this did not seem quite reasonable: he immediately undertook to prove that it was highly reasonable in him to exact as much for two horses as for three, or, if any difference were to be made, some-

C 2                                    what

what more: we were all attention.—" I will have the honour, Gentlemen, refumed he with a folemn air, of making this as clear as day light. You muft all know that travellers are often detained in the middle of their journey by an accident happening to one of the horfes in their carriage; but there is a greater chance of this happening to one of three horfes than of two."—His argument was allowed to be irrefiftible, and he was paid his full demand. "All that I ever defire of any mortal," faid the poft-mafter as he received payment, " is that he will only hear me, and liften to the voice of reafon— but thofe men who are juft gone would do neither."

I underftood that while he was proving to them that his bill was very reafonable, they had cut him fhort in the middle of his argument, and paid him with half; defiring him to recollect that falt, which before the revolution coft fourteen fols the pound, was

now

now fold at two, and that the price of tobacco had been diminifhed in the fame proportion.

Paris, October 10th.

Having left our miferable quarters a little
after five this morning, we arrived at Paris
about four in the afternoon; paffing through
the lines which have been forming in the
plains of St. Denis. Military men laugh at
the idea of defending fuch a town as Paris
by any intrenchments which could be made
before the Pruffians come, if they come at
all; and which, if made, would require a
garrifon of a hundred thoufand men, and all
the cannon in France to protect. The Parifians, however, feem pleafed with thefe
intrenchments; particularly the women, of
whom we obferved great numbers, with their
ufual gaiety, intermingled with the work-
men.

Having written to an acquaintance to in-

C 3

form

form him about what time we expected to be at Paris, we drove to the Hotel des Tuileries, where he had engaged lodgings, which were preferred on account of their vicinity to the Conventional Affembly.

It will not be improper to mention here fome things which took place in the Convention during our abfence from Paris, but of which I did not know the particulars till my return.

One moft important object, and which demanded the early attention of the Convention, was to vindicate, as far as is poffible, the French nation from the foul ftain of the late maffacres, by bringing the real authors of them to punifhment. To this the Convention was invoked by juftice, and prompted by every feeling of our nature.—In an af-fembly in which there are fome clergymen, many lawyers, and, as I am told, a confiderable number of philofophers, it was not to be fuppofed that a meafure fo neceffary and be-

coming

coming would be long delayed. But it is somewhat extraordinary, that a seaman was the first who fixed the attention of the Assembly upon it.

" Il est temps," said Kersaint, " d'élever des échafauds pour ceux qui commettent les assassinats, et pour ceux qui les provoquent, &c. . . . Il y a peut-être plus de courage qu'on ne pense à s'élever contre les assassins, mais dussai-je tomber sous leurs coups, je serai digne de la confiance de mes concitoyens*."

He then moved that four commissioners should be immediately appointed to propose the most effectual measures for the preventing and punishing assassination, and that

---

* It is full time to erect scaffolds for those who commit assassinations, or prompt others to commit them, &c. . . . Perhaps it requires more courage than might be imagined to speak against assassins, but should I fall the victim of their vengeance, I will shew myself worthy of the confidence of my fellow-citizens.

their

their plan fhould be prefented to the Convention the next day.

It could hardly be fuppofed that fuch a meafure would be oppofed.—Strange as this appears, however, it met with oppofition.

Bazire obferved, that France was ftill in the crifis of a revolution, and *very vigorous meafures* were neceffary.—It was true, he added, that many fufpected perfons had been arrefted and punifhed; thofe perfons had been endeavouring to raife a civil war; but, continued he, there are not four men to be found in all France capable to give a plan which can, in the prefent moment, reconcile the public intereft with the rights of the citizens.

Tallien (he who was fecretary to the Council of the Community on the 2d of September,) faid, that the exifting laws againft affaffination were fufficient for the fafety of

the

the citizens, and propofed the order of the day to Kerfaint's motion.

Others afked for its adjournment.

To demand the adjournment of such a motion, cried Vergniaud, is to demand impunity for affaffins, to propofe the order of the day is to propofe anarchy——There are men, added he, who call themfelves republicans, and are, in reality, the flaves of tyrants; they fpread fufpicions, hatred and vengeance among the citizens——they wifh to excite the French people, like the foldiers of Cadmus, to cut one another's throats inftead of fighting the common enemy.

He ended an eloquent fpeech by fupporting Kerfaint's motion.

Collot d' Herbois and others faid, that this motion was intended for eftablifhing *a law of blood*, and that there were men in office who would ufe it for the deftruction of the moft diftinguifhed patriots.

Some of thofe whom Collot d' Herbois meant by the moft diftinguifhed patriots are

strongly

strongly suspected of being the planners of the massacres—Collot d'Herbois himself is not clear of this suspicion, which accounts for the opposition to Kersaint's motion.

Merlin of Thionville opposed the motion, and went so far as to assert, that the baker who was murdered by the mob some months before, on a suspicion of engrossing grain to raise the price of bread, had been murdered on purpose to furnish a pretext for proclaiming martial law, and by that means to justify the troops for firing on the people, which was then intended, and afterwards performed in the Champ de Mars. The Queen, from motives of humanity, had shewn kindness and generosity to this man's widow;—in consequence of which the ridiculous falsehood, now mentioned by Merlin, was invented and propagated.

Kersaint spoke with energy against those absurd imputations; and Buzot, with strong and perspicuous reasoning, shewed

that

that the propofed law was not to fhed blood, but to prevent blood from being fhed ; and in addition propofed, that a guard fhould be formed from all the 83 departments for the immediate protection of the Convention, that each department might have the con-viction that its deputies could fpeak and vote freely, and were not influenced by fear either of the people in the galleries, or of the Council General of the Community of Paris, which had ufurped fo much power, and had exercifed it with fo much ty-ranny.

It was at laft decreed, that fix commiffi-oners fhould be appointed to form a law againft the inciters to murder and affaffina-tion, and alfo to give in a plan for the for-mation of a guard to be at the difpofal of the Convention, which was to be drawn from all the 83 departments, to prevent the Convention from being domineered over by the

the General Council of the Commune of Paris as the Legiflative Affembly had been.

This General Council exercifes its ufurped power in a dreadful manner : citizens are ftill arrefted and imprifoned by orders iffued by its members.

Two commiffioners from this council, declared at the election of the deputy at Auxerre, that the Commune of Paris poffeffed the whole power of the State ; that thofe chofen as deputies fhould put their confidence in the Commune, and not in the National Affembly, the minifters, or the generals.

Commiffioners from the fame council advifed the inhabitants of Douay to erect fcaffolds on the ramparts, and to execute all who were of a different opinion from them, as ariftocrats and traitors.

And two other commiffioners from that community raifed fuch a fpirit of infurrection at the Electoral Affembly of Seine and Marne that fourteen perfons were murdered in the tower of Meaux.——Thofe facts were announced by different members of the Convention.

Nothing therefore can be more urgent than to deprive this Community of its ufurped power; and for this purpofe it feems abfolutely neceffary that the Convention fhould have guards, and fuch executive force at its command as will overbalance and keep in awe the rabble of the fuburbs, who are at any time to be put in action by the influence of Santerre, and the money of another perfon who has a great deal at his command, which he is faid to lavifh among the fans-culottes of the fuburbs, when any meafure is to be carried for the intereft of the party.

Some time after this a moft extraordinary fcene was exhibited in the Conventional Affembly:——Merlin de Thionville, a man far more diftinguifhed for zeal than prudence, declared

declared that La Source had in private converfation said, that there was a faction in the Convention for eftablifhing a dictator, and he called on La Source to announce who this intended dictator was, that he might be inftantly poniarded.

La Source, who muft have been fomewhat furprifed to hear a private, perhaps a confidential remark, publifhed in this manner; explained what he had faid differently. He faid that he had complained of the tyranny of certain men, who flatter and deceive the citizens of Paris, and who point out the beft friends of the people as victims to the rage of affaffins : that fuch men were already dictators; that there was the greateft neceffity for an armed force to fecure the independence of the Convention, and prevent it from being dictated to by thofe who had ufurped illegal influence.——" Let thofe men of blood, he added, tremble, and know that the fame power which hurled Lewis

from

from his throne, will not long suffer the despotism of others."

But in the course of the debate Rebecqui, one of the deputies for Marseilles, in direct terms, accused the partizans of Robespierre of a design of raising him to the dictatorship. Danton, dreading that this might draw on a discussion and produce an investigation which he wished to prevent, endeavoured with some address to turn the attention of the Assembly to a different object. He moved that the pains of death should be decreed on any person who should attempt to destroy the unity of France, by dividing it into different commonwealths, bound together by a federative bond, like the United Provinces and the Cantons of Switzerland. Danton knew that Buzot, Vergniaud, Guadet, and others who were eager for the punishment of all who had been directly or indirectly concerned in promoting the murder of the prisoners, were accused of inclining

2        to

to this plan of federative republics, which is by no means the wish of the majority of the Convention—he therefore intended to intimidate them from prosecuting the assassins, by holding up the dread of being accused themselves.

Buzot, sensible of his intention, boldly opposed the insinuation. " Who is it," he exclaimed, "that thinks of disuniting France? I propose that a guard for the Conventional Assembly shall be furnished by the 83 departments, with a view to union, and thereby to signify that the Convention is equally under the care of them all ; those who oppose this measure appear rather to wish for disunion."

He put this in so clear a light, that Robespierre thought the only means to prevent its evidence from being apparent to the most short-sighted of the Assembly, was by overwhelming the argument with a torrent of words, and obscuring it in a mist of sophistry, phiftry, both of which this popular orator has at his command.

He began by expatiating on his own patriotifm, on his incorruptibility, and the fervices he had rendered the ftate while he fat in the conftituent affembly.——The theme was attractive, but becoming lefs pleafing to the audience than to the orator himfelf, one of the members called out, " *Robefpierre veux tu bien terminer cette longue kyrielle* ; declare nous franchement en quatre mots tes fentimens et non ta vie paffée\*." This, however, did not bring him to give any explicit anfwer to the accufation ; he dwelt for an hour longer on the favourite fubject with which he began, then launched into proteftations of his love for his country, and of the incredibility of his ever forming any fcheme againft that freedom for which he had fo

---

\* Pray put an end to your tedious harangue, and inform us, in two words, of your fentiments on the point in queftion, and not of all your paft life.

D long

long ftruggled; and finifhed by declaring his fufpicions that there were among their body, thofe who watched an opportunity of dividing France, and then combining it into federate ftates; and therefore he feconded Danton's motion.

Barbaroux, a young man, and deputy from Marfeilles, in fupport of what his colleague Rebecqui had afferted, declared, that on his arrival at Paris, it had been infinuated to him by certain intimates of Robefpierre, and particularly by Panis, that in the prefent emergency there was a neceffity for uniting under fome perfon of great popularity, in whom a power equal to that of the Roman dictators fhould be placed for a certain time; and that Robefpierre, from his known patriotifm and popularity, was the propereft perfon they could fix upon for that office.

Panis endeavoured to defend himfelf by faying that Barbaroux had affuredly either miftaken his words or meaning.——" Is it poffible," poſſible," added he, wiſhing to conciliate his accuſer, " that Barbároux, whom I love, be-cauſe I know him to be a good patriot, can believe I ever meant ſuch a thing ?"

This manner of denying ſuch a charge forms a ſtrong preſumption of its truth ; for a man would hardly ſpeak in ſuch terms of another, who accuſed him falſely of ſo dangerous an offence.

Barbaroux, however, was not to be ſoft-ened, but perſiſted in the charge. " Who, beſides yourſelf," cried Panis, " can witneſs that I ever made ſuch a propoſal ?"

" I can, cried Rebecqui," " for I heard you." This ſeemed to diſconcert both Panis and Robeſpierre, and to ſilence and con-found the whole party, till Marat, think-ing the exigency worthy of his intrepidity of countenance, aſcended the tribune. He no ſooner appeared than murmurs and exe-crations aroſe in every corner of the Aſſembly.

" It would appear," ſaid he, without

any

any mark of emotion, " that some in this Affembly are my perfonal enemies."

" All! all! we are all your enemies!" refounded from every quarter.

He lamented the general delusion with the accent of regret, and then affuming an air of courage, with a full swell of voice, he declared that he, and he only, had conceived the idea of appointing a dictator; that he had mentioned it to feveral, fome of whom may have repeated it, but that the thought was originally his own. That, convinced as he had long been of the plots of a perfidious court, and as he ftill was of the treafons of many citizens, he thought the exigency of the times required that the direction of the public affairs fhould be placed in the hands of an honeft and determined man, an enlightened patriot, who, without fear or refpect of perfons, would *apply the axe of juftice to the necks of the guilty.*—" Such is my own opinion," continued he ; " I have publifhed it, it, and if your ideas have not foared to the height of mine, fo much the worfe for you."

Such an inflated declaration iffuing from a little dirty mortal, whofe murky vifage fcarce overlooked the tribune, turned the indignation of the Affembly into mirth, and many of the members burft into laughter.

But Vergniaud reftored the gravity of the Affembly, by bringing forward a very extraordinary circumftance, which points out pretty plainly thofe to whom the maffacres of the prifoners, not only in Paris, but in every other part of France where they took place, are to be attributed.

He then read a letter figned by certain members of the council of the Commune de Paris, which had been tranfmitted to all the municipalities of France, immediately after the flaughter of the prifoners at Paris in the beginning of September.

This letter is of fo very fingular a nature,

that

that I think it proper to tranfcribe the whole.

Freres et amis, un affreux complôt tramé par la Cour pour égorger tous les Patriotes de l'empire François, complôt dans lequel un grand nombre de membres de l'Affemblée Nationale font compromis, ayant réduit, le 9 du mois dernier, la Commune de Paris à la cruelle néceffité de fe fervir de la puiffance du peuple pour fauver la Nation, elle n'a rien négligé pour bien mériter de la patrie.

Aprés les témoignages que l'Affemblée Nationale venoit de lui donner elle-meme, eut on penfé que des-lors des nouveaux complôts fe tramoient dans le filence, et qu'ils eclatoient dans le moment même, ou l'Affemblée Nationale, oubliant qu'elle venoit de déclarer que la Commune de Paris avoit fauvé la patrie, s'empreffoit de la deftituer, pour prix de fon brûlant civifme ?

Fière de jouir de toute la plenitude de la confiance

confiance nationale qu'elle s'efforcera de mériter de plus en plus, placée au foyer de toutes
les conspirations, et déterminée à perir pour
le salut public, elle ne se glorifiera d'avoir
rempli pleinement ses devoirs que lorsqu'elle
aura obtenu votre approbation, qui est l'objet
de tous ses vœux et dont elle ne sera certaine
qu'aprés que tous les départemens *auront
sanctionné ses mesures pour le salut de la chose
publique* ; et professant les principes de la plus
parfaite egalité, n'ambitionnant d'autre pri-
vilége que celui de se présenter la premiére
á la breche, elle s'empressera de se remettre
au niveau de la Commune la moins nom-
breuse de l'empire, dès qu'il n'y aura plus
rien â redouter,

Prévenue que des hordes des barbares
s'avancent contre elle, la Commune de Paris
se hâte d'informer ses freres de tous les départemens, qu'une partie des conspirateurs
féroces, détenus dans les prisons, a été mise à
mort par le peuple, *actes de justice qui lui ont paru*

D 4 *indispensables*

*indispensables* pour retenir par la terreur les legions de traitres cachés dans ses murs, au moment ou il alloit marcher à l'ennemi ; *et sans doute la nation,* aprés la longue suite de trahisons qui l'a conduite sur les bords de l'abyme, *s'empressera d'adopter ce moyen si utile et si nécessaire,* et tous les François se diront, comme les Parisiens: Marchons à l'ennemi, *mais ne laissons par derriére nous ces brigands pour égorger nos femmes et nos enfans.*

Signed PIERRE DUPLAIN, JOURDEUIL, PANIS, SERGENT, L'ENFANT, MARAT L'AMI DU PEUPLE, LE CLERC, DUFORTRE &c. &c. Administrators of the Committee of the Public Safety. *

The

* Brethren and friends, a horrid plot, planned by the Court, to murder all the patriots of the French empire; a plot in which a great number of the National Assembly were engaged, having, on the ninth of last month, forced the Commune de Paris to the cruel necessity of making use of the power of the people to save

The moral of this virtuous epiftle is evident——If you have any regard for your country,

fave the nation, the Commune has neglected nothing for the fervice of the country.

After the approbation which the National Affembly itfelf beftowed on the Commune, could it have been imagined that new plots were projecting in filence, which broke forth at the moment when the National Affembly, forgetting that fhe had declared that the Commune de Paris had faved the country, haftened to diffolve that very Community as a recompence for all its faithful fervices.

Proud of poffeffing the full confidence of the Nation, which we are refolved to deferve more and more; placed in the centre of all the confpiracies, and determined to perifh in defence of the public, we cannot boaft of having entirely fulfilled our duty till we fhall obtain your approbation, which is the object of all our wifhes, and of which we cannot be certain till all the Departments have *fanctioned our meafures for the public fafety.* Profeffing principles of the moft perfect equality, wifhing no other privilege but that of prefenting ourfelves the firft at the breach, we will put ourfelves on a level with the

fmalleft

try, or any tenderneſs for your wives and children, you will cut the throats of all your priſoners as ſoon as you conveniently can.

What an infernal letter! and what renders it ſtill more atrocious, is its being deliberately written by men in the character of magiſtrates.

ſmalleſt municipality in the Nation, as ſoon as the dangers which now threaten the country are paſt.

Informed that bands of barbarians are advancing, the Commune de Paris haſtens to acquaint all the departments, that part of thoſe furious conſpirators detained in the priſons of Paris have been put to death by the people ; *an act of juſtice which ſeemed indiſpenſable to ſtrike terror* into the breaſts of thoſe legions of traitors hid within her walls, at the time when the citizens were about to march againſt the enemy. And no doubt the Nation, after that long ſucceſſion of treaſons which have brought her to the brink of ruin, will haſten to adopt a meaſure ſo uſeful and neceſſary ; and all the inhabitants of France will ſay, like the Pariſians : Let us march againſt the enemy, but let us not *leave behind us a band of villains to murder our wives and children.*

It

It might naturally be expected that the reading of this invitation to murder should have filled the Affembly with fo much indignation, that a decree of accufation would have been immediately paffed againft Panis and the reft. It produced however only new clamours and confufion, with an outcry from one part of the hall for the order of the day.——At laft *Coutbon* propofed that they should turn their attention from accufations againft individuals to the more important exigencies of the ftate: this was fupported by all thofe who dreaded any inquiry or inveftigation refpecting the promoters of the maffacres; and thofe who had been at firft inclined to that meafure being fatigued, or perhaps afraid to perfift, the order of the day was agreed to——On which Marat, who remained in the tribune, pulled a piftol from his pocket, which having held to his head, he faid, " I now declare to you, citizens, that if the fury which has been difplayed on this

occafion

occasion had carried you the length of a
decree of accusation against me, I should
have blown my brains out before your
faces." What he meant by this I know not,
unless it was to vex the Assembly on being
disappointed of so desirable an event.

Next to the disorderly conduct of some of
the members themselves, nothing disgraces
the National Assembly so much as the insolence of the audience in the galleries—How
could any court or any assembly of men support dignity, if it was exposed to be applauded or hooted according to the opinions
or caprice of those admitted to hear their debates? There is, it is true, a decree against all
noises and signs of approbation or disapprobation; but notwithstanding its being broken
every day, nobody has ever been punished
on that account.

The majority of the Convention have a
great desire that a strict investigation should
be made into the massacres, that the promo-

2                                    ters

ters of them may be punished in the most exemplary manner ; and the same majority are equally solicitous to have an armed force at the command of the Convention decreed and established. But I imagine they have thrown a great obstacle in the way of obtaining the last of these objects, by manifesting a design to pursue the first. They would have shewn more policy if they had said nothing of the one till they had secured the other. A confiderable number of members of the Convention itself are fuppofed to be confcious of being directly or indirectly involved in that horrid bufinefs ; they fee their own ruin in fuch an inveftigation, and therefore will oppofe it by every means in their power. What means have they in their power fince a majority of the Convention is for the meafure ? They cannot object to a law againft affaffination, and for the punifhment of murder ; but, knowing what ufe is immediately to be made of the armed force, they

will

will raife objections to that being eftablifhed; and till fuch a force is eftablifhed, their friends in the fuburbs will be able to protect the authors of the maffacres. In fhort, the minority in the Convention, at the head of which are Danton and Robefpierre, already have an armed force at their command, in the active citizens of the fuburbs; and will in all probability ufe every means, and they are not fuppofed to be fo fcrupulous as their rivals in the means they employ, to prevent any other armed force from being eftablifhed.

The fituation of the generals who command the armies of France at prefent is difagreeable in many refpects; but particularly in their being under the control, and expofed to the cenfure of men who are no judges of their military abilities, and extremely liable to prejudice and fufpicion.—— Nothing can be more detrimental to the intereft of the ftate, than that thofe men who are rifquing their lives in the public fervice, and

and peforming their duty with fidelity to their country, fhould be expofed to calumny, and furrounded with fufpicion, the tendency of which muft be to difcourage their minds, cool their zeal, and difturb all their operations.

Talien, a young man who was fecretary to the municipality of Paris, and is now a member of the Convention, made an attack lately, in that Affembly, on General Montefquiou, who commands the army in Savoy. —He accufed him of being tainted with ariftocracy, and added, which was a pretty bold affertion for a man who was bred a clerk, that, *in his opinion*, the general was deficient in military abilities, and therefore he moved that he fhould be deprived of his command.

It is not to be imagined that much attention would have been paid to Talien's judgment of the abilities of a general officer, had he not been a creature of Danton's, and

fuppofed

supposed to act under his direction—His proposal, therefore, was supported by others, who were for passing a decree that General Montesquiou had lost the confidence of the nation.

La Riviere observed, that as it might occasion disquietude to other generals, if one of their brethren was to be cashiered with so little ceremony, it might be reasonable to appoint a committee to examine a little into Montesquiou's conduct in the first place, and defer the punishment till it should appear that he deserved it.

This observation in favour of the general was made in such very guarded terms, that one would hardly think it could have given offence even to his bitterest enemy.——Billaud de Varennes, however, said in reply, that it was not surprising that the same person should defend Montesquiou, who had formerly defended the conduct of La Fayette. In the present circumstances, this insinuation might

might have been very hurtful to La Riviere; he therefore afcended the tribune with precipitation, and declared that he was one of the 224 members of the Legiflative Affembly who had on the 8th of Auguft voted againft La Fayette ; that what Billaud had faid was falfe and calumnious, and required that he fhould be called to order, and cenfured as a calumniator by the prefident.

"Called to order! for what?" cried Danton. "In the fenate of Rome Brutus and Cato boldly fpoke out thofe plain truths which we from the pufillanimity of our manners evade as perfonalities ; for my part I am refolved to accufe, without circumlocution, every perfon whofe conduct I think fufpicious."

Although it may be granted that Billaud and Danton have as great a refemblance to Brutus and Cato as the Convention has to the Roman fenate, yet ftill there is a difference between the bold truths of the latter, and the bold falfehoods of the former ; the comparifon therefore is not quite appofite.

Danton however infifted upon General Montefquiou's being deprived of his command, for which he urged two additional reafons ; one, that when the public fafety is in danger, it is fufficient that a general is fufpected : the other, added he, is, " qu'il faut nous montrer terribles ; c'eft du caractere qu'il faut pour foutenir la liberté *."

This is certainly the character that Danton has uniformly fupported fince the 10th of Auguft, which tends to ftrengthen fome fufpicions of a terrible nature, indeed, which are harboured againft him.

The propofed decree was paffed, that General Montefquiou fhould be deprived of his command.

What renders Montefquiou obnoxious to fome leading members in the Convention,

* That we may appear terrible ; fuch is the character requifite for fupporting the caufe of liberty.

does

does him honour in the eyes of impartial
people—he ftrenuoufly oppofed the petitions for the dechéance of the King, and
was for fupporting him in the exercife
of the veto which the conftitution gave
him. He was alfo accufed by Bazire of
having faid at the extraordinary commiffion,
that if they fufpended the King's authority,
they ran the rifk of being abandoned by
the army; it is alfo imagined that he wifhes
to behave with more mildnefs to the Gene-
vois than is agreeable to certain people in
power. But what will prove more injurious to Montefquiou than all thefe charges, is, that Danton is his enemy.

It muft have been very mortifying to
Danton, and the other enemies of this gentleman, when the news arrived a little after
their decree, that he had already entered
Savoy, and was proceeding with the moft
triumphant fuccefs.—He concludes his letter
to the minifter of war with the following
words. " Je vous rends grace, Monfieur,

de

de m'avoir procuré cette maniere de re-
pondre à la calomme ; c'eft ainfi que j'aime-
rai toujours à la repouffer *."

The friends of General Montefquiou
feized this opportunity of moving that the
decree againft him fhould be recalled.

His enemies oppofed this.

Manuel feconded the motion which was
firft made by Lacroix, adding, that he hoped
they would recal this decree without lofs of
time, left Montefquiou, by gaining a new
victory, fhould put them ftill more in the
wrong. Danton, perceiving the tide flowing
in favour of Montefquiou, and being unable to turn it entirely againft him, propofed that the Affembly fhould extend the
power of the commiffioners that were fent
to his army, by leaving it to their judgment
to deprive the general of his command, or

* I return you thanks, Sir, for having put it in my
power to make this kind of anfwer to calumry; I
fhould wifh to repel her attacks alwzy ir the fame
manner.

to

to continue him in it, as they might think expedient. Danton had before given a more extenfive commiffion to an officer of Montefquiou's army, namely, to watch the conduct of the general, and, if he fhould make one retrograde movement, to fhoot him through the head.

Genfonné, with much reafon, fhewed the impropriety of the Affembly's allowing the execution of their decrees to depend on the judgment of any but themfelves; and it was obferved by Couthon, that the nation had given to the Convention the right of making decrees, but not the power of dele-gating that right to others. On which Danton, pufhing prejudice and want of candour as far as poffible, exclaimed: " They fay that Montefquiou has gained a victory, but I beg leave to obferve, that victories are not gained by a fingle man—the victory was gained by the French army."

This argument certainly does prove that Montefquiou has no better title to his vic-

tory

tory in Savoy, than Hannibal had to that at Cannæ, or Cæfar to the victory at Pharſalia.

Danton perſiſted in his motion; although, he added, that it was poſſible that an old courtier, like Montefquiou, feeing the fuccefs which attended the army of the republic in all quarters, might at laſt reſolve to adhere to it.

It was decided, however, according to the propoſal of Genſonné, that the execution of the laſt decree againſt Montefquiou ſhould be ſuſpended.

I know not whether the continued fuccefs which attends General Montefquiou, will finally overcome the envy and malice of his enemies; but, in a third letter, which came foon after the ſecond, he announces the reduction of all Savoy, from the Lake of Geneva to Mount Cenis : the progrefs of his troops, he fays, refembles a triumphant proceffion more than the march of an army; the inhabitants of towns and villages flock to him with congratulations, and the three-coloured

coloured ribbon in their hats; and adds, that the minds of the people seem disposed to a revolution like that of France; and that the proposal had been already made of forming Savoy into an 84th department of France.

On transmitting Montesquiou's letter to the Convention, Servan, the war minister, wrote to the president, that, as the expedition into Savoy had rendered that country free, it was worthy of the French Republic to solemnise so happy an event by ordering the hymn of the Marseillois to be performed in the Square of the Revolution, with the utmost magnificence, by vocal and instrumental music. He adds, " que ce chant patriotique, expression fidelle des sentimens François, retentisse dans tout l' empire, que nos voisins l' entendent, et qu'il devienne à jamais, l'espoir des peuples, et la terreur des tyrans *."

After

* Let that patriotic song, the faithful expression of the sentiments of France, resound all over the nation;

may

After General Kellermann had given the first check to the Pruffians on the 20th of September, he wrote to Servan for liberty to celebrate a *Te Deum* in his camp, on account of that important affair.——" The fong of the Marfeillois," replied the minifter, " is the *Te Deum* of the French republic ; let it be performed by the mufic of your army, and fung by the foldiers." ‏

In both inftances Servan's propofal was adopted,

To fubftitute a profane fong in preference to a religious rite, it might be imagined, would give great offence : fuch a propofal from the parliament to their army in the time of the Englifh republic, would have produced a mutiny and have fhocked the whole nation. It had no fuch effect in the prefent inftance in France, where religious zeal is wonderfully extinguifhed ; and an enthuf-

may it be heard by all the neighbouring countries ; and may it become the hope of the people, and the terror of tyrants !

afm

afm of another kind glows in its ftead, the enthufiafm of Liberty, what they call Civifme, in which an attachment to the prefent government, and an abhorrence of monarchy, are included.

This is profeffed with as much oftentation and apparent zeal as ever the Roman Catholic religion was, in the moft fuperftitious times; for, although the punifhment with which a want of civifme is attended, is not fo durable as that pronounced againft the irreligious, it is more immediate; which, on the generality of mankind, has full as great an effect. Civifme, like religion, produces both enthufiafts and hypocrites: the former deteft and abominate a king and nobility, as much as their zealous forefathers, two centuries ago, abominated the devil and his angels; and they are as zealous perfecutors of every deviation from the orthodox creed of civifme, as their predeceffors were of herefy. The enthufiafts are chiefly among the poor; the hypocrites among the rich: many of

whom

whom are juft fuch republicans in France, as the Jews are Chriftians in Portugal.

Immediately after Montefquiou's letter had been read. in the convention, Bancal, one of the deputies for the department du Puy-de-Dome, put the Convention in mind, that the Conftituent Affembly had by a folemn decree renounced every idea of conqueft ; and therefore he very wifely moved that the Convention, faithful to that facred principle, ought to rejeƈt the propofal of erecting Savoy into an 84th department of France, and fhould order it to be proclaimed all over Savoy, that France renounces conqueft, and defires no extenfion of territory.

This motion, equally juft and politic, was oppofed : it was faid, France has not given a temporary freedom to a country, that it may again fall under the yoke of its former tyrant. She ought to agree to the generous wifhes of the people fhe has freed, by accepting their union, and extending the empire of Liberty as far as poffible. " All

8                                              Europe,"

Europe," faid a member, " will gradually join you, and all Europe will be like one family.——The people of every nation will be your friends, and you will have no ene-.mies but kings—you cannot furely refufe fuch a fublime idea."

A flourifh of this kind might be applauded in a difputing club, or might perhaps be ad-mired in a vifionary declaimer on politics; but it was hardly to be imagined that fuch fentiments would make any impreffion on an affembly of legiflators, where practical knowledge and fober good fenfe prefided. It was hardly to be expected that thofe fine words would not be conftrued by all Europe into an abfolute renunciation of the decree againft conqueft, and really meant that the new republic intended, under a pretence of fpreading liberty, to overturn every govern-ment, and fubdue every nation around.

Jean Baptifte Louvet, notwithftanding the applaufe which was very liberally beftowed on the fentiments above mentioned, had the firmnefs

firmnefs and good fenfe to declare, that, without renouncing one of the wifeft decrees of the conftituent affembly, they could not interfere in the government of any other country : that they could not, without infringing the moft facred right of the people of Savoy, prefs upon them the conftitution which France might affume for herfelf. How did they know that the conftitution which was expedient for France, was alfo expedient for Savoy? and if expedient, how did they know that the Savoyards at the bottom of their hearts chofe it ?——" That which is effentially juft," Louvet continued, " is for the moft part found policy. Let it be folemnly declared to all the people who fhall be, I will not fay fubdued, but freed by your arms, that they may choofe to themfelves what form of government they pleafe, that their laws fhall be of their own making, that you not only wifh to give them freedom, but freedom in the mode which they themfelves prefer.——" I am convinced,"

convinced," added he, " that in Brabant, whither your armies intend to march, there exift ftrong prejudices againft fome of your laws, and your conftitution in general ; prejudices which it will require many years to eradicate, and which will render you more odious in their eyes than their prefent mafter, if you attempt to force your conftitution upon them. It is as expedient, therefore, as equitable, to declare the complete independence of every country into which you carry freedom."

Danton, in anfwer to this, faid, that they had affuredly the right to declare to every fuch country, that it fhould never more be governed by a king : that if the people were fo abfurd as to defire a government contrary to their intereft, it fhould not be allowed : that the National Convention of France fhould be *a committee of infurrection against all the kings in the univerfe.*

Nothing can be imagined more mad than

7

this

this propofition, the tendency of which is to force all the monarchs in Europe, in felf-defence to make war on the Republic : what private view Danton has in this, I do not know, but it evidently goes to the ruin of France.

The Affembly, however, becoming impatient to clofe the difcuffion, ordered General Montefquiou's letter to be printed, and referred the propofition refpecting Savoy to the confideration of the diplomatic and the war committees.

Notwithftanding the prudent conduct and brilliant fuccefs of Montefquiou, I am informed that there is no great probability of his being continued in his command. His enemies are of a difpofition not to forgive him for having reduced Savoy at the very time that they were afferting he would never enter it, or to forget the injuftice they have already done him. Befide thefe and the motives of diflike previoufly mentioned, they

they have another ground of hatred towards him, namely, his being a nobleman, and of a very ancient family. This appears equally unjuft and abfurd :—unjuft, becaufe a man of noble birth, who from a love of general freedom has adhered to the revolution, has more merit than they can boaft who had no fuch facrifice to make——and it is abfurd, becaufe, inftead of giving no importance to the accidental circumftance of birth, it is giving a great importance to it, which operates againft the poffeffor. But if a man's nobility is not allowed, independent of perfonal merit, to be of fervice to him, neither ought it to be allowed, independent of demerit, to injure him.

Accounts are arrived that Dumourier, having left a fufficient force to harafs the retreating army of Pruffia, has quitted his own camp, and is foon expected in Paris.

October 11.

I was prefent this day for the firft time at the

the Conventional Affembly, where a virulent attack was made on Dillon, one of the generals employed againft the German army, and who, from the lateft accounts, is now preffing upon their rear at Verdun.

As it elucidates what immediately follows, I fhall here infert a fhort account of Dumourier's memorable campaign, from the time he was appointed to the command till he left the army, although I was not acquainted with all the particulars till fome time after this date.

General Arthur Dillon commanded the French army on the frontiers of Flanders, when he heard of the infurrection of the 10th of Auguft.

Dumourier, being at that time fubordinate to him, commanded in the camp of Maulde. From the accounts which Dillon received of that affair, he conceived it to be a rafh infurrection which would be difapproved of by the nation, and that it would foon end in the

the ruin of all concerned in it. He therefore gave out an order to the army on the
13th, in which he said, that the conſtitution
had been violated by men who were the enemies of liberty; that he determined to remain
faithful to the nation, to the law, to the king,
and to the conſtitution framed by the aſſembly in the years 1789, 1790, and 1791, to
which they had all ſworn.

He tranſmitted this order from Pont-ſur-
Sambre, where he was with his army, to the
camp of Maulde, with a letter to General
Dumourier, directing him to publiſh it
there.

Dumourier had a different idea of the
tranſactions of the 10th. He ſaw that the
public opinion went in favour of the ſucceſſ-
ful party; that it would be very difficult to
wreſt the government out of the hands
which had ſeized it; that an attempt of
that kind by the army would immediately
produce a civil war, and expoſe the country

to foreign invafion; and that he himfelf
would remain fubordinate to Luckner, La
Fayette and Dillon. Dumourier was nearer
to Paris than Dillon, and had received earlier and, as is fuppofed, more diftinct information from his friend Genfonné, of the ftate
of affairs. In his anfwer to Dillon's letter,
he regretted that general's precipitancy, affured him that he would not publifh the
order in his camp, and advifed Dillon to
retract it without lofs of time.

He fent at the fame time an account of
what he had done, and was difpofed to do,
to his friends at Paris; and when the three
commiffioners from the National Affembly
arrived, he not only took the oath of Equality himfelf, but perfuaded Dillon to do the
fame. That officer found no difficulty in
explaining his conduct to the commiffioners,
affuring them, that it had proceeded from the
mifreprefentation which had been made to
him of the affair of the 10th, but that he was

2                                              zealous

zealous to serve the French nation, whatever form of government they should think proper to adopt.

The National Assembly were so much pleased with this conduct of Dumourier, that they gave him the supreme command of the army formerly under M. de la Fayette, placing Dillon, who is an elder officer, under him. Having no pretext for putting Dumourier above Luckner, and desirous at the same time that the former should be the efficient commander, they ordered Luckner to Chalons, to form an army there of the men who were marching from all parts to that place, where they were to be clothed, armed and sent in detachments wherever the exigencies of the state required. Kellermann was, at Dumourier's recommendation, ordered to replace Luckner as commander of the army in Lorraine; Biron and Custine commanded the army on the Rhine, and Montesquiou that which was ordered against

F 2

Savoy:

Savoy : all thefe officers took the oaths required by the Affembly, and made the armies under their orders take them alfo.

Dumourier fent Dillon to command the army of the Ardennes, which comprehended all the troops placed in that part of the frontiers of France, between Rocroy and Montmedy. The two generals afterwards met at the town of Sedan, with a view to fix on future meafures.

The enemy had already entered France, was in poffeffion of Longwy, the firft fortified town on the frontier next to the dutchy of Luxembourg, and feemed at once to threaten Montmedy, Verdun and Thionville.

The Duke of Brunfwick's army was above 50,000 ftrong : General Clairfait had joined him with 15,000 Auftrians, befide a confiderable body of Heffians and French emigrants, amounting in all to 90,000 men.

After leaving the frontier towns tolerably garrifoned,

garrifoned, Dumourier had not above 17,000 men to act immediately againft this immenfe force; and thefe 17,000 had been ufelefsly encamped between Sedan and Stenay, the Meufe being fordable in numberlefs places between Stenay and Verdun, where the enemy had no oppofition.

On comparing the ftrength of the invading army with the weaknefs of that which was to oppofe it, it was at one time imagined that all direct oppofition would be vain, and that the moft effectual meafures would be, by a fudden irruption into Auftrian Flanders, to endeavour to divert the enemy from advancing againft Paris: but the fmall probability there was that fuch an expedition, however fuccefsfully conducted, would have the defired effect, foon made that fcheme be laid afide; and Dumourier, infpired by an immenfe defire of renown, and trufting to the refources of his own genius, and the enthufiafm which animated his

F 3 country-

countrymen, refolved, by the defending of pofts, and every other poffible means, to attempt to check and retard the progrefs of the enemy, till he fhould be reinforced by the army of Kellermann from Lorraine confifting of 20,000 men, by that which Bournonville was leading from Flanders which amounted to 13,000, and what Luckner had fent to him of the new levies which were affembling at Chalons.

Small as Dumourier's force was, he had the courage, on the 29th of Auguft, to detach from it two battalions of infantry, under the command of M. Galbaud, an excellent officer, who had orders to throw himfelf into Verdun, and affift in the defence of that town.

Dumourier gave the command of the advanced guard of his army to Dillon; it confifted of five battalions of infantry, with fourteen fquadrons of light horfe. Dillon was ordered to march to Stenay, where
Dumourier

Dumourier intended to join him on the firft of September, and difpute the paffage of the Meufe with the enemy.

Dillon, with a thoufand horfe, pufhed on before the reft of his troops, to Stenay, and was making arrangements for the defence of the place, when the advanced guard of the Auftrian army, four thoufand ftrong, with feveral pieces of cannon, appeared. Convinced of the impoffibility of defending the town without infantry, and without cannon, he evacuated Stenay, croffed the Meufe, and drew up his troops upon the oppofite fhore of that river, fending notice to his infantry, who were advancing, to return to the camp at Mouzon. When he himfelf retired to join them there, his rear was attacked by the Auftrian cavalry, who were repulfed with confiderable lofs, and Dillon arrived in fafety at Mouzon in the middle of the night *.

* Compte rendu au miniftre de la guerre, par le Lieut. General A. Dillon.

F 4 Dumourier

Dumourier advanced with his small army to Mouzon on the first of September, and then marched on to Beaumont en Argonne, where Dillon had previously traced out a camp.

Finding that it was now too late to dispute the paffage of the Meufe, Dumourier determined to make himfelf mafter of the various ftraits in the foreft of Argonne. This foreft extends from the Chene le Populeux to Paffavent, a fpace of about forty miles; the German army, in marching to Paris, was under the neceffity of going by fome of thefe ftraits, or making a confiderable circuit by bad roads, and turning the foreft. Dumourier detached Dillon with fix thoufand men, to feize upon the very important pafs of Biefme, near the Grandes Iflettes, in the foreft of Argonne. It is about feven or eight miles from Verdun, on the direct road from that city to Paris by Chalons. He had at this time heard nothing from Galbaud, and had no doubt of of Verdun's holding out a much longer time than would be neceſſary for Dillon to perform this ſervice. But Verdun ſurrendered by capitulation on the ſecond of September, without having made any reſiſtance, and Dillon would in all probability have arrived too late, had it not been for the ſagacity of M. Galbaud. When that officer came near to Verdun, he found it ſo completely inveſted by the Pruſſians, that it was impoſſible to execute the orders of Dumourier. He conſidered, in the next place, how he could employ the two battalions under his command moſt effectually for the public ſervice; and, anticipating the intentions of his commander, he marched them to Bieſme, and immediately ſent a meſſenger to Dumourier, to inform him of what he had done, and to demand a reinforcement. The army at Verdun, in advancing to Paris, were now under the neceſſity of forcing this poſt, or making a

circuit

circuit of forty miles, by Varennes and Grand Pré on the north, or one ftill larger by Bar-le-duc on the fouth: Dumourier thought the former the moft probable, for he pofted himfelf with the body of his army at Grand Pré. This is alfo a pafs in the foreft of Argonne, requiring however a much greater force to defend it than that of Biefme ; to which Dillon marched with redoubled efforts, in the dread that Galbaud, who he had heard was in poffeffion of it, fhould be forced before he arrived *.

While Dumourier remained at Grand Pré, he detached General Miranda with a body of two thoufand cavalry, to protect a convoy he expected, and alfo to reconnoitre the Pruffian army, whofe movements at this time feemed equivocal. Miranda performed this fervice with ability and fuccefs; an advanced guard of Pruffians, confifting

* Compte rendu au miniftre de la guerre, par le Lieut. General A. Dillon.

of

of four thousand, were posted in such a manner that they must have intercepted the convoy—He attacked and defeated them, and the convoy arrived in safety at Dumourier's camp *.

The march of Dillon from Mouzon to Biefme, through a forest exceedingly difficult to traverse, and so near to a superior army, required military skill in the commander, and steadiness in the troops, especially as they were assured by the municipal officers of a village through which they passed, that Galbaud, discouraged by the terror spread among his troops by those who came from Verdun, had quitted Biefme, and fallen back towards Chalons, and that the town of Sainte-Menehould was in the possession of the enemy. Dillon, however, having sent couriers to all quarters to ascer-

* Rapport des Commiffaires de la Convention aux Armées reünies.

tain

tain thofe facts, foon difcovered that they were not true, and on the afternoon of the fifth of September effected his junction with Galbaud.

The troops were immediately employed in fortifying, by all the refources of art, the natural ftrength of this poft, which was done fo effectually that, when the King of Pruffia in perfon, with the Duke of Brunf-wick, reconnoitred the place from the heights near Clermont, they thought it too ftrong to be forced.

Some people have ventured to cenfure the Duke of Brunfwick for neglecting to attack this poft of Biefme before Galbaud was reinforced by Dillon, or for not order-ing Dillon to be oppofed in his march from Mouzon to it.

It belongs to military men only, and fuch as are acquainted intimately with the fitua-tion of the country, and the circumftances

6

in which the German army was at that time, to decide on this point; but any one may naturally conclude, that a general of so high a reputation as the Duke of Brunfwick muſt have had fufficient reaſons for acting as he did.

M. Gobert, adjutant general of Dumourier's army, and probably better qualified to judge of the conduct of the Duke of Brunfwick than moſt who have cenſured it, obſerves, that Galbaud was in poſſeſſion of the paſs on the 31ſt of Auguſt, that the garriſon of Verdun had joined him on the ſecond of September, and that the Duke of Brunfwick might naturally believe that many peaſants from the neighbouring villages would immediately reſort to Galbaud, and aſſiſt in defending the paſs, this being a kind of ſervice in which new troops might be as uſeful as veterans.

Whatever were the Duke's reaſons for
waving

waving the attack of this post, the possession of it enabled Dillon to afford protection to a number of villages situated on the river Aire, and put the Prussians to the necessity of long and most fatiguing marches, by Grand Pré to the camp of La Lune near St. Menehould, instead of going directly through Biesme.

Dumourier was in possession of the defiles of Grand Pré for some time before he was disturbed, and at last became persuaded that the Duke of Brunswick meant to avoid the forest of Argonne altogether, and march to Chalons by Bar-le-duc. Under this conviction he wrote to Dillon that he was preparing with a strong advanced guard to harass the rear of the enemy's army, who, he understood, were endeavouring to pass by Dillon's right to Chalons. He directs him to leave 2000 men to guard the pass; and then to assemble all the troops, and order them to

St. Mene-

St. Menehould, where he would endeavour to join him, and, with their united force, afterwards form a junction with Kellermann. He concludes his letter in thefe words :

" Faites raffembler, par le tocfin, tous les payfans pour aller border les abattis : portez-vous tout-à-fait à votre droite, et dirigez-y tout ce qui fe raffemble à St. Menehould. Après notre jonction, nous nous arrangerons enfemble pour couvrir cette place et pour fuivre le mouvement fur Chalons. Faites fonner le tocfin fur toute votre route, j'en ferai autant, et cela deconcertera un peu la marche des Pruffiens. Je commencerai mon mouvement à minuit *.

DUMOURIER.

*Le Général en Chef de l'Armée du Nord.*"

It

---

* Affemble all the peafants by the alarm bell, that they may line the abatis †. Direct your march to the

† An abatis is formed by trees cut down and arranged with their branches towards the enemy, fo as to form a kind of fortification.

right,

It is probable that the Duke of Brunf-wick had made fome movements which indicated an intention of marching by Bar-le-duc to Chalons; or had otherwife con-trived to fpread this impreffion, on purpofe to conceal his real defign, which was to force the defiles of Grand Pré.

Kellermann and Luckner were both de-ceived in this point. The former was fo much convinced that the Duke's movement was a feint, that he had thoughts of marching from Sainte Dizier, where he then was, to Chalons, fo as to arrive before the enemy.

right, and order all the troops who fhall affemble at St. Menehould to move in the fame direction. After our junction we will fix upon meafures for covering that place, and attending the march of the enemy to Chalons. Order the alarm bells to be rung during your march, I will do the fame; this will fomewhat difconcert the march of the enemy. I will begin my march at midnight.

(Signed)     DUMOURIER.

Luckner

Luckner had fent reinforcements to the army of Kellermann where they were not needed, inftead of fending them to Dumourier at Grand-Pré, by a fhort route which Dillon had indicated.

Dumourier was foon convinced of his miftake, and wrote the following letter to Dillon.

Grand-Pré le 12 Sept. l'an
4me de la Liberté.

LES enemies vous ont abandonné, mon cher Général, pour fe porter fur moi; ils me font une attaque dans le moment; je ne fais pas encore fi c'eft la véritable, je crois que ce n'eft qu'une feinte pour attaquer la Trouée du Chêne-le-Populeux *, ou je porte du renfort. Envoyez moi du

* This is a poft on the north end of the Foreft of Argonne, which Dumourier meant to defend. By the Trouée de Clermont he means the Straits of Biefme.

G fecours,

fécours, fans cependant dégarnir la Trouée de Clermont.

Je vous embraffe.

*Le Général en Chef de l'Armée du Nord.*
Signé        DUMOURIER *.

On the following day Dillon received another letter from Dumourier, who, being affured that the enemy intended a fecond attack with more force than that of the day before, and having received no fuccours from Chalons, gave a pofitive order to Dillon to fend him directly all the troops he could poffibly fpare without endanger-

* The enemy have left you, my dear General, to come againft me; they begin an attack at this moment. I am not quite convinced that they are in earneft, I rather fufpect that this is a feint to divert my attention from the paffage of Chêne-le-Populeux, where they mean a real attack, and whither I am actually fending reinforcements. Send me fuccour, without however too much weakening the Strait of Clermont.

Comte Rendu par le Lt. Gén. A. Dillon.

ing

ing his own pofition. Dillon accordingly fent him about 3000, the fourth of which was cavalry; and this was the only rein-forcement which Dumourier received before he was obliged to quit Grand-Pré: but fmall as this aid may be thought, it was as much as Dillon could in prudence fend, becaufe the body of Pruffians which had marched under the Duke of Brunfwick to Grand-Pré had been immediately replaced by 15,000 Auftrians and Heffians, who were afterwards reinforced to the number of 20,000, by whom he expected to be at-tacked every day.

It is probable that Dillon had emiffaries near the perfon of the Duke of Brunfwick, who gave him notice of what paffed, for his information is in general juft; and in a letter to Kellermann, dated the 13th of September, he informs him, that Dumourier had been attacked the day before, and that the attack had been renewed the morning

G 2

of

of the 13th, without fucce{s ; and he adds, " Je fais qu' hier le Duc de Brunfwick furieux a dit au Roi de Pruffe—Je perdrai bien du monde, mais j'y pafferai *."

The Duke of Brunfwick was as good as his word—On the 14th of September the attack of the Pruffians was irrefiftible. During the time that Dumourier was himfelf attacked, he was informed that a poft called La Croix aux Bois, which General Chazot defended, was forced. Dumourier therefore was obliged entirely to abandon the paffes of of Grand-Pré, and to direct his march to Sainte-Ménehould, where he had previoufly traced a camp in a very ftrong pofition.— On his march, his army was fo violently preffed by the advanced cavalry of the Pruffians, that it was thrown into confufion, and part fled in a fhameful man-

* I know that the Duke of Brunfwick faid to the King of Pruffia yefterday in a violent paffion—I fhall lofe a great many men, but I am refolved to pafs.

ner,

ner, quite to the town of St. Menehould, which they entered, crying, " All is loft !" and fpreading difmay on all fides. Dumourier, in the account which he fent to the Convention, feems to think that if the Pruffians had pufhed on with vigour during this panic, his army might have been difperfed.

Dillon happened to be at St. Menehould when the fugitives arrived—he did every thing in his power to prevent the terrour from fpreading—he fent detachments of horfe to the neighbouring villages to ftop thofe who fled, and prevent the alarm reaching Chalons, where it might have had the worft effect on the new levies affembling under Luckner.

By Dillon's exertions, and the animating prefence of Dumourier, the army regained order, fpirit, and confidence in their officers.

Thofe who had diftinguifhed themfelves in this fhameful manner were fent in dif-

G 3                                grace

grace from the army, which on the morning of the 15th entered the camp at St. Menehould, and began with all diligence to fortify it, in the perfuafion that it would very foon be attacked. Bournonville, at the head of a body of 13,000 men, joined Dumourier on the 17th. The Duke of Brunfwick knew that Kellermann was near at hand with a greater force, and formed the plan of attacking him before he could join Dumourier. Kellermann, by forced marches, gained the heights of Valmy on the evening of the 19th. Valmy is within lefs than a mile of other heights, on which was the ftrong camp of Dumourier. Kellermann received intelligence of the march of the Pruffians during the night, which convinced him that he would be attacked the following morning. He made his difpofitions accordingly, and ufed every poffible means of encouraging his foldiers. He walked through the lines with fome of the

moft

moſt popular officers, to animate them by their diſcourſe. The army anſwered them by huzzas, and the cry of Vive la nation ! Kellermann's army extended from a village called Dammartin la Planchette, along the heights of Valmy. A free communication was kept up between his army and that of Dumourier, who ſent 8000 men to his aſſiſtance during the cannonade, which laſted the whole day. The Pruſſians manœuvred with their uſual coolneſs and addreſs, ſometimes forming into columns, as if their intention had been to attack with the bayonet, and ſometimes moving with an intention to ſurround Kellermann, and cut off his communication with Dumourier. The firmneſs of the French, under the ſkilful direction of their Generals, prevented the Pruſſians from accompliſhing either. Dumourier was in perſon at the batteries during ſeveral hours of the cannonade, and at the head of

his

his own troops to oppofe the Pruffians when they attempted to furround Kellermann. The fuperior addrefs of the French cannoneers was apparent during the whole action; and the army in general fhewed a degree of fteadinefs which difciplined troops alone have been fuppofed to poffefs, and rivalled the Pruffians in fteadinefs and obedience to their officers, while their natural vivacity appeared in fongs and cries of Vive la nation! amidft the carnage of the cannonade. In Kellermann's army there were above four hundred killed, and between five and fix hundred wounded. The General himfelf narrowly efcaped, his horfe being killed under him. It is faid, and it is moft probable, that the lofs of the Pruffians was confiderably greater. What military men peculiarly admire in the conduct of Kellermann, was the fkill he difplayed that evening in changing his pofition in the prefence of the

the enemy, to one ftill more advantageous; by which his right wing touched the army of Dumourier, his left was protected by heights eafily defended, while in his front was a rivulet greatly fwelled by the recent rains *. That he was not attacked during this manœuvre is not only a proof of the ability with which it was performed, but alfo forms a ftrong prefumption of the great lofs which the Pruffians had fuftained, and of their being difcouraged by this unfuccefsful attack.

At the fame time that the attack was made on the army of Kellermann, the 20,000 men which had been left at Clermont made an attempt on Dillon's camp at Biefme.—— The Duke of Brunfwick had been under the neceffity of leaving this ftrong party

* Obfervations fur la Compagne de 1792, par Gobert, Adjutant Général.

behind,

behind, otherwise Dillon would have intercepted all his convoys; so that Dillon, with about five or six thousand men, had detained 20,000 from the Prussian army when it marched against Dumourier and Kellermann. Those 20,000 now marched to the attack of Biesme; they were so confident of their own success, and that Dumourier would be routed by the Prussians, that they made their whole equipage and baggage of every kind follow them, in the expectation that after they had forced the post of Biesme, they would be ordered to join the Prussians and accompany them to Paris. Dillon's defence, however, was attended with the same success as Kellermann's——the Austrians and Hessians were repulsed and obliged to retire in great disorder.

After these unsuccessful attacks, the Duke of Brunswick encamped his army at La Lune, near the army of Dumourier, and

and between St. Menehould and Chalons. Here the Pruffians, who had already fuffered by ficknefs, were greatly diftreffed from a want of provifions. Bournonville, detached with a body of 4000 men
by Dumourier, had intercepted feveral convoys that were advancing from their magazines at Grand-Pré. He intercepted in particular feveral droves of cattle going to the
Pruffians, and ordered them to be flaughtered for the ufe of his own army: for this
laft exploit, joined to his courage and
ftrength, he was called the French Ajax.——
Nothing could bribe the French peafants
to carry any kind of neceffaries to the
Germans, while they flocked with fupplies
to the camp of Dumourier. It alfo was
difficult and moft expenfive for the Duke of
Brunfwick, or any officer who commanded
his detached parties, to procure intelligence,
as they were furrounded with fpies, who
informed Dumourier of all their movements.

ments. As the Pruffians could procure no
provifions but from their own magazines,
the fcarcity was increafed by the exceffive
rains which fell at this time, and rendered
the roads uncommonly deep, and in fome
places almoft impaffable; in the mean time,
the Pruffians were more expofed to the in-
clemency of the weather, and fuffered more
from cold, moifture, and want of provifions, than the French, who were protected
in fome degree from thofe evils by the care
and attention of their countrymen. To
thefe diftreffes were added the vexation and
difcouragement which the Pruffians muft
have felt at finding the whole country
united againft them, inftead of a great
proportion being difpofed to join them, as
they had been made to expect.

There are profeffions in which men fometimes acquire great reputation with little
merit; this may happen either from the
public being no judges of the merit of
thofe

those particular professions, or because success in the profession may arise from the merit of others who direct the measures of the individual who acquires the reputation.

This is often the case in the military profession, at the top of which men are placed from the circumstances of birth, independent of all idea of merit, and frequently in spite of the most glaring proofs of incapacity. In this profession, likewise, men have acquired fame from successes that have been entirely owing to the superiour valour of their troops, and the superiour skill of some subordinate officer.

But if the commanders of armies may on some occasions acquire fame without deserving it, no set of men are more exposed to censure on account of sinister events, which no sagacity could foresee, and no human power could prevent.

Few men have experienced this more than the Duke of Brunswick, who has

been

been blamed for not marching directly to Chalons, or Rheims, as soon as he found himself between those cities and Dumourier's army. Those who make this criticism do not think of the danger and difficulty of marching with an enemy hanging on the rear, and intercepting the convoys of the advancing army.

But without taking farther notice of such random censures, it is the opinion of many of the military profession, that instead of remaining inactive at his camp at La Lune after the cannonade of the 20th of September, he ought to have attacked Dumourier at St. Menehould. Those who hold this opinion say, that from the superiority of the Prussians over the raw troops of France, he had a great probability of beating and dispersing them, which would have spread such an alarm that the levies which were marching against the Duke would have joined in the flight; and in-

5                                         stead

ſtead of enemies, he would have met only friends on his way to Paris; for nothing is ſo efficacious as a victory, in converting enemies into friends.

I have been aſſured, that this meaſure was propoſed by the Marechal de Caſtries, in a Council of War held at La Lune; and his opinion was ſupported by that of M. de Poilly, a General Officer in the French army, who had reſided in that province, and had an accurate knowledge of the country; and that this attack of the camp of Menehould was alſo greatly deſired by the whole corps of French Emigrants.

Without any pretenſions to military knowledge, it is not difficult to conjecture what may have determined the Duke of Brunſwick againſt riſking ſuch a meaſure.

He certainly had entered France with a perſuaſion that he would be favoured by a great part of the country who diſliked the conſtitution: he had reaſon to believe

that

the events of the 10th of August, and the third of September, would render the people more averse to the new government, and more favourable to his expedition. The easy conquest of Longwy and Verdun tended to confirm him in those sentiments. He found no very great difficulty in forcing the Straits of Grand-Pré.

Thus far therefore every thing rather had a tendency to encourage the Duke to proceed; but the action of the 20th of September, and the disposition in which he found the country, must have had a very different effect on his mind. By the former he had the proofs of a firmness in the French army, and a skill in the General which he did not expect; and in the country, so far from any favourable disposition towards his enterprize, every appearance was hostile in the highest degree. At his camp at La Lune his convoys were sometimes intercepted; he could obtain no pro-
visions

visions from the inhabitants, and his army was suffering under the complicated distress of want, and a dangerous epidemic ; it is said there were near ten thousand sick in his camp, and at Grand-Pré. In such circumstances an attack on Dumourier's army, now 70,000 strong, and whose strength he had already experienced, was not very promising of success ; and if unsuccessful, would have been attended with the entire ruin of his own. But even upon the supposition that he had been victorious, the remains of the French army after a defeat, with the troops at Chalons, Rheims, Soissons, and in every part of the country, would have rendered the retreat of his army, diminished by victory and enfeebled by sickness, very dangerous if he had marched much farther into France.

As soon as it was evident that the country was against him, the Duke of Brunswick's enterprize might have been considered as having failed. He had nothing to think of but to effect a retreat, which he finally conducted with a fkill equal to the higheft reputation.

But he firft propofed a truce; during this a conference took place between the chiefs of the oppofite armies. It has been faid, that Dumourier agreed to this with a view to promote defertion among the German foldiers, by diftributing the decree of the National Affembly for the encouragement of deferters, and alfo in the hopes of in-ducing the King of Pruffia to break with the Auftrians, at this moment of indignation and difappointment; and it has been af-ferted that Dumourier proved himfelf a much better politician than the Duke of Brunfwick on this occafion. The reverfe of this however feems to be the truth; for if what is mentioned above were really Dumourier's objects in agreeing to the truce, he failed in both. There was no defertion from the Pruffian army, and the

King

King did *not* break with the Emperor; but it was of infinite importance to the Duke of Brunfwick, who had already determined on a retreat, to have a few days of truce, which he employed in conveying his artillery and heavy baggage undifturbed from the camp of La Lune to Grand-Pré.

Nothing can be more uncandid and inconfiftent than the manner in which the Duke of Brunfwick's conduct has been criticifed—It is afferted in the firft place, that he inconfiderately led his army into a fituation fo defperate, that if they advanced, they muft be all either killed or taken prifoners; if they retreated, one half muft be cut in pieces ; and if they remained where they were, they muft be ftarved.——Taking this account to be the true ftate of the cafe, one would imagine that he fhould be allowed fome credit for having extricated his army from fo perilous a fituation——inftead of which, we are told, that even in this, he fhewed

lefs

lefs addrefs than the enemy, from whom he delivered them.

In confirmation however of my own opinion on this fubject, I fhall only add, that it was the Duke of Brunfwick who firft propofed the truce, and not Dumourier— that during the whole time it co .tinued, his artillery and baggage were moving to Grand-Pré, and that as foon as he knew they were fafe there, he renewed his original manifefto, which he muft have known would put an end to the truce. All thofe circumftances render it probable that, however acute and able Dumourier may be, the truce was more advantageous to the Duke of Brunfwick than to him.

On the thirtieth of September the Duke raifed his camp at La Lune, and retreated with his whole army by Grand-Pré to Bufancy. The Auftrians, under the command of General Clairfait, feparated from the Pruffians, and paffed the Meufe at Stenay, and took the
neareft

nearest way to the county of Luxembourg; while the Pruſſians paſſed at Dun, and purſued the courſe of the river to Verdun. Their march was ſlow, on account of the number of their ſick, as well as of the badneſs of the roads; but in ſuch order, that although purſued by numerous detachments of French, no conſiderable advantage was gained over them during this whole march.

When Dumourier ſaw the enemy in full retreat, and that they could attempt nothing of importance in that quarter this ſeaſon, he determined to go to Paris. He wiſhed to ſettle with the Executive Power a plan of operations for an immediate expedition into Auſtrian Flanders, whither he has ordered a great part of his army, and where he expects to gather freſh laurels. What gives a high idea of Dumourier's vigour of mind is, that in adhering to the plan of operations which he

had

had traced out for the defence of France, he refifted the injunctions which he frequently received from the adminiftration at Paris— and took the whole refponfibility upon himfelf. At Paris there was fo great an alarm, on hearing that fome German irregulars had been near Rheims, that they wifhed him to fall back. And Servan, the war minifter, has the following expreffions in a letter to Dumourier, dated the 27th of September.

" J'efpere toujours, mon cher Général, que vous refterez convaincu, ainfi que nous, que vous n'avez plus un moment à perdre pour vous rapprocher de la Marne, afin de couvrir par la Chalons, Rheims, et les fuperbes campagnes du Soiffonnois et de la Brie; que nous import actuellement que l'ennemi occupe les plaines arides de la Champagne!" —And he ends the fame letter with thefe words, " Perfonne ne vous voit tranquillement à Sainte Menehould tandis que les houlane houlans viennent infulter les fauxbourgs de Rheims*."

When we reflect on the character of the people Dumourier was accountable to for his conduct, and how little they are difpofed to forgive what they confider as reprehenfible, we muft the more admire his fteadinefs. It is now generally faid, that if he had fallen back to Chalons and Rheims, the enemy might have got poffeffion of a plentiful country, and perhaps wintered in France.

He left Bournonville to harrafs the Pruffians during their retreat. That General

* I hope, my dear General, that you are as much convinced as we, that you ought, without a moment's delay, to move towards the department of La Marne, on purpofe to protect Chalons, Rheims, and the fertile fields of the Soifonnois and La Brie. Of what importance is it to us that the enemy are in poffeffion of the barren plains of Champaigne?

We cannot with patience think of your remaining at St. Menehould, while the Hulans are infulting the fuburbs of Rheims.

H 4                                                        followed

followed them as far as Bufancy; and then being ordered to the army intended againſt Flanders, he was replaced by the Generals Kellermann and Valence, who, with all their zeal and activity, were not able to gain any advantage over this retreating and ſickly army.

Dillon, on his part, followed that body of Auſtrians and Heſſians who had attacked his poſt at Biefme, and were now retreating by another route towards Verdun.

He had about 16,000 men with him, and the army he purſued was more numerous, and conſiſted of well diſciplined troops. Having heard that the Auſtrians and Heſſians were irritated againſt each other, and having been informed that the Landgrave himſelf had ſpoken with anger againſt the conduct of the Auſtrians, he wrote a letter from Domballe to that Prince, which he ſent by M. Gobert his Adjutant General, at the ſame time that he diſmiſſed M. Lindau,

dau, an Heffian officer, who had been taken prifoner. In this letter, after fome general reflections refpecting the right of nations to change their governments, which it is not probable the Landgrave will think conclufive, Dillon affures him that he is furrounded in fuch a manner that it will be very difficult for him to efcape ; but that if he will fet out the following morning for his own country, and entirely evacuate the French territories with his troops, that he will be allowed to pafs undifturbed by certain pofts which were at that time occupied by the French.

Dillon faw, that it was not in his power with 16,000 men to prevent the retreat of 20,000; but he thought if he could perfuade the Heffians to feparate from the Auftrians, he might cut off the latter.——It was not very likely indeed that the Landgrave would be fo far deceived as to accept of Dillon's offer; but whatever may be thought

thought of the depth of the ftratagem, it is evident that Dillon meant to ferve, not to injure France; for he fhewed the letter to General Galbaud before he fent it, and he alfo gave a copy of it, with the Landgrave's anfwer, to Sillery, Carra, and Prieur, the Commiffioners of the National Convention *.

But what puts Dillon's intentions out of all queftion is, that on the 4th of October he intercepted a letter from the Director of the diftrict of Etain, to the Landgrave of Heffe, dated the firft of October, by which it appeared that the Landgrave was expected to take his head quarters at Etain; on which Dillon fent a courier from his camp at Sivry-la-Parche to General Favart at Metz, to inform him, that he intended to attack the enemy on their retreat, and that they were to retreat by Etain; to prove which he tranfmitted the intercepted letter to Favart, and defired

* Rapport des Commiffaires de la Convention.

him

him to fend, a detachment from the garrifon of Metz to co-operate in haraffing them.

He adds, " Faites avertir tous les villages, que tous les citoyens reprennent de la confiance, que l'on fonne le tocfin par-tout, toutes les armes feront bonnes pour harceler l'ennemi, et tomber dans chaque defilé fur fes equipages. Faites proclamer que tous ceux que lui fourniront une livre de pain, font traitres à leur pays. Je le purfuivrai fans rélache s'ils fe retirent ; je les combattrai s'ils reftent," &c.*

General Dillon's letter to the Landgrave of Heffe Caffel, and the Landgrave's anfwer,

* " Let this be proclaimed in all the villages, that the citizens may recover their fpirits ; let the alarm be founded every where : all forts of arms will ferve to harrafs the enemy, and to affift in attacking their carriages in every defile. Let it be proclaimed, that all who furnifh them with a fingle pound of bread will be confidered as traitors to their country. I will purfue them without relaxation if they fly—I am determined to fight them if they remain," &c.

were

were tranfmitted to the Convention without any commentary. They were read in the Affembly, and, inftead of appearing meritorious or innocent, they had the moft malignant and moft unnatural conftruction put on them by fome of the members. Merlin of Thionville exclaimed, that this letter was a complete proof of Dillon's being a traitor.——This Merlin is a moft zealous accufer; he feems to think that by murdering the reputation of others, he fhall accumulate a vaft flock of fame to himfelf, as the Indian imagines that he becomes the immediate poffeffor of all the courage and dexterity of the enemy he kills. Merlin, not fatisfied with the interpretation he had given to this letter to the Landgrave, reverted to Dillon's proclamation at Pont-fur-Sambre and other parts of his conduct previous to the 10th of Auguft; on all which he put the moft malignant conftruction, and

and finished by proposing a decree of accusation against him.

"One general officer," said Kersaint, "has already answered your decree of accusation by a victory—How do you know that Dillon was not obeying the orders of Dumourier when he wrote the letter in question?"

Couthon, in answer to Kersaint, declared that no decree of accusation could be better founded than that now proposed against Arthur Dillon—He said, he would not take into consideration any thing laid to his charge before his letter to the Landgrave, but in the same breath he recapitulated whatever was most likely to injure him in the mind of the Convention respecting his conduct long before that time; and immediately after the tenth of August.

Couthon labours under a disease which renders him unable to walk, or even to stand; and which seems to have communicated its malignity to his disposition. He

He is always brought in the arms of his
fervant from his carriage into the Affembly, and is indulged in the liberty of
fpeaking without rifing from his feat—He
has the reputation of being a man of acute
parts; there is a mildnefs in his countenance that is not found in his opinions,
which are generally violent and fevere.
His fpeech rendered the enemies of Dillon
more furious—One member faid that he
feemed inclined to make no other ufe of
the army committed to his charge but as
a fafe-guard to conduct the enemies of
France out of the country; another obferved, that it was highly expedient that the
Convention fhould charge the Executive
Power to take particular care that Dillon
did not make his efcape. And a third afcended the tribune and made a motion
which terminated the climax of intem-
perance and injuftice—He propofed that
the three Commiffioners fhould be immediately

diately arrested as traitors for not having fuspended Dillon from his command, the moment he fhewed them a copy of the letter he had written to the Landgrave. Nothing could be more uncandid and cap- tious than the fpirit fhewn by thófe men on this occafion; they muft have known that Dillon had purfued the Heffians and Auf- trians with indefatigable activity to Ver- dun, and that it was in confequence of the batteries which he loft no time in erecting againft that town, that it foon after fur- rendered, but they could not forget Dillon's conduct on his firft receiving the accounts of the proceedings at Paris on the 10th of Auguft. Prudence and good policy indi- cate a different conduct; the beft way furely to conciliate men to a revolution, is to prefent them with greater advantages under the new government than they en- joyed under the old.——But thefe furious reformers, whilft they declaim againft the

2                                              tyranny

tyranny of the ancient government, prefent nothing in fupport of the new, but
accufations, poniards and guillotines.
With much difficulty, inftead of an immediate accufation, they at laft came to a refolution, that the Executive Council fhould
to-morrow ftate to the affembly all the circumftances relative to General Dillon's
conduct to the Landgrave of Heffe Caffel,
before they made any decree refpecting
him

October 14.

I went this morning to the Conventional Affembly, and was admitted into the
box where, on the 11th of Auguft, I had
feen the unfortunate family, now prifoners
in the temple, feated.

The hall and galleries were uncommonly
crowded, becaufe Dumourier, who arrived
in Paris laft night, was expected to come to
the Affembly this day.

The forenoon was fpent in debates, in
which

which Buzot, Vergniaud, and some other of the most distinguished members of the Convention took part. About one o'clock I saw one of the huissiers go to the President, and I heard him acquaint him, that Dumourier attended in the adjoining room.

The President, however, did not interrupt the debate, which continued for at least an hour after this information was given. It was known to some in the Assembly, that Dumourier was waiting to be called in; several members thinking the President was ignorant of that circumstance, went up and whispered him—he signified by a nod that he already knew it, and allowed the debate to continue.

It struck me as singular, that a General who in such critical circumstances had rendered the most important services to his country, and was just returned victorious, should be treated with such coolness.—I have no doubt it was done on purpose, and, in the republican fpirit, intended as a hint to the General not to overvalue his importance.

At laft, however, the Prefident read a letter from General Dumourier, in which he informs the Convention, that he defires to pay his duty to them, and waits their orders. A member moved that he fhould be admitted directly; and the General, attended by feveral officers, appeared at the bar, amidft the applaufe of the Affembly, and the acclamations of the galleries.——He is confiderably below the middle fize, of a fharp and intelligent countenance, and feems rather above 50 years of age. He pronounced the following difcourfe, throwing his eyes occafionally on a .paper which he held in his hand.

" Citoyens Legiflateurs —— La liberté triomphe par tout : guidée par la philofophie. elle parcourra l'univers, et s'affeoira fur tous les trônes, après avoir écrafé le defpotifme,

potifme, aprés avoir eclairé les peuples. Les loix conftitutionelles auxquelles vous allez travailler, feront la bafe du bonheur et de la fraternité des nations. Cette guerre-ci fera la derniére; et les tyrans et les privilégiés, trompés dans leurs criminels calculs, feront les feules victimes de cette lutte du pouvoir arbitraire contre la raifon.

"L'armée, dont la confiance de la nation m'avoit donné la conduite, a bien merité de la patrie: réduite, lorfque je l'ai jointe le 28 Août, à 17,000 hommes, déforganifée par des traitres que le châtiment et la honte pourfuivent par tout, elle n'a été effrayée ni du nombre, ni de la difcipline, ni des menaces, ni de la barbarie, ni des premiers fuccés de 80,000 fatellites du defpotifme. Les defilés de la forêt d'Argonne ont été les Thermopyles, où cette poignée de foldats de la liberté a prefenté, pendant quinze jours, à cette formidable armée une refiftance impofante. Plus heureux que les Spartiates, nous avons été fecourus par deux armées

I 2

animées

animées du même esprit que nous. Nous nous sommes rejoints dans le camp inexpugnable de Sainte Menehould. Les ennemis, au désespoir, ont voulu tenter une attaque, qui ajoute une victoire à la carrière militaire de mon collègue, et mon ami, Kellermann.

" Dans le camp de Sainte Menehould, les soldats de la liberté ont deployé d'autres vertus militaires, sans lesquelles le courage même peut être nuisible : la confiance en leurs chefs, l'obéissance, la patience et la persévérance. Cette partie de l'empire Français presente un sol aride, sans eau et sans bois, les Allemands s'en souviendront : leur sang impur fécondera, peut être, cette terre ingrate qui en est abreuvée. La faison étoit très pluvieuse et très froide : nos soldats étoient mal habillés, sans paille pour se coucher, sans couvertures, quelquefois deux jours sans pain, parceque la position de l'ennemi obligeoit les convois à de longs detours,

detours, par des chemins de traverse très *mauvais* en tout tems, et *gatés* par des pluies continuelles ; car je dois rend re justice aux regisseurs des vivres et des fourrages, qui, malgré tous les obstacles des mauvais chemins, de la saison pluvieuse, des mouvemens imprévus, ou que j'etois obligé de cacher, ont entretenu l'abondance autant qu'il leur à été possible ; et je suis bien aise de publier que c'est à leurs soins qu'on doit la bonne santé des soldats. Jamais je ne les ai vus murmurer. Les chants et la joie auroient fait prendre ce camp terrible pour un de ces camps de plaisance, ou le luxe des rois rassembloit autrefois des automates enrégimentés pour l'amusement de leurs maitresses ou de leurs enfans.

" L'espoir de vaincre soutenoit les soldats de la liberté ; leurs fatigues, leurs privations, ont été récompensées : l'ennemi a succombé sous la faim, la misére et les maladies ; cette armée formidable fut diminuée de moitié ; les cadavres et les chevaux morts jalonnent

lonnent

lonnent la route; Kellermann les pourſuit avec plus de 40,000 hommes, pendant qu'avec un pareil nombre je marche au ſécours du départément du Nord, et des malheureux et eſtimables Belges et Liégeois.

" Je ne ſuis venu paſſer quatre jours ici que pour arranger avec le Conſeil les details cette campagne d'hiver. J'en profite pour vous preſenter mes hommages. Je ne vous ferai point de nouveaux ſermens; je me montrerai digne de commander aux enfans de la liberté, et de ſoutenir les loix que le peuple ſouverain va ſe faire à lui même par votre organe *."

The

---

* Citizen Legiſlators—Liberty is every where tri-umphant; directed by philoſophy, ſhe will pervade the world, ſhe will cruſh deſpotiſm, open the eyes of man-kind, and ſeat herſelf on the throne of the univerſe. Thoſe conſtitutional laws which you are about to frame will ſerve as a baſis for the union and happineſs of nations. The preſent war will be the laſt of wars, and the tyrants of the world, deceived in their crimi-nal

The loud applause of all the deputies and spectators was renewed several times after

nal calculations, will be the sole victims of this contention between arbitrary power and reason.

The army entrusted to my command by the public confidence has deserved well of their country : reduced, when I joined it, to 17,000, and weakened by the machinations of shameless traitors, who I hope will one day meet the punishment they deserve, it was never intimidated by the numbers, the threats, the barbarity, or even by the first success of 80,000 slaves of despotism. The straits of the forest of Argonne was the Thermopylæ in which that handful of the soldiers of liberty, for fifteen successive days, presented a resistance which kept that formidable army in awe. More fortunate than the Spartans, we were succoured by two armies animated by the same spirit with ourselves; they joined us at the impregnable camp of Saint Menehould. The enemy, prompted by despair, hazarded an attack, which adds a victory to the military career of my friend and colleague Kellermann.

At St. Menehould the soldiers of freedom displayed other military virtues, without which valour itself may become hurtful, namely confidence in their officers,

I 4                                    obedience,

after Dumourier had concluded, before the
Prefident could make a reply, which he did

at

obedience, patience and perfeverance. That part of
France is barren, and deftitute of wood and water.
The Germans will remember it. Their flavifh blood
with which it is drenched, may perhaps render it more
fertile. The weather was uncommonly wet and cold,
our foldiers were ill clothed, they had neither ftraw to
lie upon, nor blankets to cover them, and fometimes
they were for two entire days without bread ; for fuch
was the pofition of the enemy that our convoys were
obliged to make a circuit, by crofs roads, at all times
bad, but then rendered worfe by the late exceffive
rains. Here I muft do juftice to the commiffaries of
ftores and forage : notwithftanding all the obftacles of
bad roads, bad weather, and of fudden movements, which
I could not always forefee, and, when I did, was often
obliged to conceal, they fupplied us as well as poffibly
could have been expected. And it is with pleafure I
take this opportunity of declaring, that the health of
your army is owing to their extraordinary care and diligence. Amidft all the difficulties I have ftated, the
foldiers were never heard to murmur : on hearing the
fongs of joy which refounded from every corner of our
warlike camp, it might have been miftaken for one of

thofe

at length in the following terms—" Citoyen General—L'accueil que vous venez de recevoir de la Convention Nationale, exprime

thofe camps of pleafure in which luxurious monarchs formerly affembled regimented automatons to manœuvre for the amufement of their children and miftreffes.

The hope of victory fupported the foldiers of liberty. Their fatigues and hardfhips have been fully compenfated. The enemy funk under fatigue, famine and difeafe. That formidable army was diminifhed one half; directed by the dead bodies of men and horfes, Kellermann purfues them at the head of forty thoufand men.

I purpofe to march immediately with the fame number to fuccour the department of the North, and to the relief of our efteemed and unfortunate friends, the inhabitants of Brabant and Liege.

I am come hither, for four days, to fettle with the council the plan of our winter campaign—I avail myfelf of the opportunity to pay my duty to you. I bind myfelf by no new oaths; but I will fhew myfelf worthy of commanding the fons of liberty, and faithful in fupport of thofe laws which the fovereign people are now about to frame through you.

mieux

mieux que je ne le pourrois faire sa satisfaction de vos services, et la haute opinion qu'elle a conçue de vos talens et de votre patriotisme. Continuez, Citoyen General, continuez à diriger les soldats de la liberté dans le chemin de la victoire; continuez a vous couvrir de lauriers; continuez a bien servir la patrie, et vous acquirerez de nouveaux droits a la reconnoissance de la république.

" La Convention Nationale vous invite, ainsi que vos fréres d'armes à la seance *."

One of the deputies then moved, that the

---

* Citizen General—The reception you have met with from the National Convention is a stronger testimony than any expression of mine could be, of their approbation of your conduct, and of their high opinion of your talents and patriotism. Citizen General, continue to lead the soldiers of liberty in the road of victory—continue to gather laurels—persist in serving your country, and you will acquire new claims to the gratitude of the republic.

Con—

Convention fhould authorize the Prefident to demand of General Dumourier what he thought refpecting the affair of Dillon.

This was done accordingly, and Dumourier readily anfwered, that he had read a copy of the letter in queftion; that he confidered it merely as a bravado on the part of Dillon, and of little importance, efpecially as General Dillon had foon after purfued the Heffians with the utmoft vigour.

Having faid this, Dumourier, with the officers who accompanied him, entered the hall—Many of the deputies rofe and faluted him, after which he feated himfelf among them.

Two officers then appeared at the bar, one of whom addreffing the Affembly faid, " Legiflators, the Adjutant General of the army of the North prefents you with a ftandard taken in the midft of fire and flaughter from the French emigrants; as foon as it was feen by the foldiers of liberty, they

they broke through the fquadrons of thofe traitors, and tore it from them."

The Prefident having made a fuitable anfwer, Vergniaud obferved, that feveral ftandards which had been won from defpotifm were already hanging in the hall; that as thofe were honourable trophies of the victories of the republic, they were worthy of being expofed to the view of the citizens:——but as for this, he added, around which the enemies of their native country, a fet of affaffins whom you have deftined to the fcaffold fought:——this odious flag ought not to fhock your fight; I move, therefore, that it be delivered into the hands of the executioner, and publicly committed to the flames.

This propofal was applauded and adopted. Dumourier remained in the Affembly till it broke up. He was dreffed in the uniform of a General Officer, blue and gold lace; he is faid to be a great deal lefs

5                                                    attentive

attentive to drefs than is ufual in France;
but in any drefs I fhould know him to be a
Frenchman. He poffeffes the peculiar vivacity of air and manner that diftinguifhes
the natives of this country. I underftand
that he is remarkably entertaining and
agreeable in converfation; that though he
has indulged in pleafure, and yielded to
diffipation, yet he is capable of the moft
indefatigable exertion, both of body and
mind, when the importance of the object
requires it; that he has always been fonder
of pleafure than of money; and ever ready
to facrifice both for renown. His enemies,
who allow that he poffeffes great acutenefs
of mind, and the moft unfhaken courage,
throw doubts upon his fteadinefs in other
refpects. His military talents have been
fufficiently evinced in the courfe of the laft
memorable campaign: without the fingular
circumftances which raifed him to command, and drew them into action, the
man

man who with inferior force baffled the attempts of the moſt renowned Generals of the age, would have remained undiſtinguiſhed and ſubordinate to thoſe on whom birth without talents, or age which has not profited by experience, ſo often devolves the command of armies.

Paris, October 13.

The minds of the Pariſians are greatly elevated by the wonderful ſucceſs of the French arms. The repulſe of the Auſtrians at Lille, the fortunate expedition of General Anſelme into the county of Nice, the reduction of Savoy, the rapid progreſs of Cuſtine on the Rhine, and above all, the retreat of the Pruſſians, are events of a nature to have raiſed the national vanity of a people leſs ſuſceptible of its influence than the French.

They ſeem convinced that their arms are irreſiſtible, and they begin to indulge the

moſt

moſt romantic ideas. Of all failings to which mankind are liable, vanity is the moſt comfortable; and perhaps it may be fortunate for a people entangled in circum-ſtances rather vexatious, to have this for a compenſation. But ſhould the Convention be affected in the ſame way, it may be attended with afflicting conſequences to the country. I heard ſome things this day in the Aſſembly, and alſo from one of the deputies, with whom I had ſome converſation ſince, that give reaſon to ſuſpect that the romantic notions above alluded to are not confined to the people without doors.

The late ſucceſſes are imputed, beſide the valour of the troops, to the ſuperiour dexterity, ſagacity, and natural quickneſs of the French cannoniers over thoſe of all other nations.

It has been propoſed to erect a monument in the town of Varennes in commemoration

tion of the flight of two kings, meaning Lewis XVI. who fled to that town, and the King of Pruffia, who lately retired through it; thofe who make the propofal give this infcription for the monument, *Regibus fugatis;* and add this reflection, *Dans peu, chaque état aura fa Varennes.*

Every ftroke of fatire directed againft kings is fure of being well received by the Convention.

The War Minifter feems fenfible of this—He tranfmitted to it lately an intercepted letter, which he pretends is from fome perfon at Berlin, addreffed to the Pruffian Minifter, Bifchofswerder, in which the writer afferts, that the people are highly difpleafed at the part their fovereign has taken againft the French nation, and that the following epigram on that fubject is read with delight—" Un jour Dieu voulut épargner une ville a caufe d'un jufte qui y étoit;

y étoit ; aujourd'hui un prince Allemand veut faire périr toute la France pour un imbécille couronné qui s'y trouve."

But in the midſt of this exaltation on account of their ſucceſs againſt external enemies, and of all this ſeverity againſt kings, the repreſentatives of the people ſeem not to have it in their power to puniſh the inſolence of certain perſons within the city of Paris.

The Convention decreed, that the election of the municipal officers of Paris ſhould be by ballot. Certain turbulent people, who wiſh the electors to be overawed by the mob, diſapproved of this, and prevailed on the ſection of the Theatre François to proceed according to the old method of voting aloud.——For this act of diſobedience and contempt the Preſident and Secretary of the ſection were ordered to appear at the bar of the Aſſembly.——Being queſtioned by the Preſident, they anſwered in a ſtyle that by no means indicated repentance; yet as they did not avow an intention of perfisting in their disobedience, a very slight apology was accepted, and the two culprits were admitted to the honours of the sitting—of course this feeble attempt to maintain authority will encourage disobedience. Buzot took this occasion to urge the necessity of adopting the measure of having a body of troops at the command of the Convention, to ensure obedience to its decrees, and protect the persons of the deputies.

There are certain members of the Assembly, who, deriving their importance entirely from the favour of the rabble, are prepared to oppose this measure; but as the majority approve of it, their opposition, it is thought, will be soon overcome.

October 14.

I was sitting this morning in the Conventional Assembly, when suddenly the

8

firing

firing of cannon was heard——This produced some signs of emotion among the deputies, who, like me, were ignorant of the caufe.

Having been accuftomed to fuch founds on account of victories, or fome other occafion of public rejoicing, a noife of this nature was formerly apt to excite chearful and agreeable ideas only. The impreffion I had in the prefent inftance was of a very different nature. The firing which took place when the Royal Family were fitting in the fame box on the 10th of Auguft, inftantly fprang up in my mind; an idea clofely linked with that of the execrable fecond of September, and the dreadful peal which was the harbinger of three continued days and nights of blood and flaughter.

Thofe unpleafant reflections were removed when I was informed that the firing in the prefent cafe was on account of the feftival which had been decreed for the

fuccefs

fuccefs of the arms of the Republic in Savoy.

I immediately left the Affembly, and went through the gardens of the Tuileries to the Place de Louis XV. now called the Place de la Revolution.

A ftatue, with the emblems of Liberty, was placed on the pedeftal on which the equeftrian ftatue of Lewis XV. formerly ftood. On the eaft and weft fide of the pedeftal was infcribed, République Françoife, 1792 : on the fouth fide, Entrée de Montefquiou à Chambéry, Capitale du Duché de Savoye; on the north, Entrée d'Anfelme, dans le Comté de Nice et Montalban.

A large body of the national guards, with a number of armed citizens from all the different feétions of Paris, with difplayed banners, marched in proceffion to the place.

A deputation from the National Convention,

tion, and another from the Municipality of
Paris, attended at an amphitheatre erected
for the purpofe, near the ftatue of Liberty.
A great number of Savoyards of both fexes
and all conditions, holding each other by
the hand, and with every appearance of joy,
preceded by a band of mufic, marched
between two long ranks of men armed
with pikes, to the fquare, and were received by the acclamations of an immenfe
number of fpectators. All the colours and
banners of the different regiments affembled
in the fquare were arranged around the
ftatue of Liberty. A numerous band of
mufic then performed the hymn of the
Marfeillois, and that favourite fong was
fung by fome chofen fingers of the band;
and moft of the people with whom this vaft
and magnificent fquare was crowded joined
in the chorus. After which the cannon
were repeatedly fired, and in the intervals

the

the fky refounded with univerfal fhouts of Vive la République!

The hymn of the Marfeillois is called for every evening at every theatre in Paris, and nothing can exceed the enthufiafm with which it is heard.

I went laft night to a new mufical piece called the Ephefian Matron. The houfe was pretty full, but the appearance of the audience was very different from what I re-collect to have been ufual on fuch occafions before the Revolution.

The women ftill difplay fancy and fome degree of elegance in their drefs, but the men are univerfally dreffed with the utmoft fimplicity. I fat in the parquet next to a remarkably tall man wrapt in a drab co-loured great coat, who feemed between fixty and feventy years of age. On his withdrawing, I was told that this was Admiral d'Eftaign, who commanded the

French

French fleet and army in America and the West Indies in the laſt war.

The conduct of the Count d'Eſtaign was more univerſally approved of during the late war, than ſince the Revolution.

He was Commander of the national guards of Verſailles in October 1789, when a mob from Paris broke into the palace, murdered ſome of the guards, and committed many ſhameful exceſſes.

M. d'Eſtaign appeared to be at once a friend to the principles of the Revolution, and an aſſiduous courtier.

In a nation whoſe conſtitution is mellowed by time, and where the ſubjects have experienced the bleſſing of that liberty which the ſpirit of their anceſtors obtained, united to the tranquillity ariſing from the monarchical form of their government; a love of freedom not only is compatible with attachment to the monarch,

K 4

but,

but, as long as he governs according to the principles of the constitution, those sentiments mutually strengthen each other.

But, in a nation on whose government the scions of freedom are but newly engrafted, at the expence of the monarch, and without having hitherto produced any palatable fruit, the case is different. The struggles and animosities between those who produced the alteration, and those who opposed it, are too recent; mutual suspicion and a sense of mutual accusations are still existing; and he who attempts to be the friend of both parties, is trusted by neither.

M. d'Estaign has taken no part in the latest transactions; he seems to desire to live unnoticed, and hitherto he has been undisturbed.

October 15.

The emigration of the noblesse has been so very extensive, that it is rare to meet with any person of name within the walls of Paris, particularly any who have ever been

been employed or entrufted with the ancient government. Yet thofe of this defcription, who venture to remain in France, are perhaps in lefs danger in Paris than in a provincial town; becaufe in the capital there is always a fufficient force to fupprefs *partial* and *incidental* tumults, provided the magiftrates are difpofed to call it forth, and make ufe of it; whereas in the villages and provincial towns a tumult may be excited, which the magiftrates, were they ever fo much inclined, are unable to quell.

A groundlefs fufpicion, or a calumny invented and propagated by an enemy, may kindle the fury of a few fanatics, and the head of the perfon who is the object of it, may be fixed on a pike before the magiftrate can affemble force to protect him.

His innocence is made apparent when it is too late; every body laments his fate: the murderers however are excufed, becaufe they were mifled (*egaré* is the palliative word

word used on such occasions) by the no-
bleft of all errors, too much zeal for their
country's good; and tranquillity is reftored
only till frefh fufpicions and calumnies excite new murders.

I heard a petition read in the Convention from the widow of a fword-cutler of
Charleville. A report had been fpread
that he furnifhed arms to the enemy: this
immediately roufed the people, and in the
firft fury of their civifme, as it is called,
they cut off his head. Very foon after it
appeared that the report was falfe, and that
the unfortunate fword-cutler had always
been a zealous patriot. Some of the deputies feemed very much fhocked at this; but
I heard one obferve, with great coolnefs,
that he was forry for what the people of
Charleville had done; and then added, with
an air of fagacity, " but the beft people in
the world are liable to be miftaken."

However ready the French are to accufe
individuals,

individuals, the inhabitants of the moft defpotic country are not more afraid of fpeaking treafon, than the French are of faying
any thing to the difadvantage of the *people :*
no nation was ever more indulgent to the
caprices of its tyrant, than France is at prefent, to that moft capricious and bloody of
all tyrants, Le Peuple Souverain.

Some of the battalions which have been
lately raifed at Paris, though retained in
tolerable fubordination while they continued within the capital and furrounded
with the national guards of all the fections,
have been guilty of great exceffes fince they
left it——The firft divifion of the gendarmes
à pied de Paris, on entering lately into the
town of Cambray, broke open the prifon,
and fet all the prifoners at liberty except
one man, whom they, in their wifdom,
thought juftly confined.——On thefe troops
leaving the town, all the prifoners whom
they had fet free were again confined by
order

order of the magiftrates ; but the fecond divifion paffing through the fame town the day following, threw open the prifons once more, and beheaded the unfortunate perfon whom their companions had kept in confinement when they gave freedom to all the other prifoners. They murdered, in the fame manner, feveral of their officers, who were endeavouring to prevent their exceffes, and bring them to order. An official account of thofe alarming tranfactions has been read to the Convention, and was immediately referred to the war committee ; but what makes it doubtful whether any effectual meafures will be taken to punifh thofe affaffins, is, that Marat continues to palliate, and almoft to juftify every crime of this nature that is committed, whether by the populace or foldiers : until the Affembly are able and willing to fupprefs his Journal, and punifh the Author, what hope is there that they will have it in their power to remedy

or

or prevent that blood-fhed and anarchy to which the fpeeches and writings of this man fo greatly contribute?

October 16.

The committee appointed to fuperintend the camp and entrenchments forming near Paris, made fome propofitions yefterday to the Convention. They were not agreed to: one member faid, that the pitiful farce of *la precautione inutile* had been acted too long, and propofed that an immediate ftop fhould be put to that work, which, after fome debate, was decreed.

All ideas of defence are now thought ufelefs.——Nothing but attack, and taking vengeance on the enemies, and maintaining the dignity of the Republic, is now fpoken of.

If, however, there be dignity in affuming fome degree of loftinefs in tranfacting with the powerful Potentates who invaded the country, there furely is none in affecting a dictatorial tone with the weakeft of their neighbours.

neighbours. This domineering fpirit however appears too much in the conduct of the Convention towards Geneva, the comfortable condition of whofe citizens for a feries of years has fufficiently proved that the happinefs of the fubject does not depend on the extent of the State's territories. Geneva has been confidered as the nurfery of freedom, and has long maintained, by the prudence of her councils, that independency which was obtained by the valour of her citizens, whofe prudent conduct the French would do well to imitate, if they wifh the Republic of France to be as durable as that of Geneva.

Some members of the Convention have taken offence, becaufe Geneva lately thought proper to demand thofe fuccours from the cantons of Berne and Zurick, to which they are intitled on emergencies like the prefent by exifting treaties.

Although France had not invaded Savoy, the

the ftate of diforder in which the former has been, the exceffes which have been committed by the French army in various parts of the country, in fpite of the decrees of the Convention at Paris, rendered it highly expedient for the Republic of Geneva to take every meafure in her power to fecure the town from a fudden attack. For, however well difpofed the Convention might be, who could fay that a band of patriots, fome independent portion of the peuple fouverain, would not, without confulting the Convention, feize on Geneva? But meafures of precaution became ftill more neceffary when France declared war againft the King of Sardinia, and when a French army was ready to invade Savoy; for, as the poffeffion of the city of Geneva might be advantageous to either of the armies, in order to preferve a ftrict neutrality, it was neceffary to guard it from both. The Republic therefore received within the walls of Geneva

1609

1600 men of the militia of Zurick and Berne ; a force which, joined to that of the citizens, might fecure the town from being feized by a fudden affault, but could not be confidered as an act of hoftility againft France, even although there had been no previous treaty between Geneva and the Swifs cantons by which fhe was entitled to claim this fuccour.

Geneva is acknowledged by all the powers of Europe as an independent ftate : it feems contradictory to acknowledge fovereignty and independency in a ftate, and then complain of fo natural an exercife of it as the calling in the aid of neutral powers to enable it to maintain ftrict neutrality.

The Convention feems, however, to have been guilty of this contradiction, and at the fame time difplayed unbecoming pride in fupercilioufly paffing to the order of the day at the meeting of yefterday, after hearing the explanations from the council of

4                                    Geneva

neva read, and in approving of the haughty conduct of their commissioners towards that state. This ill accords with the prudent and pacific tenor of the declarations which the National Assembly formerly made, and stamps credit on the assertions of the enemies of the Revolution, that the treatment which Geneva now receives from the new Republic is a specimen of what all the neighbouring States may expect.

Although it may be thought natural that a monarch, particularly an arbitrary one, should, from motives of vanity, avarice, or ambition, endeavour to extend his dominions by war and conquest; yet the vanity or avarice of a private citizen of Paris, Lyons, Marseilles, or any other part of France, can be little gratified by the accession of new provinces. France, therefore, being now a Republic, the ambitious and restless spirit of her kings, that fatal source to which the other States of Europe have imputed almoſt all the wars of the two laſt centuries, being now dried up, long peace and tranquillity is to be expected when this new form is acknowledged and eſtabliſhed.

This reaſoning ſeems plauſible *a priori :*— it is unfortunate, however, that the hiſtory of the world ſhews that Republican States have been inſpired with as violent a deſire of conqueſt, and as reſtleſs an ambition, as any monarch from the age of Alexander to that of Lewis XIV. And the ſpirit which the new Republic of France begins already to manifeſt, gives no reaſon to expect that the philoſophy from which ſhe boaſts her origin, has taught her more moderation than her predeceſſors.

Independent of the diſlike one naturally feels of an act of power unſupported by juſtice, I confeſs I could not ſee my old friends, the citizens of Geneva, treated in this manner without indignation.

When the Convention is conſidered as main-

maintaining the independency of their country againſt a powerful league, and undiſmayed by the idea that all the powers of Europe may join in the combination; it is impoſſible not to reſpect their firmneſs. But when they are ſeen behaving with haughty injuſtice to a neighbouring people devoid of the power of reſiſtance or retaliation, and reſpectable from their talents and virtues only, the conduct of the Convention excites a very different ſentiment.

October 16.

The Convention ſhewed more moderation this day in their conduct towards the Republic of Genoa, than they had manifeſted towards Geneva ; although for many obvious reaſons it might have been expected they would have been partial rather to the latter.

The miniſter for foreign affairs informed them, that in a quarrel which had happened

L 2

in

In the port of Genoa, between some Venetian soldiers and the crew of the French frigate Juno, the flag of the frigate had been pulled down and torn in pieces; in consequence of which the Venetians had been imprisoned, and condemned, by a decree of the Senate of Genoa, to provide the frigate in a new flag before they should be set at liberty. The minister gave it as his opinion, that as he understood the French sailors were the aggressors, no farther notice should be taken of this affair, but that the Convention should remain satisfied with the decision of the Senate of Genoa.

Several of the members differed in opinion from the minister. One deputy said, that the decision of the Senate of Genoa would have been considered as sufficiently satisfactory under the ancient government, because then ships of war were given by the favour of princes, of their mistresses, and of their valets; and those appointed to command

mand them were of as frivolous characters
as thofe by whofe influence the appointments
were obtained. But France being now formed into a Republic, where talents, exertion,
and the manly virtues alone can lead to pro-
motion, or fituations of confidence, and
above all, at this time, when the caufe of
freedom is triumphant, more ample redrefs
fhould be infifted on.

I perceive that many people expect a
great improvement, both in the army and
navy, in all effential points, from the new
order of things which began in France on
the 20th of laft September.

It will foon be put to trial whether the
rough Republican qualities will render men
better officers than that gallant fpirit and
delicate fenfe of honour, which, in fpite of
effeminacy and corruption, always formed
part of the character of the French nobleffe.

I have had frequent converfations with
deputies who are fuppofed to have con-

fiderable

fiderable weight in the Convention, concerning the probable fate of the King: they feem
to be perfuaded that the majority of the Affembly, including the moft refpectable members, are inclined to banifhment, and are endeavouring to poftpone every motion tending to bring on the trial till the people have
cooled fo far as to be fatisfied with fuch a
fentence, which they fear is not the cafe at
prefent. A remark made by one of the deputies, it is thought, had great effect on the
Convention: the remark was, " Charles I.
eut des fucceffeurs, les Tarquins n'en eu-
rent point *."

It is a dreadful thing to think that a judi-
cial or legiflative affembly, fuppofed to be fupreme, and which ought to be influenced
by no confiderations but thofe of juftice
and public good, fhould, in a matter of this

* Charles the Firft had fucceffors, the Tarquins had
none.

moment to their country, and to their own confciences, be under any kind of conftraint.

As far as I can perceive however, the real çitizens, or bourgeoife of Paris, by no means defire the death of the King; and if by the people is underftood the profligate idle rabble of the fuburbs, and the wretches who are hired to clamour in the public places, what probability is there that they will ever cool, or be fatisfied with any decifion except what thofe who hire them, or their own favage difpofitions, fuggeft ?

This very day, in the Convention, I had an opportunity of judging how little the hopes given by the deputies above mentioned are to be relied on. For at a time when there was no queftion regarding the King, a member afcended the tribune and faid, " He was going to remind the Convention of a part of their duty to their country, of the higheft importance, namely, the procefs of

L 4 Lewis

Lewis Capet (this is the name they generally give the King), which had been too long postponed; he therefore demanded that a day might be fixed for his trial, that the wrongs of the nation might be avenged by the blood of that traitor."

By trial it is evident he meant execution. I understand his name is Hardy, deputy of the department de Seine Inferieure.——He is a well-looking young man; but the harshness of his sentiment formed a strong contrast with his countenance. This gave rise to many intemperate and foolish expressions from other members who supported the motion for the trial, which they also used as synonimous with execution. One talked of the martyrs of Liberty who had fallen before the palace on the 10th of August, whose ghosts called for vengeance on the perjured Lewis. And when another suggested that " the papers respecting the King's treachery should be printed and delivered

livered to the members, and that it would require a confiderable time before judgment could be pronounced; a third afferted, that " Lewis Capet could not be confidered as King, becaufe royalty was abolifhed in France—What is he then? why, a fimple individual, in a ftate of confinement for trial : but the law, continued he, exprefsly fays, that every perfon confined for a crime fhall be brought to his trial within the fpace of 24 hours of his being arrefted ; the affaffin Lewis has been too long confined, and ought to be brought to trial and punifhed as foon as poffible."

On this, as on other occafions, I obferved that the people in the galleries redoubled their applaufe as often as cruel things were faid, and violent meafures propofed. This feemed to become a motive with thofe who wifhed to ingratiate themfelves with the multitude, to proceed in making new propofals; the laft always more violent than the

2                                        former.

former. Yet the difcuffion was not premeditated, at leaft it feemed to me to arife accidentally.

Ruhl, one of the members for the department of the Lower Rhine juft arrived from Strafbourg, informed the Convention, that he had on the road paffed a party of dragoons who were conducting thirteen Emigrants to Paris, who had been taken in arms on the frontiers——He was afraid that thofe unhappy men were in danger of being deftroyed by the populace as foon as they fhould arrive, and thought it his duty to acquaint the Convention that meafures might be taken for their fafety until they fhould be legally tried. Whether Ruhl introduced the Emigrants with an intention to divert the Convention from the trial of the King, I know not ; but for fome time it had that effect, the debate turned to the fubject of the Emigrants——But one member feemed difpleafed with this, and abruptly exclaimed

exclaimed, There are others more guilty than all these Emigrants, and whose trial is more pressing. " Je veux parler de Louis XVI. je demande que son procés commence."

The debate recommenced respecting the trial, and soon became as intemperate as at first. From the hard unfeeling things that were uttered, one might have thought that the hearts of the disputants were of flint: they struck fire from each other so fast, and wrought themselves into such heat, that I expected some violent resolution would have been taken directly.

Téte à téte, or in a very small circle, the French are nearly as calm, and generally more ingenious, than most of their neighbours; but a numerous assembly of Frenchmen almost always become turbulent.

Barbaroux of Marseilles then rose, and had the address to put an end to the debate: the argument which proved effectual, did

little

little honour to thofe on whom it had influence. He began by afferting the right of
the Convention, in confequence of the
power tranfmitted by the people, to judge
the King.——After having expatiated on this
topic at fome length, he added, " But it is
expected by all Europe that you will proceed in a bufinefs of that important nature
with all poffible prudence and deliberation :"
[Here fomething of a murmur was heard in
the gallery]—becaufe, added he raifing his
voice, perhaps Lewis and Marie Antoinette
are not the only criminals whom the fword
of juftice has to ftrike."

He no fooner uttered this, than the in-
cipient murmur ended in acclamations of
applaufe.——The certainty which this implied
not only that the king and queen would
be tried, but condemned and executed, and
that feveral others would meet with the
fame fate, feemed to pleafe them fo much,
that they were fatisfied with a delay, which
perhaps

perhaps would not have otherwise been carried, and which was all that the moderate part of the Convention (who were convinced of the injustice and imprudence of proceeding against the King) durst at that time propose, or had reason to expect.

October 17.

General Dumourier set out early this morning to take the command of the army destined against Austrian Brabant. Some nights ago, accompanied with some of his officers, he attended the meeting of the Jacobins: it is good policy in the General of a French army to pay this piece of respect to a society which has so great and such extensive influence.——He addressed them to this purpose : " Citizens, you have torn the history of despotism, you have saved France, your efforts in the cause of Freedom are engraved by the hand of Liberty on the hearts of all good Frenchmen :

we

we are going to finifh what we have begun, and we will fulfil your expectations, or perifh in the attempt."——Danton, who was prefident, anfwered him to the following effect: " Citizen General, when La Fayette took flight, you did not defpair of the fafety of the Republic ; you rallied our troops weakened by treachery and divifion ; you repelled with a few foldiers the numerous armies of tyrants ; you have deferved well of your country :——under your direction the republican pike fhall break the regal fceptre, and the cap of liberty fhall annihilate the diadem——We are your brethren and your friends, and your name fhall make a fhining figure in our hiftory." Other members fpoke in praife of Dumourier, who at length retired amid the applaufe of the fociety.

I went this evening to the fociety of the Jacobins, and was witnefs of a fcene of a different kind, and which was little to be

5
expected

expected fo foon after what is above de-
fcribed.

It will be proper to mention here an affair
which happened about eight days before the
General's arrival at Paris.

Dumourier had written a letter to the Convention, informing them, that the Parifian
battalions of Mauconfeil and Republicain had
committed a crime which threw difhonour
on the French nation, by maffacring four
Pruffian deferters in the town of Rethel, in
the department of Ardennes. The particulars of this fhocking affair he tranfmitted
to the minifter of war, and they appear in a
letter from General Chazot to Dumourier,
which was read in the Convention. The
four men in queftion were dragoons, who
deferted from the Pruffians to Rethel, where
they inlifted in the French army. Some
foldiers of the battalions above mentioned,
having met the four deferters in a tavern,
picked a quarrel with them, abufed them as
traitors to their country, dragged them into
the

the ftreets, and threatened to behead them. Chazot, who was in the town, hearing of this, fent orders to protect the men; but the greateft part of the foldiers of both battalions being now joined, formed foo ftrong a body for any force the General had to ufe againft them : all that his meffengers could obtain of thofe mutineers therefore was, that they fhould carry the deferters before the General, which was done accordingly. He ufed every argument and every perfuafion (for no other means were in his power) to prevail on thefe mutinous madmen to ufe no violence to the deferters : fo far from fucceeding, fome of the wretches cried out, *Si le Général s'oppofe à nos defirs, il faut l'expédier \*.*

Chazot, finding that his remonftrances only rendered them more furious, pufhed through the crowd, and with difficulty efcaped to his horfe and rode away. He was no

---

\* If the General oppofes our wifhes, he muft be cut off.

fooner

fooner gone than the wretched deferters were cut in pieces.

The abfurdity of this abominable deed almoft equals its barbarity, and this remark may be made with juftice on many tranfactions in this country fince the 10th of Auguft. Common prudence might have prevented fome of the moft unjuftifiable, without the fuggeftions of humanity, and humanity would have prevented them, even where prudence did not exift. This atrocious deed deftroyed the hope of weakening the Pruffian army by defertion, which had been fo great an objedt with the Convention, that a penfion of 100 livres had been decreed to every foldier who fhould defert from the Pruffian army to the French; and while it put an end to every expectation of this kind, it alfo deftroyed every hope of quarter, or mercy, when any of themfelves fell into the hands of the Pruffians *.

To

* I have heard it afferted fince my return to Eng-land,

To expiate this guilt, and vindicate the character of his army, Dumourier had given orders to General Bournonville to march a body of troops with some pieces of artillery against the two battalions, who were ordered to ground their arms, and submit, on pain of being immediately put to death. They submitted accordingly, their colours were sent to their Sections, their arms and uniforms taken from them, and the men themselves ordered in that disgraceful state to Paris, there to wait the pleasure of the Convention.

It afterwards appeared that the unfortu-

land, that there was a considerable desertion from the Prussians to the French at the Camp of St. Menehould, and that a fear of its increasing was the chief reason of the Duke of Brunswick's retreat; which reason he took great pains to conceal. But as the Duke's retreat is sufficiently accounted for independent of that, I have allowed the account of it to remain as it was in my Journal, according to the intelligence I received at Paris.

nate

nate men who had been thus murdered, were not native Pruffians, but Frenchmen, who had enlifted in the Pruffian army before the Revolution, and had feized the firft opportunity of returning to their countrymen.

Marat having heard of this circumftance, publifhed in his journal, and pofted on the walls, accufations againft the General, and vindications of the affaffins. The former he defcribes as a debauchee, as an old valet of the court, and, which includes every thing that is wicked, as an ariftocrate. The latter he reprefents as worthy men, full of patriotifm, which prompted them to anticipate by a few hours the blow of the executioner on the necks of four traitors. He afferts, that Dumourier, Chazot, and others, calumniate thofe innocent battalions, on purpofe to render the citizens of Paris, and particularly the General Council of the Commune, *to whom France owes the revolu-*

M 2 *tion*

*tion of the tenth of August,* odious to the country; that the four deferters were not Pruffians, as had been perfidioufly publifhed by Dumourier, but French Emigrants, taken in arms, and therefore defervedly put to death by the patriotic battalions.

He likewife accufes Dumourier of having connived at the efcape of the Pruffians out of France, when he might have forced their camp, and obliged them to lay down their arms; and alfo for having quitted his own army at this critical time, on purpofe to caroufe with drunkards and opera girls.

I never was more furprifed in my life than when Marat, having afcended the tribune at the Jacobins, began to repeat thefe affertions. The man's audacity is equal to any thing, but what I thought full as wonderful was the degree of patience, and even approbation, with which he was heard. The houfe was crowded, and it contains a very

numerous

numerous audience. When Marat is in the tribune, he holds his head as high as he can, and endeavours to assume an air of dignity—He can make nothing of that; but amidst all the exclamations and signs of hatred and disgust which I have seen manifested against him, the look of self approbation which he wears is wonderful—so far from ever having the appearance of fear, or of deference, he seems to me always to contemplate the Assembly from the tribune, either with the eyes of menace, or contempt.

He speaks in a hollow croaking voice, with affected solemnity, which in such a diminutive figure would often produce laughter, were it not suppressed by horror at the character and sentiments of the man.

After having insisted for some time on the guilt of the murdered, the innocence of the murderers, and the cruelty of Dumourier, he informed the society, that he had

M 3                                    thought

thought it his duty to question the General in perfon, that he might learn from himfelf what he had to fay in defence of his conduct towards thofe two meritorious battalions. Marat then gave a very circumftantial account of his having called on Dumourier the night before he left Paris; that he had been accompanied by two members of the National Convention, one of them I think he called Bentoble, the name of the other I do not recollect. At Dumourier's they were informed, that the General was at the Theatre des Variétés, and was not to fup at home. " A number of carriages, and brilliant illuminations," continued Marat, " indicated to us where this fon of Mars was fupping with the fons and daughters of Thalia; we found foldiers within and without: after traverfing fome chambers filled with pikemen, mufketeers, dragoons, huffars, the warlike fuite of the General, we came to a fpacious room full of company, at the door

of

of which was Santerre, commander of the Parisian guards, performing the functions of a lackey, or an usher. He announced me aloud, which I was sorry for, because it might have made those persons disappear whom I should have wished to have seen; but I *did* see some, whom it is of use to mention for the better comprehending the operations of the ruling party in the Convention, and letting the public know who are the state jugglers with whom the commander of our armies is most connected. To pass over the officers of the national guards, the aid-de-camps, and others, who paid their court to the great Dumourier, continued he, I saw in this august company the ministers Roland and Le Brun, attended by Kerfaint and La Source. As my name had thrown the company into confusion, I probably did not remark all who were present, I only remember these conspirators whom I have named; but it was early, and

it

it is probable that Vergniaud, Buzot, Ra-
baud, Lacroix, Guadet, Genfonner, and
Barbaroux, were also at this entertainment;
for they all belong to the fame gang. At
fight of me, continued Marat, looking very
fierce, Dumourier was appalled."

At this a number of the fociety of Jacobins burft into laughter; and one perfon
near me faid, "That is what he was not at
the fight of the Pruffian army."

When the laugh was over, Marat, with an
unaltered countenance, refumed, "At fight
of me Dumourier was appalled; which is
not to be wondered at," continued he, erecting his head, ftanding on his tiptoes, and
looking very fierce, "fince I am known to
be the terror of all the enemies of my country." He proceeded to inform the fociety,
that he had defired to fpeak with Dumourier in another room; and being there, had
afked an account of all the particulars relative to the four deferters: that the General
had

had told him he had already fent thofe particulars to the War Minifter, and to the Convention, and had no other account to give." Marat concluded by faying, " that he had put other queftions to the General, which difconcerted him fo much that, inftead of attempting to anfwer them, he was forced to fneak away abruptly with affeincluded difdain; and fo, having made it clear that he could not juftify his conduct, I left this affemblage of generals, and actors, and minifters, and mountebanks, to pafs the night together.

Marat endeavoured to enliven this recital with a few jokes, which excited laughter in the Jacobin Society, but had not that effect on me.—Marat attempting pleafantry, increafes the horror which his appearance creates; it gives fomething of the fenfation which I imagine I fhould have, if a murderer, after cutting a man's throat by a

dexterous

dexterous ftroke of a knife, fhould fmile in my face, and tip me the wink.

When I went to the Convention this morning, the firft thing that ftruck me was the murky figure of Marat ftanding on the fteps which lead to the tribune, watching an opportunity of entering it: there was a great unwillingnefs to hear him, and he waited near two hours before he obtained the right to fpeak, fome other member being always pointed to by the Prefident.

Marat often exclaimed againft this to no purpofe, and feizing a moment when the tribune was empty, he began to addrefs the Affembly without the Prefident's permiffion; but his voice was drowned in the outcry againft him from all corners.—— At length I heard De la Croix, the prefident, fay to thofe near him, " Je crois qu'il vaudroit mieux laiffer parler ce gueux là ;"

and

and raifing his voice, he added, " Marat je vous donne la parole, mais je ne vous promets pas de vous la maintenir *.

Marat then entered the tribune, and began the fame invective againft Dumourier that I heard him pronounce laft night at the Jacobins.——He was interrupted by cries of indignation from all fides : one member addreffed the Prefident to filence him, and not permit a man who was a difgrace to the Affembly to calumniate citizens of the greateft worth : another added, that his calumnies were praife ; all feemed to hold him in execration.

During the uproar, Marat ftood with an undifturbed air, looking down on the Affembly. When the clamour abated fo that his voice could be heard, he faid, with an air of irony, and in a tone of forrow,

* I believe we had beft allow the fellow to fpeak.

Marat, I give you the right to fpeak, but I cannot promife to maintain it with you long.

" I am

" I am really grieved to behold such inde-cent behaviour in the Affembly——Is it not fingular that the perfon whom you try to overwhelm with unjuft clamours, fhould be more concerned for your honour than you are yourfelves? Is it not extraordinary that you fhould be fo much prejudiced againft a man animated with patriotifm?"—— Here there was an univerfal laugh; but when he attempted to refume his invectives againft Dumourier and Chazot, the clamour re-commenced, and the Affembly fhewed the utmoft impatience.

Kerfaint then informed the Affembly that the foldiers of the battalion called Re-publicain, fenfible of their error, had of themfelves delivered up the traitors who had excited them to mutiny and murder, and had promifed to their general to efface the memory of their crime by their con-duct againft the enemy.

Marat, feeing that every body rejoiced
in

in the punifhment of the ringleaders, had the boldnefs to affert that he never had juftified the conduct of the battalions. The cry in contradiction of this affertion was fo univerfal that he could not proceed, and a member immediately exclaimed: " A man, whofe name it is difagreeable to pronounce, dares to affert, from that tribune, that he never juftified the affaffins of the unfortunate deferters ; in contradiction of which, I do now affert, that laft night, at the Jacobins, he faid that they merited a civic crown.— Citizens, you may judge of the character of this man from what I have told you. Since he has been chofen as a deputy by the people, and fince we are doomed fome-times to hear him, I now move, that as often as he comes out of that tribune, it may be purified before another member en-ters it."

After this, the Affembly paffed to the order of the day. Marat defcended, and
strutted

strutted through the hall, affecting to
despise the murmurs which arose against
him.

It seems extraordinary that a man so
odious, and whose acquaintance every body
seems to shun, should venture to attack,
in such an abusive manner, a popular and
successful general. Yet the difference between the manner in which Marat was
heard in the Jacobin Society, and in the
Conventional Assembly, is remarkable; and
I see people who are persuaded that Marat is
supported in secret by those who in public
disavow any connection with him.——The
same people have also observed, that the
prevailing opinion in the Jacobin Club
always becomes sooner or later the prevailing opinion in the National Assembly, and
that those suspicions which Marat endeavours to raise against Dumourier, are spread
at the instigation of one who has very
great influence in that society. That person,

6

son, however, would do well to remember the words of Orosmane in Zayre :

" Quiconque est soupçonneux invite à le trahir."

The presidency of De la Croix ended this day; and Guadet, of the department of the Gironde, was elected by a great majority. Guadet seems to me one of the most acute men in the Convention; his speeches are always perspicuous and correct, and sometimes finished with an epigrammatic neatness.

October 19.

Two days ago a letter was read in the Convention from the commissioners to the army of the North, acquainting the Assembly, that a great number of volunteers had applied for liberty to retire at the end of the campaign.

Some members had represented the danger of permitting this in the present circumstances, and proposed a decree against it.

it. But this meafure having been thought harfh to men who had, as volunteers, rifked their lives in defence of their country, in a time of great danger ; inftead of a decree, it was moved, that the Convention fhould fend an addrefs to all their armies, inviting the volunteers to prolong their fervice until the country was declared to be out of danger.——A committee of four, namely, Condorcet, Danton, Hercault de Sechelles, and Vergniaud, had been accordingly appointed to draw up the addrefs ; and I heard Danton read it to the Convention this morning. It was rather too long; and although applauded by a few, it was very evident that the generality of the Affembly did not much relifh it.

A member then rofe, and, taking a paper from his pocket, faid, that he had compofed an addrefs, which he begged leave to read.——This furprifed me a good deal ; but I did not obferve that it produced the

5 fame

fame effect on any member of the Convention :—it feemed to me a ftriking inftance
of that eafe with which the natives of France
do certain things which would mightily difconcert fome of their neighbours. I hardly
think, that, in any public affembly in England, after a committee had been appointed
to draw up an addrefs, any individual of
the affembly would offer to read a compofition of his own, as preferable to that of
four of the moft diftinguifhed members in
it. —This gentleman, however, afcended
the tribune, and read his performance
without embarraffment. It had the fate
of moft productions which are read by
their authors, whether in public or private
affemblies ; it gave far more fatisfaction to
the reader than to the audience ; with this
difference, that here the audience did not
take the trouble of pretending to admire.

The air of indifference with which this
was heard did not difcourage another member from offering a third addrefs.—By the

ftyle of this performance, and the folemn manner in which it was read, it was evident that the author wifhed to be confidered as a man of depth and learning : he pronounced fome fentences with a warmth, which he, no doubt, thought would prove victorious : the warmth with which they were delivered, however, was furpaffed by the coldnefs of their reception.——Towards the conclufion, refuming his addrefs to the volunteers, he faid, Enfin foldats *philo-fophes.*

This unexpected epithet raifed a laugh that overpowered a yawn which had been gaining very faft on the audience for fome confiderable time.

I fully expected that fo many unfortunate attempts would have prevented any new fpecimens from being offered, and confequently, that the addrefs of the committee would have been adopted. I was miftaken in both conjectures, for the Affembly had no fooner recovered their gravity, than

*Faure,*

*Faure*, deputy from the department of Lower Seine, defired leave to read one of his compofition. He is a man of about fixty years of age, very plain in his drefs, and devoid of affectation in his manner.— His addrefs was in the following words :

Citoyens Soldats,

La loi vous permet de vous retirer: le cri de la patrie vous le defend. Les Romains ont-ils abandonné leurs armes quand Porfenna étoit encore aux portes de Rome ? L'ennemi a-t-il paffé le Rhin ? Longwi eftil repris ? Le fang François, dont il a arrofé la terre de la liberté, eft-il vengé ? Ses ravages et fa barbarie font-ils punis ? A-t-il reconnu la majefté de la République et la fouveraineté du Peuple ? Soldats, voila le terme de vos travaux : c'eft en dire affez aux braves defenfeurs de la patrie. La Convention Nationale fe borne à vous recommander l'honneur François, l'intérêt

de

ce la République, et les foins de votre propre gloire*.

The laconic energy of fome expreffions in this addrefs, pleafed the Convention; it was adopted, ordered to be printed, and tranfmitted to the armies.

October 20.

This was a day of exultation in the Na-

* Citizen Soldiers,

The law allows you, but the voice of your country forbids you, to retire. Did the Romans quit their arms, when Porfenna was ftill at the gates of Rome? Has the enemy yet repaffed the Rhine? Is Longwy retaken? Has the blood of your countrymen, with which the enemy has bedewed this land of liberty, been avenged? Have his ravages and his barbarities been punifhed? Has he acknowledged the Majefty of the Republic, and the fovereignty of the People?

Soldiers, thefe are the end of your labours: nothing more need be faid to the brave defenders of their country. The National Convention has only to recommend to your care, the honour of the French Nation, the intereft of the Republic, and your own perfonal glory.

tional

tional Affembly.—Letters were read from their commiffioners, giving an account of the retaking of the town of Longwy, and that the Germans were now entirely driven out of France. Flattering accounts alfo came from the army of Cuftine, and that of the South : and a paper entitled, "Addreffe de la Societé des Amis de la Liberté, et de l'Egalité féante à Chamberri," was read.—It begins with this expreffion—"Legiflateurs du Monde * :"—and, in the middle of the addrefs to the Affembly, the King of Sardinia is apoftrophized in the following terms : " O Roi de Jérufalem et de Chypre affez long-temps tes fatellites ont appefanti fur nos têtes ton joug de fer !—il eft tombé, nous l'avons foulé aux pieds, &c. &c †."

* Legiflators of the World.

† O King of Jerufalem and Cyprus, too long have thy fatellites oppreffed our necks with thy yoke of iron —it is fallen at laft, and we have fpurned it under our feet !

It

It is much in the fame ftrain throughout; and what will appear more extraordinary, this piece of bombaft was ordered by the Affembly to be printed in French, Spanifh, and German, and tranfmitted to the departments and to the armies.

But a fcene took place in the Convention yefterday, after I left it, which forebodes more mifery to the country than can be compenfated by the moft brilliant fuccefs. An addrefs was read by deputies from the 48 fections of Paris, againft the armed force which was fome time fince propofed, and the modification of which is now under the deliberation of a committee. By this addrefs the Convention is told, " That it would be putting the members on a footing with tyrants, to furround them with guards —Pretorian guards.——That Paris made the Revolution of the tenth of Auguft—and that Paris would maintain it." They alfo admonifhed the Convention, that there are

thofe

those present who contemplate their conduct, and weigh their decisions; and finally, that the sections of Paris consider the project of a guard to the Assembly as dangerous and odious.

The answer of Guadet, the President, was sensible and spirited. He said, that the exercise of the sovereignty of the French people, and all the rights of the Republic, resided in the Convention, which knew how to defend them, and which, though always willing to receive counsel from good citizens, would receive orders from the nation only.

But, in asserting that the Convention can defend the rights of the Republic, he asserts more than is true:—that an address, in such insolent terms, should be allowed to be read, is a proof not only that the Convention has *not* that power, but that the authors of the address know this, and are determined to do all they can to prevent

N 4         its

its ever having it, and for that reafon oppofe
the eftablifhment of the guard in queftion,
yet nothing can be more evident than that,
until the Convention has the power of im-
pofing filence on the galleries, of protecting
the perfons of the deputies, and of enforcing
its decrees, there can be neither wifdom
nor ftability in their government.——For,
were we to fuppofe that a few members of the
Convention, of diftinguifhed capacity, were
fupported by a majority in meafures of
wifdom and moderation ; yet if they are
liable to be infulted by a mob, thofe deputies who fupport them one day from conviction, will defert them another through
fear, and produce that confufion, and
thofe contradictory meafures which have of
late occurred, and which, if not remedied,
will end in complete anarchy and ruin.

A fufficient body of guards, under the
entire difpofal of the Convention, would
prevent this.——But it appears by this address

drefs from all the sections, that those who oppose the establishing any guard for the Convention, have not only the direction of the General Council of the Commune, but also of all the sections of Paris. It is true that the majority of the other departments of France, and of course the majority of the deputies, are for this guard ; but I sometimes converse with those who are able to form a much juster notion of what is likely to be the consequence than I can—who are of opinion, that Paris will carry the point against all the other departments ; and that whatever the *opinion* of the deputies may continue to be, the majority of their *votes* will, in a short time, be against the armed force.

Indeed it is evident, that, although all the departments of France are, in theory, allowed to have an equal share in the government, yet, in fact, the single department of Paris has the whole power of the

4                                        govern-

government; the other departments govern by reprefentation——Paris rules in perfon. The Majefty of Le Peuple Souverain refides in the capital, and by dint of infurrection, which is always in the power of certain leading perfons here, Paris gives the law to the Convention and to all France, and will continue to do fo till an armed force is eftablifhed, and placed entirely under the command of the National Convention.

October 21.

The city of Marfeilles, on hearing of the danger to which the Convention is expofed from the mob, and the people in the galleries, raifed a battalion, which was ordered to march to Paris for its protection. The intrepid and decifive behaviour of the Fédérés from that city, on the tenth of Auguft, have made a ftrong impreffion on the minds of the Parifians; and a body of feven or eight hundred men from Mar-

fcilles

feilles are confidered as equivalent to a
much greater number raifed elfewhere. As
this battalion comes for the exprefs purpofe
of protecting the Convention, its approach
has given difquietude to that party who wifh
the Affembly to be overawed by the people
in the galleries : endeavours have been
ufed, therefore, to create a prejudice againft
the Marfeillois in the minds of the populace of Paris—and particularly in the patriotic Sans Culottes of St. Antoine and St.
Marcelle.——It is circulated that they are
brought to the capital for fome purpofe of
ariftocracy. The name of Marfeillois is
in fuch high eftimation, that this infinuation
has hitherto had little effect.

The battalion is arrived, and this day
fent a deputation to the Convention. A
member of the deputation pronounced a
fpeech full of energy at the bar.——" We
fet out," faid he, " from the fhore of the
Mediterranean, to offer our lives in defence
of

of our brethren of Paris, then threatened by the foldiers of defpotifm, but that danger is over, and the only enemies which remain for us to fight, are thofe who defire to erect a *tribunitial* or *dictatorial* power in France.——Legiflators, you are delegated by the eighty-three departments, we have as great an intereft in you, therefore, as the citizens of Paris——We know that certain men tell the Parifians that the Convention has a defign of eftablifhing pretorian guards around them for the purpofes of tyranny—— one word is a fufficient refutation of that calumny.——*We* fhall belong to thofe guards.

Reprefentatives, the children of Marfeilles how to obey, as they know how to fight, they hate *dictators* as they hate kings, and you may count upon them for the maintenance of your laws, and of your authority."

Another perfon came afterwards to the bar of the Affembly and accufed Marat in the

the fevereft terms.—" That blood-thirfty man," faid he, " after having preached murder and carnage within the city of Paris, now difperfes his journals among the armies, to excite the foldiers to mutiny. The electors of Paris have difhonoured themfelves in choofing fuch a perfon, and you will partake of that difhonour; you will cover yourfelves with the blood which Marat has caufed to be fhed, if you do not expel him from among you, and punifh him for his crimes."

Some members endeavoured to interrupt the fpeaker, and the Prefident reminded him that he ought to fpeak with refpect of a reprefentative of the people.

" It is not Marat, the reprefentative of the people, I attack," refumed the fpeaker; " it is Marat the journalift, the incendiary, againft whom the French Republic, and human nature, calls for vengeance."

A member faid, that this petition againft
Marat

Marat was not in due form; that before the accusation could be sent to the Committee of General Safety, they ought to collect all the proofs that were against him.— " If you insist upon *all*, they must be brought in a waggon," said another.

The protectors of Marat, for it is evident that this man has protectors in the Convention, said every thing they could to persuade the Assembly to pass to the order of the day, without further notice of this petition, or accusation ; but in spite of all their efforts it was ordered to be transmitted to the Committee of General Safety.

The address from the Sections of Paris against the armed force, is a manœuvre of Danton and his friends, and their having the influence to obtain it, gives a higher idea of their strength than has been hitherto entertained.

The deputation of the Marseillois is considered as a measure of Roland and the
Girondists,

Girondifts, to give the Convention an idea of the protection it has to expect, till fuch time as a more regular armed force fhall be decreed.

October 22.

A very fhort time after the 10th of Auguft, thofe who had been united againft the court divided, and became hoftile to each other. Roland had been chofen minifter for the home department. He has the appearance of a man of fincerity, and, whether he deferves it or not, he has the reputation of a man of probity, is fupported by a great number, who are confidered as the beft intentioned in the Affembly, and alfo by fome who are diftinguifhed for their talents; among the latter are, Vergniaud, Guadet, Buzot, Briffot, Rabaut de St. Etienne, Jean Baptifte Louvet, La Source, Kerfaint, Petion, Lanjuinais, and Barbaroux.

Roland was likewife intimately connected with Claviere, Servan, and Le Brun; the two firft had formerly been in the adminiftration

ftration with him, and Le Brun was placed as Minifter for Foreign Affairs, after the 10th of Auguft.

The confidence which the people, and the majority of the Affembly put in the integrity of Roland, and the fupport he had from fo many men of the beft abilities in the Affembly, excited the jealoufy of certain members, particularly of Danton, who could not bear to fee a man, whom he confidered as far inferior in underftanding to himfelf, in poffeffion of fo much credit.

It is imagined that Danton had formed a plan for preventing Roland from continuing in adminiftration, and which, if it had fully fucceeded, would alfo have excluded him from being of the Convention.

It is even believed by fome that he was elected a deputy to the Convention without his own application or knowledge; according to the Conftitution, no member of the National Affembly can hold the office of minifter,

it

it was imagined that Roland would refign the fituation of minifter, that he might be of the Convention; and it has fince appeared, that there were certain flaws in his election as a deputy, which, as is fuppofed, were known to thofe who had brought it about, and which would have rendered it void : and thus, had he refigned his office of minifter, as Danton did, he might afterwards have found himfelf precluded from the Conventional Affembly. But before this could be brought to trial, it was propofed in the Convention that Roland fhould be *invited* by the Affembly to remain in adminiftration. This propofal had not been forefeen by Danton; he oppofed it with all his might, and in this he was joined by all his friends. The good qualities of Roland having been enumerated by thofe who were for the invitation, that very circumftance, with the popularity of the man, were laid hold of, as grounds of jealoufy, and reafons againft his being in-

O
vited.

vited. One deputy put them in mind, that a Greek, in the fenate of Athens, had declared that he would not give his vote for Ariſtides, becauſe he was tired of hearing him called *the juſt* : another deputy ſaid, that as often as he heard any member of the Aſſembly greatly applauded, he trembled for his liberty.

If theſe reaſons were uſed as pretexts, and in the expectation that they would have the effect to prejudice the Aſſembly againſt Roland, thoſe who urged them muſt have a poor opinion of the underſtanding of their audience.—If, on the contrary, they really thought that a man's being conſidered as a juſt man, rendered him dangerous as a miniſter, their audience had a right to think meanly of theirs.—I perceive an affectation in the Convention to adopt maxims and uſages from antiquity, which, however juſt and applicable they might be at a former age, and in a different country, are by no

means

means fuitable to France in the prefent circumftances. This difpofition of mifapplying
general maxims, very often renders the
weak the dupes of the worthlefs.

Notwithftanding the oppofition, however,
the Convention was on the point of decreeing, that Roland fhould be invited to
remain in adminiftration; which Danton
perceiving, he could no longer reftrain his
ill humour, but peevifhly faid, " If you are
determined on this meafure, I move that
the invitation be extended to Madame Roland, who is known to affift her hufband
with her counfel * ."

This illiberal fally was heard with difap-
probation by the Affembly, and would have
had no effect in preventing the invitation
which had been propofed, had not Cambon
fpoken againft it : he obferved, that to *invite*
a minifter to continue in office, was in fome

* Madame Roland has the reputation of being a moft
accomplifhed and amiable woman.

degree

degree to weaken his refponfibility; and Buzot declaring that this obfervation had fo much weight with him as to make him alter his opinion, the invitation was no more infifted on.

The day following, Roland, in a letter to the Convention, expreffed his concurrence in fentiment with thofe who thought that to invite a minifter to continue, would be derogatory of the rigorous principles of republicanifm, and tended befides to render him lefs refponfible than he ought to be: that, however, the Convention having even deliberated on fuch a meafure, he confidered as highly honourable to him, and a motive to engage him to retain his office of minifter, and to wave that of deputy: that the danger which he plainly perceived would attend him in the firft fituation, was another inducement for his retaining it; but that his chief motive, however fuch a declaration might be conftrued by his enemies,

8                                                        was,

was, that he thought his continuing minifter would, in the present circumftances,
be advantageous for his country.

Perhaps nothing but confcious integrity
could induce a man of fenfe to hold fuch
language : but certainly nothing but a ftrong
conviction of its truth on the mind of the
Convention, and a fentiment of high efteem
for the perfon who ufed it, could prevent it
from being thought prefumptuous. Roland's
letter excited no fuch fenfation.——The inftant it was perceived that he had refolved to
continue in office, the greateft joy appeared
in the Affembly, and his letter was ordered
to be printed, and fent to all the departments.

Roland has continued minifter for the
home department ever fince. I have feen
him frequently in the place appointed for
the minifters, which is immediately within
the bar, and oppofite to the Prefident.
None of them ever come to the Affembly

unlefs

unlefs they have been fent for, or when they have fomething to ftate, on which they wifh to have the inftructions of the Con-. vention—and they withdraw as foon as they have made their report, without taking any part in the debate.

On fuch occafions I have feen fome of them obliged to remain feveral hours before they were heard. For, if a debate is already begun when a minifter enters, he is generally allowed to fit unnoticed in his place till it be finifhed. Some of Roland's addreffes to the Convention are diftinguifhed for correct-nefs and elegance. It is faid, that they owe the latter to his wife : this report is founded entirely on prefumption, Mrs. Roland being a woman of tafte and literature ; and it is circulated not fo much with a view to add to her reputation, as to detract from that of her hufband.

When he enters, there is generally a whifper

whifper of approbation in the Affembly, and, while he is fpeaking, I have often heard the deputies near me fay, with fervour—*Ah le digne homme ! le brave miniftre!* What proves that he and thofe connected with him enjoy the confidence of the majority of the Convention, is, that the Prefident and the fecretaries have hitherto been chofen from among his friends.

Roland was the popular minifter, whofe difmiffion raifed fo great a clamour againft the Court. One of the pretexts for the fhameful irruption of the populace into the King's palace, on the 20th of June, was to prefent a petition for his recall : if Roland himfelf had any hand in promoting that infurrection, he has little claim to the epithet which was applied to Ariftides. Thofe who wifh to fucceed him and his friends in their offices, reprefent them to the people as in all points as dangerous to liberty as ever the Court was : fo that it

O 4

is

is not improbable but that Roland and his friends may fall the victims of the example given on the 20th of June, of over-awing the legiſlative power, and attacking the executive, by a mob.

The duke of Rochefoucauld was at that time Preſident of the Department of Paris, and was zealous to bring the authors of that inſurrection to puniſhment—the zeal he ſhewed upon that occaſion was thought to be the remote cauſe of his murder.

The aſſaſſinations formerly mentioned, that were committed at Clermont, at Cambray, at Charleville, by the volunteers as they paſſed through theſe places, ſeem to have proceeded from want of diſcipline and from the caprice, prejudice, and cruelty, which are ſo apt to gain upon vulgar and uninſtructed men, aſſembled in great numbers, and under no controul. Great pains have been taken to ſpread the opinion, that ſome other murders which have been committed

committed in the provinces, were entirely owing to a fudden, unpremeditated commotion of the people — particularly the horrid affaffination of the Duke of Rochefoucauld. It is generally believed, however, that the murder of this nobleman originated in more diftant caufes, and more concealed promoters.

M. de la Rochefoucauld was a man of humanity and candour. Unfeduced by the advantages enjoyed by thofe of his own rank, he felt with generous fympathy for the diftreffed fituation of others : he beheld with fatisfaction the overthrow of the old arbitrary fyftem of government, in the hopes of feeing one more agreeable to juftice erected in its ftead—A friend to monarchy as well as freedom, M. de la Rochefoucauld had in his contemplation a monarchy of milder afpect than his country had ever enjoyed—more limited in its nature, but with fufficient power in the

Prince

Prince to defend his prerogatives, and sufficient means in the people to resist tyranny; more agreeable to humanity, more conducive to the general-happiness, not only of the people, which is infinitely the most important object, but also of the Monarch himself, if he happens to be a man of sense.

The Duke of Rochefoucauld was President of the Department of Paris on the 20th of June 1792, and did all in his power in the first place to prevent, and afterwards to discover and bring to punishment, the instigators of the scandalous irruption of an armed multitude into the King's palace.

Having made frequent allusions to the transactions of that day, I shall here give a short account of them.

For several days before the 20th of June it was known all over Paris, that the inhabitants of the Fauxbourgs of St. Antoine and St. Marcelle

St. Marcelle intended to march in arms to the Tuileries, on pretence of prefenting a petition to the King—but in reality with the defign of intimidating and forcing him to fanction two decrees of the National Affembly, which he had hitherto refufed.

The council of the department of Paris, of which M. de Rochefoucald was Prefident, did every thing in their power to prevent an attempt of a nature fo unjuftifiable, fo contrary to the principles of the conftitution, and which might be attended with the moft fatal confequences.

This council made reprefentations to the Mayor of Paris, to the Procureur of the Commune, and to Santerre, who at that time was commander of the battalion of Les Enfans-trouvés.

But unfortunately thofe to whom the council of the department made thefe reprefentations, and whofe peculiar duty it was to prevent the intended proceffion,

were

were the very people who had planned it, and were fecretly promoting it with all their influence.

The inhabitants of the two fuburbs began to affemble in arms, on the morning of the 20th of June, at the place where the Baftile formerly ftood. As accounts of this came from all quarters, to thefe fecret inftigators, fome of whom were magiftrates, they could not decently avoid making a fhew of oppofing it. When the multitude were at the height of enthufiafm, and ready to march, thofe magiftrates appeared in their municipal fcarfs, and gravely *admonifhed* the people to depart peaceably home, lay up their arms, and go to bed. " You have acted *your* part," faid one of the rabble ; " move out of the way, and let us act ours." The proceffion began at nine in the morning ; the battalion of St. Antoine marched firft : between it and that of St. Marcelle banners were carried, fufficiently expreffive of the defign of this ceremony,

mony, if it had been at all doubtful. On
one was inscribed these words,

Tyrans, tremblez; ou soyez justes,
Et respectez la liberté du peuple *.
On another,
Louis, le peuple est las de souffrir †.
On a third,
Tremblez tyran, ta derniere heure est
venue ‡.
On a fourth,
Le rappel des ministres, la sanction ou la
mort §.

Other banners were carried, ornamented
with vile allegorical figures, and suitable
inscriptions.

They marched to the hall of the National Affembly, and required permiffion to
walk through it in proceffion. A member

---

* Tyrants, tremble, or be juft,
  And refpect the liberty of the people.
† Lewis, the people are weary of fuffering.
‡ Tremble, tyrant, thy laft hour is come.
§ The recall of the minifters, the fanction, or death.

made

made a speech against the granting of this request, giving for his reason, that the petitioners were armed, and in great numbers; but, as this orator's eloquence, while it opposed the mob's being let in, proved that they could not be kept out, the Assembly graciously granted the prayer of the petitioners, and, in consequence, was amused for three hours with a procession of armed men, accompanied by women and children, marching through the hall. Among other ingenious emblems, a pair of old black breeches were carried on a pole, with this comfortable inscription, Libres—et sansculottes *.

From the National Assembly the armed multitude went to the palace, where there was a considerable number of troops on duty ; but no orders having been given to resist, and many portions of the multitude who formed the procession being conducted

* Free—and without breeches.

by

by men dreffed in municipal fcarfs, the gardens and courts of the Tuileries were crowded in an inftant. One body marched with more regularity than the reft, dragging fome pieces of cannon with them, and con-ducted by Santerre, and Legendre the butcher.——The multitude foon after rufhed into every apartment, calling aloud, that they muft fee the King ; they had a peti-tion to prefent. M. Acloque, commandant of the fecond legion of national guards, having placed fome grenadiers at the door of the apartments neareft to the King's, told two municipal officers that if they would prevent the mob from proceeding, he would inform the King of their requeft, and that he was perfuaded his Majefty would receive twenty of their number, according to the law——He then went to the door of the King's apartment, which he found fhut—— he knocked, and begged that he might be inftantly admitted, faying, that he came to fave the King's life——The door of the cham-ber

ber was opened; he found the King, with the Queen, the Prince, the Princess Royal, Madam Elizabeth the King's sister, and the following gentlemen: the Marechal de Mouchy, Beaulieu, Minister of the Finances, Lajard, Minister of War, Terrier de Monciel, Minister of the Home Department, the Count d'Hervilly, Marechal de Camp and Commander of the Horse Guards.

M. Acloque, perceiving that they had their swords drawn, and seemed determined to sacrifice their lives in defence of the royal family, entreated them to sheath their swords, otherwise they would increase the danger in which the King was—In a short time a great noise was heard at the door, the rabble were breaking it open, with pikes, axes, and the butt end of musquets. The King himself ordered the doors to be thrown open:—before this was done, the ends of some of the musquets and pikes had been driven through the door—twenty or thirty of the mob burst into the room.

M. Acloque

M. Acloque accosted them with a firm voice: " Citizens, respect your King—the law commands it; and we will all perish rather than suffer his being insulted."—One of the company at the same instant calling out, Vive la nation ! Vive le Roi ! the intruders stopped short.

It was then proposed to the King, that he should stand on a seat in the room commonly called L'Œil de Beuf, to prevent his being pressed upon, and that he might be seen by the people, who were entering in great numbers; to which he consented.— The Queen, at the King's desire, with the royal children, went into the adjacent room; but Madame Elizabeth kept constantly by his side, rejecting every entreaty that was made by the King himself and others to quit him for an instant.

On the sixth of October 1789, when the mob marched from Paris to Versailles and broke into the palace, the Princess Eli-

P zabeth

zabeth attached herself to the perſon of the Queen, whoſe life ſhe knew was at that time more threatened by thoſe ruffians than that of her brother; and on the preſent occaſion, as he was in greater danger, ſhe adhered to him.

Four grenadiers of the national guards appearing at the door, the Princeſs, who had betrayed no ſymptom of fear on her own account, burſt into tears at ſight of them, and ſaid, " *Ah! Meſſieurs, defendez le Roi.*"

Thoſe four grenadiers, an officer of chaſſeurs, a cannonier, with the gentlemen above mentioned, placed themſelves around the King and the Princeſs Elizabeth, and with admirable conſtancy kept off the preſſure of the crowd, and protected the perſon of the King for above three hours; the Marechal de Mouchy, in ſpite of his great age, remaining the whole time. All the adjacent rooms, mean-while, ſwarmed with

with a mixed rabble of men and women,
armed with pikes, fabres, fticks with knives
fixed at their ends, fufils and piftols ; many
of them calling, " En bas le veto, au diable
le veto!" and fome of them fhewing fo much
fury, that thofe around the King's perfon
had difficulty in keeping them off.

One fellow, mounted on a chair, fpoke
to the King in the moft audacious manner,
requiring the recal of the patriot minifters,
meaning Roland, Claviere, and Servan,
whom the King had a little before difmiffed;
he alfo required that the two decrees fhould
obtain his approbation.——To which his Majefty anfwered with firmnefs, " Je ferai ce
que je croirai devoir faire ; mais ce n'eft pas
ni le lieu, ni le moment, de me faire une
pareille demande *."

A red cap was reached to the King at

* I will do what I ought ; but this is neither the
place nor the time to make a requeft of that nature.

the

the end of a pike, by a man who cried, Vive la nation !—The King faid, " La nation n'a de meillieur ami que moi *." On which the other infolently added, " Eh bien, donnez nous en la preuve en mettant le bonnet rouge, et en criant "Vive la nation ! †"

On attempting to put on the red cap, it was found too fmall for the King's head ; but a grenadier having ftretched it upon his knee, the King put it on, and wore it as long as the mob remained.

At one time, when the noife and con-fufion was greater than ufual, a grenadier, addreffing the King, faid, " Sire, n'ayez pas peur." On which he anfwered, " I am not in the leaft afraid, friend." So faying, he preffed the foldier's hand to his breaft, that he might feel that his heart beat calmly.

---

* The nation has no better friend than I am.

† Prove it then, by putting on the red cap, and by crying " Vive la nation !"

Among

Among thofe armed with various weapons, one ruffian brandifhed a pike with the heart of a calf ftuck on the point, from which hung a label, with this infcription, " Cœur des ariftocrates *."

To the noify requifitions that were made from all corners of " Otez le veto! rappellez le miniftres !" the King anfwered, that he would do what was juft.——Legendre the butcher, thinking this expreffion rather equivocal, took this opportunity of giving the monarch a fpecimen of his eloquence.—— " *Monfieur*," faid Legendre——the King feeming a little furprifed at this new ftyle and manner, for this man's manner is as extraordinary as his ftyle—" *Monfieur*," repeated Legendre, " ecoutez nous ; oui *Monfieur*, vous êtes fait pour nous ecouter, vous etes un perfide, vous nous avez toujours trompés, vous nous trompez encore ; mais prenez

* The heart of ariftocrates.

P 3

garde

garde à vous Monſieur, la meſure eſt a ſon comble, et le peuple eſt las de ſe voir votre jouet *."

In a company lately, where the converſation turned on the conduct of Legendre, every body preſent blamed it, except one young Frenchman, who, although of high birth, diſtinguiſhes himſelf by violent democratic principles : he urged, by way of defending Legendre, that he did not ſpeak in his own name, but in that of the nation ; that he repreſented *the majeſty of the peuple ſouverain*. The company ſmiled ; ſome of them were deputies, who, however expedient it might be to uſe this language in the tribune, did not expect to hear it in private ſociety.——I ventured to repeat a

* Sir, liſten to us—yes, Sir, it is your duty to attend to us ; you have always deceived us, you deceive us ſtill ; but take care what you are about, Sir, the meaſure of our patience is full, and the people are tired of being your dupes.

ſtory

ſtory I had heard, of an Engliſh gentleman celebrated for wit, that, walking in the ſtreets of London with a democratic acquaintance of his, who frequently uſed the expreſſion *the majeſty of the people*, they met a couple of chimney-ſweeps ; the gentleman took off his hat, and made them a very formal and low bow as they paſſed. His acquaintance aſked what he meant—I was only ſhewing the reſpect, replied the other, which is due from every loyal ſubject to two princes of the blood.

This gentleman, it is probable, judged of their affinity merely from their external reſemblance to the Sovereign; but Legendre could boaſt of an affinity in more eſſential points, an unyielding firmneſs of heart, a deciſive promptitude of execution, a diſpoſition which, ſo far from being depreſſed, finds matter of mirth and pleaſantry in ſcenes of horror, when they are thought

neceſſary

neceſſary to promote the great cauſe : theſe are features of energy which have diſtin-guiſhed the Peuple Souverain ſince the be-ginning of the Revolution, and in which Legendre bears a ſtriking likeneſs to the monarch he was ſaid to repreſent.

A deputation conſiſting of twelve mem-bers of the National Aſſembly, among whom were Iſnard and Vergniaud, at length ar-rived——Iſnard addreſſing himſelf to the people who filled the room, endeavoured to prevail on them to withdraw, repeating fre-quently, that he would be anſwerable on his life that they ſhould be ſatisfied.——This had little effect, the noiſe and exclamations of " Rappellez les miniſtres! ôtez le veto!" * recommenced.

Vergniaud alſo ſpoke to the ſame pur-poſe, and with as little ſucceſs.

* Recal the miniſters, remove the veto.

The

The noife and confufion continued till paft five in the evening, when Petion arrived, accompanied by Sergent, a municipal officer. Petion approaching the King, faid, " Sire, I was only this moment informed of the fituation in which you are."

That is extraordinary, replied the King, for I have been in this fituation above three hours.

Petion then ftanding on a chair advifed the people to retire, ending his harangue with the following very curious expreffions, which one who was prefent wrote a little after and allowed me to copy : " Citoyens, vous venez de faire entendre vos vœux au reprefentant héréditaire, avec l'énergie et la dignité d'un peuple libre qui connoit fes droits. Le Roi fait maintenant les intentions du *Souverain*, et fans doute il y aura égard. Il convient que vous vous retirez

avec

avec calme et décence, afin qu'on ne puisse pas calomnier vos intentions*."

After this, the people at the Mayor's repeated request began to withdraw :——when a fecond deputation from the National Affembly arrived, one of the members of which addreffed the King in a refpectful manner, affuring him that each member was ready to prefent his body as a fhield to cover his Majefty's.

It could not efcape the King, however, that he might have been cut in pieces three hours before the fhields arrived.

While thefe things were paffing in the

---

* Citizens, you have now made your defires known to the hereditary reprefentative, with that energy and dignity which becomes a free people who underftand their rights. The King at prefent knows the intentions of the fovereign, and undoubtedly will pay a proper regard to them. You ought now to withdraw with calmnefs and decency, that your intentions may not be calumniated.

ŒiÎ

Œil de Beuf, the Queen entered the council-chamber, attended by the Prince and Princess Royal, by Madame de Lamballe, Mme. Tourzelle, Mme. de Mau, Mme. de Soucy. Her Majesty shewed much uneasiness on account of the situation in which she had left the King, till the Adjutant General of the first legion of Parisian guards, with some soldiers, came and assured her that the King was in safety, and surrounded by faithful servants.

M. de Wittengoff, a general officer, entered the room followed by a number of people of both sexes, among whom was a woman with a red cap in her hand. She presented the cap to Wittengoff, desiring him to give it to the Queen to wear, adding, that she had just left the King, who at that moment had the cap of Liberty on his head.

It would appear that the General did not think it expedient to reject the woman's proposal; which the Queen perceiving, and being shocked at the idea of wearing the cap, said to Wittengoff, " Vous voyez Monsieur, que ce bonnet ne peut aller sur ma tête :" she then put it on the head of the Prince. This satisfied the woman and her followers.

Santerre entered the council-chamber soon after, followed by a new crowd, who having already seen the King, now demanded a sight of the Queen, which Santerre had undertaken to procure them.——He immediately required that those who stood immediately before her Majesty should open to the right and left, that the people who followed him might have a full view of her and the rest of the royal family ; which was done, Santerre *graciously* assuring the Queen that she had nothing to apprehend from the people, who were *wonderfully good*, and only wished to be gratified with a sight of her as they walked out ; and perceiving that

that the Prince was heated with the cap, he added, " Otez le bonnet à cet enfant *."

Santerre's affurances, however, did not prevent fome of the people, who were not quite fo good as the reft, from infulting the Queen, as they paffed, with very abominable language.

The crowd having moftly retired, and the King having left the Œil de Beuf to go to what are called the petits apartemens, the Princefs Elizabeth was going to wait on the Queen in the council-chamber, when a group of the mob which ftill lingered in the palace, miftaking her for the Queen, began to in-fult her ; on which one of the Princefs's at-tendants was going to undeceive them, but fhe with noblenefs of mind prevented this, left the people who were infulting her, being informed of their miftake, fhould have tranf-ferred their abufe to the unhappy Queen.

* Take the cap from that child's head.

It

It appeared from the witnesses examined on this business, that great pains had been taken with the inhabitants of St. Antoine, for a considerable time previous to the 20th of June, to work them up to this criminal measure : for it merits that epithet in a high degree, even although what is by no means clear were entirely admitted, namely that no more was intended than to prevail on the King to recall the former ministers, and to remove the negative he had given to the two decrees ; because, to prevail on the King by such means was open rebellion against the government, and ruinous to the Constitution, and might have been attended with the immediate massacre of the royal family, and other dreadful consequences, all of which the promoters of this procession were answerable for.

The active and apparent promoters of it (for others are strongly suspected who were not sworn against by the witnesses) were,

Santerre,

Santerre, at that time commander of the battalion of Enfans trouvés, Legendre, Fournier an American, Rotondo an Italian, Buirette a glafs-maker, Rofignol a goldfmith, Gonor who was called the conqueror of the Baftille, Brierre a wine-merchant, and St. Huruge, who rendered himfelf more notorious afterwards in the month of September, and Nicolas, fapeur or miner to the battalion which Santerre commanded. Thefe men had frequent nightly meetings at the houfe of Santerre, where they drew up the motions that were to be made in the groups at the Tuileries, the Palais-royal, the Place de Gréve, and to the multitude which affembled in the Place de la Baftille. They fometimes met alfo in the chamber of the committee of the fection of Enfans trouvés, to compofe placarts to be pofted on the walls ; and at thofe meetings Chabot had frequently made harangues, the tendency of which was to encourage the audience to promote

promote the intended proceffion, which he
affured them the National Affembly expected, and would receive with fatisfaction.

From the evidence it alfo appeared,
" that after coming from the National Affembly, the people fhewed no difpofition to force
their way into the palace, till Santerre, accompanied by Saint Huruge, came among
them, and afked why they did not enter the
palace, as it was for that purpofe alone that
they had affembled ; and that it was in confequence of directions from Panis, and another municipal officer, that the gates of
the Tuileries had been broken open."

In confequence of the proof of thefe facts,
the Council of the department of Paris decreed, that the Mayor of Paris, and the Procureur of the Commune, who had been frequently advertifed by the Council of the intended proceffion, had not done what their
duty required to prevent, but had rather
countenanced it, and therefore fhould be fufpended

pended from the exercife of their offices; but this decree requiring the fanction of the King, his Majefty wifhed to give no opinion nor decifion on the fubject, as he was perfonally concerned in it. He therefore referred the whole matter to the National Affembly; but his enemies there being refolved to drive him to the difagreeable alternative of either difapproving of the decree of the Council, or incurring the odium of being the immediate caufe of fufpending the popular Mayor, had fufficient influence to get the Affembly to refufe giving any opinion on the fubject, until the King fhould confirm or annul the fentence of the Council. His Majefty therefore confirmed the decree; which he had no fooner done, than the National Affembly took the whole matter into their confideration, and reinftated the Mayor and Procureur in their offices.

From this time it was clear that the con-

Q ftitution

ſtitution was at an end, that a plan was formed for the deſtruction of royalty, and that the beſt meaſure the King could adopt was to attempt at any riſk to remove himſelf and his family out of the reach of the mob of Paris. To this he was often preſſed by his friends, who thought, that if he were even removed as far as Fontainebleau, there was ſuch indignation in the minds of the moſt reſpectable citizens all over France at the ſcandalous tranſactions on the 20th of June, that they would have united againſt the anarchiſts of Paris, and given ſuch force to the executive power, as, without injuring freedom, would have ſuppreſſed them, and prevented the dreadful diſorders which have ſince taken place. But his Majeſty, probably deterred by the ill ſucceſs of his flight to Varennes, could not be prevailed on to make a ſecond attempt of the ſame nature.

Diſguſted with a ſeries of crimes which he could neither prevent nor puniſh, and

finding

finding that his presence in Paris was neither of use to his country nor to the King, the Duke of Rochefoucauld withdrew from the capital to his villa in Normandy, from whence, on account of his health, he soon after went to the medicinal waters of Forges, where he was during the dreadful period of the massacres in September, and where a commissioner from the general council of the Commune of Paris arrived with an order to arrest and conduct him to the capital. This commissioner was a man of more humanity than those usually employed by the council on similar occasions; he readily agreed to the proposal of accompanying the Duke in the first place to his own house at Roche-Guyon, with a view that the agitation which existed at Paris might have time to subside before he should arrive, and in the hopes that the Duke's friends might be able to have the order recalled.——In company with Mr. de la Roche-

Q 2

foucauld,

foucauld was the Ducheffe D'Anville his mother, and the Duchefs his wife. On the road between Forges and Roche-Guyom, they ftopped at Gifors : during this period, moft unfortunately a battalion of National Guards arrived, among whom fome of the Paris affaffins, as is fufpected, were mixed.

These villains immediately fhewed a dif-pofition to murder the Duke, who, being more folicitous for the fafety of his mother and his wife than for his own, and fearing that they might be injured or infulted if he remained with them, he perfuaded them to go on. The Duke himfelf afterwards walked to his carriage under the protection of the Mayor of Gifors, the Commiffioner, and fome of the national guards ; but he was, notwithftanding, followed by the affaffins loading him all the way with abufive lan-guage, till one of them having found means of coming very near the Duke, threw a ftone with fuch force that, ftriking him on the

the temple, it killed him on the fpot, and fome of the wretches immediately, on feeing him fall, cried, " Vive la Nation !"

The French nation is difgraced by fuch an exclamation on fuch an occafion ; and, were I not convinced that the majority deteſt the aĉtions and ficken at the exclamations of fuch wretches, I fhould join in fentiment with thofe who wifh it wafhed from the furface of the globe.

October 24.

In a converfation which I had this day with a member of the Convention, I delivered my fentiments pretty freely upon the fubjeĉt of the murder of Mr. de la Rochefoucauld, and fome fimilar events which have taken place of late in France : he expreſſed the utmoſt horror at them, but added that fcenes of the fame kind had been aĉted in every country of Europe in times of revolution and diſſention, when great intereſts

Q 3

were

were at ftake, and when the human paffions were inflamed and agitated in the higheft degree. He mentioned certain barbarous cruelties which had been committed, on both fides, during the conteft between the white rofe and the red in England : he enlarged on the maffacre in Ireland in the reign of Charles the Firft, and on the perfidious affair of Glenco in Scotland in the reign of King William. He added that, every thing confidered, perhaps it belonged lefs to one of my nation than of any other, to complain of the exceffes of revolutions or civil diffenfions ; and with a fmile he quoted from Juvenal :

Quis tulerit Gracchos de feditione querentes ?

I did not choofe to pufh the argument farther, although, with refpect to the reciprocal cruelties which were committed during the conteft between the white rofe and the red, the remark was obvious, that what

a nation

a nation had done during an age of barba-
rifm and fuperftition, is not to be compared
with that of another in the days of knowledge and refinement—and perhaps it would
not be difficult to fhew that the barbarities
he enumerated which had been committed
in Great Britain and Ireland, were equalled
by thofe committed in France at the fame
periods ; in which cafe, there has been fuch
an accumulation here of late, that, on comparing accounts, a moft dreadful balance
of horrors would remain with this country.

I find fome people believe, or pretend to
believe, that the murder of the Duke of
Rochfoucauld was the accidental effect of the
fudden frenzy of a few volunteers ; but many
circumftances do not admit of that opinion.
The magiftrates of Gifors, although they
wifhed to protect the Duke, did not feize and
punifh his affaffins, which looks as if they fufpected that the affaffins acted under the direction of fome men whofe enmity the magi-

Q 4                                          ftrates

ftrates were afraid of incurring: and when we recollect that the Duke's conduct, immediately before and after the 20th of June, was highly offenfive to thofe who fpirited up the fhameful infurrection of that day; when we recollect the characters of fome of them who were afterwards members of the new formed council of the Commune de Paris, and the orders for arreft which they iffued previous to the 2d of September; it will feem much more probable that the death of the Duke of Rochefoucauld proceeded from inftructions from fome of *them*, than from a fudden impulfe of the actual murderers.

If any thing could render this crime more atrocious, it would be, that a man who lies under the higheft obligations to the Duke, was the planner of his affaffination. This idea has been propagated notwithftanding its enormity, and perhaps is circulated the more on that very account; for the minds of fome people are peculiarly attached

tached to the wonderful, and they are ſo fond of repeating what creates the greateſt emotion, of whatever nature that emotion is, that the very circumſtance which renders a ſtory leſs credible, is an inducement for one ſet of people to repeat it, and another to believe it. Much ſtronger preſumptive proof than any I have heard, is neceſſary to induce me to think any man capable of ſuch aggravated wickedneſs, particularly if the purſuits of his life have been of a nature to humanize the heart as well as to enlighten the underſtanding, and if the fact can be fully accounted for, without ſuppoſing him to have had any direct or indirect hand in it.

October 26.

The party which is formed againſt Roland and the Girondiſts * manifeſt already

as

* Vergniaud, Genſonné, Guadet, and ſome others diſtinguiſhed for their talents, are deputies from the department

as much enmity to them as the fame party did to the court for turning Roland out of office. What renders them very formidable is the influence their leaders have in the Jacobin fociety, which begins to murmur againft Roland and all his friends. To Briffot they fhew fuch peculiar diflike, that he was lately expelled from the fociety : he

partment of Gironde, and fupport Roland ; many others have joined them, and the whole are called Girondifts or Rolandifts ; and Marat, who has a determined hatred to Briffot, fometimes calls them in his journal Briffotins, and the whole clafs Roland Briffotins. Although Condorcet is of more eminence in the literary world than any I have enumerated as the friends of Roland, I have not mentioned him, becaufe his conduct of late is thought equivocal ; it is not quite clear whether he means to attach himfelf to Roland or Danton.

Barrere, deputy from the department of the High Pyrenées, who was a member of the conftituent affembly without being much diftinguifhed, begins to be thought of more importance in the Convention : he has not hitherto taken a decided part with either party, but, I am told, he is courted by both.

probably

probably obtained this diftinction on account of fome paragraphs which have lately appeared in the daily paper fuppofed to be conducted by him. Marat is there treated with a contempt which may be due to his talents, but which it is not prudent to fhew for a man who is ftill a favourite of the rabble, and has fome of the moft defperate of them under his direction. In the fame paper Danton is glanced at with feverity, and Robefpierre is turned into ridicule, in a manner that would not be readily forgiven by a man of a lefs implacable difpofition.

Briffot is a little man, of an intelligent countenance, but of a weakly frame of body.

While many of the Deputies, even thofe who are no way obnoxious to the violent party, carry pocket-piftols, or canes which contain fwords ; Briffot walks through the ftreets, at all hours, without fo much as a fwitch in his hand.

-An

An acquaintance of his told me that he had spoken of this to him as a piece of great imprudence, confidering the number of his enemies, many of whom he thought capable of affaffination. To this remonftrance Briffot anfwered with a carelefs air, " S'ils font décidés à m'affaffiner, ils en trouveroient aifément le moyen de quelque manierre que je fuffe armé : d'ailleurs je fuis d'une conftitution fi foible, que ne pouvant faire qu'une trifte défenfe, je préférerois l'honneur de n'en point faire du tout."

But timidity is not to be placed among this man's failings, nor prudence among his virtues.

If Briffot is too little affected by the rancour of his enemies, Roland fhews too much

---

* If they are determined to affaffinate me, they will find the means whatever arms I may carry ; befides, I am of fo feeble a conftitution, that, confcious of being unable to make a good refiftance, I think it more honourable to make none.

fenfibility

fenfibility to the attacks which are made on him, and this is one reafon perhaps for their being continued with fuch fpirit and perfe-verance. Infinuations tending to render him unpopular, not only appear in certain daily journals, but accufations against him are fometimes pafted on the walls. He alludes to thefe rather too often in his addreffes to the Convention, which are fometimes thought laboured and pompous. . While one of this kind was reading in the affembly, I heard one of the deputies fay peevifhly, " Cet homme pretend nous gouverner par des phrafes*." Another, fhrugging up his fhoulders, faid, " Il ne cherche qu'à faire admirer la beauté de fon ftile †." To which the member who fat next him replied,

* This man thinks to govern us by fine fentences.

† His only object is to make us admire the beauty of his ftyle.

6

" Auffi

" Auffi y réuffit il quelquefois avec l'aide de
" fa femme*."

The tendency of thefe addreffes and letters generally is, after exculpating himfelf
from the charges above mentioned, to prove
the neceffity of order and fubmiffion to
law.

But if a Minifter takes the trouble of an-
fwering, in the National Affembly, all ano-
nymous accufations made againft him, neither he nor the Affembly will be able to do
any other bufinefs; and if he has no other
means of producing order and fubmiffion
to law than by fpeeches and addreffes, there
is no probability of their being produced
foon.

Some of thefe compofitions however are
very good in themfelves.

*Sed nunc non erat his locus.*

* In which he fometimes fucceeds, with the affiftance
of his wife.

—Can

—Can it be thought that the men who ftormed the King's palace, or thofe who inftigated to the maffacres, will be moved from their defigns by eloquence or argument?

At the head of the party in oppofition to Roland are Danton and Robefpierre; after them are Couthon, Bazire, Thuriot, Merlin de Thionville, St. André, Camille Defmoulins, Chabot, Collot d'Herbois, Sergent, Legendre, Fabre d'Eglantine, Panis, Marat.

Robefpierre is a man of fmall fize, and a difagreeable countenance, which announces more fire than underftanding; in his calmeft moments, he conceals with difficulty the hatred and malignity which is faid to exift in his heart, and which his features are admirably formed to exprefs. He diftinguifhed himfelf in the Conftituent Affembly by the violence of his fpeeches, and much more fince, in the Jacobin fociety, by the violence of his meafures. His eloquence is employed in invectives againft tyrants and ariftocrates, and in declamations in praife of Liberty.

Liberty. His fpeeches are barren in argument, but fometimes fertile in the flowers of fancy.

Robefpierre is confidered as an enthufiaft rather than a hypocrite: fome people think him both, which is not without example; but, to me, he feems to be too much of the firft to be a great deal of the fecond.

He has always refufed every office of emolument: his paffion is popularity, not avarice; and he is allowed, even by thofe who deteft many parts of his character, and are his enemies, to be incorruptible by money.

Roland is not fuppofed to poffefs all the energy of character that belongs to Danton; in many other refpects they differ. Roland is believed to be a thorough republican: Danton, it is thought, does not lay much ftrefs on the form of government, and would have no objection to monarchy, provided the monarch were a creature of his own; for I do not find that it is fufpected that he afpires to reign in perfon.

Roland

Roland and Danton were often in oppofition with each other when joined in the
fame adminiftration. Roland ftruggled with
all his might againft the ufurpations of
the General Council of the Commune of Paris after the 10th of Auguft : Danton favoured and abetted them. Roland exclaimed againft the maffacres in September,
did every thing he could to put an end to
them, and on that account was himfelf in
imminent danger. Danton, though he was
then minifter of juftice, is accufed of having
been criminally paffive on that very preffing
occafion. Roland ufes his whole influence
to bring the authors of thofe favage fcenes
to juftice : Danton ufes his to ftifle all inveftigation of that nature.

In external appearance and manner, thofe
two men differ as in all the reft : Roland is
about fixty years of age, tall, thin, of a mild
countenance and pale complexion. His
drefs, every time I have feen him, has been

the fame, a drab-coloured fuit lined with green filk, his grey hair hanging loofe.

Danton is not fo tall, but much broader than Roland; his form is coarfe, and uncommonly robuft : Roland's manner is unaffuming and modeft—that of Danton fierce and boifterous; he fpeaks with the voice of a Stentor, declaims on the bleffings of freedom with the arrogance of a tyrant, and invites to union and friendfhip with the frown of an enemy.

He muft be fenfible of the infinite importance of internal union, of ftrengthening the executive power, and overawing the factious at the prefent crifis. Thefe might poffibly avert fome of the evils that threaten his country, and tend to the happinefs of twenty-four millions of human creatures. But what muft then become of Danton? he would dwindle in point of importance, and fhare only the proportion of an individual in the general profperity.

In

In the comprehenfive vortex of this extraordinary Revolution, this man, originally placed in the lower ranks of life, has been whirled fo near the fummit as to have the chief direction of government within his hope—He thinks himfelf, no doubt, better qualified for that office than thofe who, according to the prefent fyftem, are likely to retain it; and if his hopes fhould be accomplifhed, he perhaps has it in fpeculation to promote the aggrandifement of his country, and would exert himfelf for that purpofe as long as it went hand in hand with his own. But if the gratification of his own ambition is to be had at no other price than the facrifice of his country's good, he will not refufe the purchafe. This, no doubt, will be thought very profligate; yet in this, perhaps, Danton differs lefs from other ftatefmen than in fome other features of his character.

A perfon who is thought to be well ac-

R 2
quainted

quainted with the characters of the leading deputies of both parties, and capable of forming a juſt judgment of their views, lately hinted to me that there was a probability that Danton and his friends would overſet their opponents.

" I thought that Roland had the majority of the members of the Convention with him ?" ſaid I.    -

" The majority of the members, if left to follow the dictates of their conſciences," reſumed he, " are certainly inclined to ſupport Roland; but Danton may fall on means which have been found efficacious in removing ſcruples of conſcience."

" I had no idea of his being ſo very rich. Where will he find the money ?" ſaid I.

" Money, it muſt be confeſſed, is the readieſt and moſt effectual," replied he, ſmiling, " but not the only means— Danton makes uſe of it the leaſt, he has it not always at his command ; for what he

does

does ufe on preffing occafions belongs to another."

" What other means has he?"

" Why, eloquence," rejoined he. " Do you count that for nothing in your National Affembly? I can affure you it has confiderable weight in ours, and Danton may pour it forth with profufion, having at command not only his own noify torrents, but alfo the popular ftream which flows from the lips of Robefpierre."

" Will not the effect of their eloquence," I refumed, " be greatly overbalanced by that of Vergniaud, Buzot, and other friends of Roland?"

" Perhaps it may," faid he; " but the ally on whom Danton has the greateft reliance has not been yet mentioned.

" Who is he?"

" Terror! Terror!" repeated he, " who has acted fo important a part fince the beginning of this Revolution. Do you not

R 3                     think

think that his gigantic form ſtalks ſometimes before the eyes of the Deputies? Do you imagine that their ſleep is never diſturbed with the viſions of heads carried on pikes, of murdered priſoners, and the mangled bodies of thoſe victims of cowardly revenge, Briſſac, Montmorin, Deleſſart, and Rochefoucald?"

"I ſhould imagine," ſaid I, "that ſuch viſions would rather diſturb the conſciences of Danton and ſome of his friends."

"They have none," rejoined he; "and Danton ſeems to have nearly as little fear as conſcience."

He then told me, that he was convinced that Danton's plan was to terrify a majority of the Deputies into his meaſures, by means of the rabble of the ſuburbs, which he expects to have at his diſpoſal, through Chabot, Marat, and other emiſſaries and tried conductors; in which view the ſections of Paris were prevailed on to preſent the addreſs

3                                                                      already

already mentioned, to the Aſſembly, which it is believed was drawn up by Danton himſelf.

His emiſſaries, I have been ſince told, are very active in circulating every report that they conceive can render Roland and his friends, particularly the Girondiſts, odious in the eyes of the people. As many of this party are republicans, and were abuſed by their enemies on that account when ſuch ſentiments were not ſo popular as they are at preſent, it was not to be imagined that they would now be accuſed of being royaliſts ; but as this is the heavieſt charge that can be brought againſt any ſet of men, the ſame perſons who formerly accuſed them of being republicans, without any regard to conſiſtency, and truſting to the abſurd credulity of the multitude, now accuſe them of being royaliſts—and not entirely without effect.

The friends of Roland brought to Paris

the

-the battalion of Marfeillois, which arrived lately, and unqueftionably with no other view than to ferve as a check to the fans-culottes of the fuburbs, who are at the command of Danton; their addrefs, which was read in the Convention, is thought to be the compofition of Barbaroux.

Monfieur Egalité is at prefent feldom heard of: he appears however almoft every day in the Affembly; he generally ftays about half an hour, feems to intereft him-felf little in what is going on, and to intereft the Affembly as little. It has been faid that a weak or wrong-headed man of very high rank, or in an eminent fituation in life, is like a man on the top of a fteeple, from whence all the world feem *little* to him, and where he feems *little* in the eyes of all the world——Whether M. Egalité, when in his original elevated fituation, regarded mankind, or was regarded by them in this light, I will not fay; but he certainly has

been

been at great pains and expence to bring himfelf low enough to be feen and eftimated at his juft value by all the world.

October 27.

According to a late decree all emigrants who are taken in arms are to be tried by a court-martial, and executed where they are taken. Notwithftanding this decree, thirteen were lately conducted to Paris. They were the fame whom Ruhl had paffed on the road as was mentioned above. When they came near Paris, new fears were ex-preffed in the Convention, of their danger of being maffacred in the ftreets.

If there is really any danger of fuch an event, the inhabitants of Paris muft be the worft of favages ; but the only people I fee of a favage difpofition, are certain members of the Convention, and of the Jacobin Club, and a great majority of thofe who fill the tribunes of both thofe affemblies ; but the fhop-keepers and trades-people (and I take

fome

some pains to be acquainted with their way of thinking) seem to be much the same as I have always known them; and I am persuaded that there is no risk of massacres or assassinations, but from a set of wretches who are neither shop-keepers nor tradesmen, but idle vagabonds, hired and excited for the purpose.——When I hear it asserted from the tribune of the Convention, or of the Jacobin Society, that the people are impatient for the death of the King, or inclined to murder unfortunate men while they are conducted to prison, and yet can perceive no disposition of that nature among the citizens, I cannot help suspecting that those orators themselves are the people who are impatient for those atrocities, and that they spread the notion that this desire is general among the people, on purpose to render it easier to commit them, and to make them more quietly submitted to, after they have been committed.

I remember,

I remember, that for feveral days before the 2d of September, frequent mention was made of the unaccountable delays of the courts of juftice with regard to the trial of the prifoners—Certain members of the National Affembly threw out hints of the people's impatience on that account; and I heard a man at the Jacobins threaten, that if the fword of juftice was withheld much longer, the people would exercife it themfelves; and yet, at that time, I could perceive no figns of fuch a difpofition among the citizens of Paris.

The dreadful fcenes in September began—the citizens were ftruck with terror—they repeated to each other, " We often heard that the people would be driven to this!" Each of them believed that all the city had rifen againft the prifoners, except the quarter which he himfelf inhabited, and from which his anxiety for his family made him afraid to move—They were told that all who fpoke

in

in favour of the prifoners were maffacred by the people, and that many fufpected perfons were taken up in the ftreets. By thefe means the citizens of Paris remained panic-ftruck, while a handful of villains, in their name, committed the moft fhocking enormities.

Reflecting on this, naturally creates a fuf-picion that fomething of the fame nature is intended by the fame means with refpect to the King.——It is expected, perhaps, that by dint of repeatedly afferting that the people in general are defirous of his death, they will be driven to fome violent meafure if his trial is delayed, alfo that they look upon all who are of contrary fentiments as arifto-crates and enemies to the Revolution ; and that the citizens will be brought at laft to defire, or pretend to defire, what otherwife they would never have thought of.

Whatever there may be in this conjecture, the unhappy emigrants above mentioned were

4                                        conducted

conducted to the prison without any attempt on the part of the people to murder them. They were tried by a court-martial the day before yesterday; if there really existed in the minds of the people any eagernefs for the execution of thefe unfortunate men, their patience was not put to a long proof: nine of the thirteen prifoners were beheaded this morning, four were officers in the army, one a lieutenant in the navy, one a counfellor in the late parliament of Guyenne, the other three belonged formerly to the Garde du corps.

The four who were acquitted were fervants, and had not been taken in arms.

What renders it more probable that there are people who wifh to renew the fcenes of September is, that a rumour was induftrioufly fpread that the Prince of Lambefc was in the difguife of a footman among the prifoners; which occafioned a rabble from the fuburbs of St. Antoine,

to

to affemble around the Conciergerie, who exclaimed for the head of Lambefc *; but on the affurances of Commiffioners from the municipality that there was no fuch perfon in the prifon, the mob difperfed.

It is more difficult at prefent to execute any great atrocity than it was in the beginning of September, becaufe a great number of profligate and idle fellows, who were at that time in Paris, have been fent to recruit the armies, and in the mean time Marat and his gang are kept in check by the arrival of the Marfeillois.

* The Prince of Lambefc is peculiarly obnoxious to the mob of Paris, becaufe, in the year 1789, when the infurrection of the Parifians began, and the bufts of Necker and of the Duke of Orleans were carried in triumph, this prince was at the head of fome dragoons in the fquare of Lewis XV. Some ftones being thrown at them from the gardens of the Tuileries, he charged with his dragoons on the multitude, fome of whom were wounded.

October 28.

While I was in the Affembly two days ago, a decree was paffed, which is fevere and unjuft in the higheft degree, and the reafoning in fupport of it was as fophiftical as the decree itfelf is cruel. The queftion regarded the French emigrants; it was firft ftated, that there is an effential difference between thofe who have gone into countries at war with France, to affift with their arms or counfel the enemies of their country, and thofe who have paffed into neutral ftates, fimply with a view to their own fafety—" The former," it was faid, " are traitors, and ought to be punifhed with death; the latter are cowards, who have abandoned their country in the hour of danger, for which they deferve only to be banifhed." Accordingly, by the decree they are banifhed, with this additional penalty, that if they ever return, they fhall be punifhed with death——not for having emigrated (on that

account

account they are only banifhed), but for having broken the law which condemned them to perpetual banifhment."

This is furely a diftinction without a difference ; for by this cruel and unjuft decree, the perfon who leaves his native country merely from fear, and takes no part againft it, is in effect fubjected to the fame penalty with thofe who have joined the invading armies, and may be taken in arms—The former is liable to be put to death if he returns to his native country, and the latter cannot fuffer any punifhment till he does the fame.

It is as if two fervants in a family were tried as accomplices with incendiaries who had fet their mafter's houfe on fire : the one is clearly proved to have aided and abetted the incendiaries; nothing appears againft the other, but that he leaped out of the window to fave himfelf from the flames. According to the fpirit of this decree, the judge might

pronounce

pronounce fentence in the fuppofed cafe to the following effect : "There is a wide difference between the crimes of thefe two men, and fo there fhall be in their punifhments. The one muft be hanged as an accomplice of the incendiaries ; and as for the other who jumped out of the window, he ought to have been afhamed ever to have fhewn his face ; and if he had ftaid out of the way and never appeared, I acknowledge it would be unjuft to hang him : but fince he is taken, that alters the cafe ; he merits now to be hanged, and I fentence him to that punifhment accordingly ; but obferve, it is not for jumping out of the window, but for the aggravating circumftance of being taken."

By this abfurd and iniquitous decree, many women are punifhed for that timidity which is natural to the fex ; and many men are ruined in their fortunes, and reduced to abfolute want, whofe only view in emigrating was to fave their lives, not from the fword of juftice, but from the poniards of affaffins.

That two parties in a ftate who are contending for the conduct of government fhould diflike each other, is common ; but that rancorous degree to which it is arrived in France is beyond any thing of the fame kind that I ever knew in England, and, I fhould hope, for the credit of mankind, beyond any thing ever known before in any other country. I made this obfervation to a gentleman who pretends to know the French thoroughly.—" The French," faid he, " have been accufed of being very inconftant *lovers* : I know nothing of that ; but I do affure you," continued he, playing on an expreffion recorded of Dr. Johnfon, " that they are very fincere and conftant *haters*."

In confirmation of this obfervation, I perceive every day the ftrongeft marks of violent

lent hatred between the leaders of the two oppofite parties. They feem to agree in nothing but in a mutual hatred againft the unfortunate emigrants, which however does not in the leaft degree diminifh their reciprocal hatred: and I am told, that the fame hatred prevails among the emigrants themfelves in all the different countries of Europe ; that thofe who emigrated at one period of the revolution hate thofe who emigrated at another, as cordially as all of them have very good reafon to hate the men who form this Convention, and are paffing fuch fevere decrees againft them.

October 26.

Marat has carried his calumnies fuch a length, that even the party which he wifhes to fupport feem to be afhamed of him; and he is fhunned and apparently detefted by every body elfe. When he enters the hall of the Affembly, he is avoided on all fides;

S 2                          and

and when he feats himfelf, thofe near him generally rife and change their places. He ftood a confiderable time yefterday near the tribune, watching an opportunity to fpeak. I faw him at one time addrefs himfelf to Louvet; and, in doing fo, he attempted to lay his hand on Louvet's fhoulder, who inftantly ftarted back with looks of averfion, as one would do from the touch of a noxious reptile, exclaiming! " *Ne me touchez pas!* "

Nothing can difconcert Marat; he perfevered in foliciting the privilege of being heard *pour un fait* \*. The Affembly fhewed the greateft unwillingnefs to hear him: he exclaimed that it was *un fait qui intéreffoit le falut public* †.

They were at laft under the neceffity of hearing him; he elevated his head as ufual when he fpeaks from the tribune, furveyed

\* For a fact.
† A fact regarding the public fafety.

the

the audience with compofure and audacity, and in a hollow voice and with folemnity of cadence faid, " It is not the citizen who now addreffes you, that provokes to murder, or puts public freedom in danger, but thofe in office, men who make ufe of their authority to opprefs the people ; *they* are the tyrants, who, under the pretence of maintaining the tranquillity of Paris, arreft and murder the moft innocent and meritorious citizens." He then accufed Roland of having given orders for arrefting an excellent patriot whom he named.

This turned out to be entirely a mifreprefentation ; but before Marat defcended from the tribune, Barbaroux informed the Affembly that Marat had paid a vifit at the barracks of the battalion of Marfeillois lately arrived ; that, at fight of their accommodations, he had lamented that fo many brave fans-culottes were fo ill lodged, while a regiment of dragoons, compofed of ancient va-

let-

let-de-chambres and coachmen of the nobility, with a mixture of the King's gardesdu-corps, all anti-revolutionifts, were fuperbly quartered in the Ecole Militaire: that he had infinuated many things tending to raife a jealoufy between the Marfeillois and this regiment of dragoons, and had hinted that it was owing to the Convention that the former were fo ungratefully treated: and, that he had invited fome of them to breakfaft with him.

It was evident that Marat's defign in this was to have feduced the Marfeillois from thofe who had engaged them to come to Paris, to attach them to his own party, and to engage them, inftead of oppofing the turbulent behaviour of the mob of St. Antoine, to act with them as their townfmen did on the 10th of Auguft.

The Marfeillois however refufed his invitation. But Barbaroux's narrative occafioned a violent outcry in the Affembly againft Marat:

rat: the epithets *fcélérat*, *affaffin*, were often repeated, and one member faid that Marat had lately been heard to declare that there would be no tranquillity in the ftate till two hundred and fixty-eight heads were cut off.

" I am the perfon," cried another member, " who heard him fay fo."

I threw my eyes on Marat, to obferve how he would look on hearing fuch an accufation.

" Very well," faid Marat ; " I did fay fo, " and it is my opinion."

I fhould have thought I had miftaken or heard indiftinctly, if he had not refumed—— " I repeat it," faid Marat: " That is my opinion, you will not pretend that men are to be punifhed for their opinions ; and as for the filly ftory of Barbaroux," continued he, " it is a malignant mifconftruction of my patriotic civilities and hofpitality to the Marfeillois. What then does the whole of this mighty bufinefs amount to ? why, that I

faid,

said, you would not enjoy peace or tranquillity till the oppressors of the people lost their heads, of whom there are two hundred and sixty-eight at the most moderate calculation. I am also accused of having shewn more attention to the battalion just arrived from Marseilles, than any other member of the Convention—If these are crimes," added he, sweeping the edge of his right hand across his throat, " égorgez-moi !"

This new denunciation against Marat was transmitted to the same committee who have the former under their consideration ; and Marat's accusation of Roland was considered as invidious, and an attempt to obstruct the course of justice.

I have never heard of any other of his good qualities — but this man certainly possesses a great deal of courage both personal and political : no danger can terrify him, no detection can disconcert him ; his heart, as well as his forehead, seems to be of brass.

October

October 29.

I was prefent when Ruhl of Strafbourg, whom I formerly mentioned, informed the Convention, that being in the commiffion for examining certain letters in the German language, which had been intercepted, he had found one from a corporal in the Pruffian army to his wife in Silefia.   In this letter he faid there were many expreffions of conjugal love and parental affection, while in the fame letter the French were painted in the blackeft colours.  " This poor corporal," continued Ruhl, " has had the perfeverance and generofity to fave two ducats out of his pay, which he inclofed in the letter to his wife, who, it appears, was then in child-bed.   I defire to be authorized to tranfmit the money, with what addition I pleafe, to this honeft corporal's wife, with a letter affuring her that the French do not deferve all the ill names which her hufband gives them."

Ruhl

Ruhl is a man about feventy years of age; there is a great appearance of naïveté in his manner. I happened to mention this ftory of the corporal to a Frenchman of my acquaintance :—" Le conte eft beau," faid he, " et ne manque que la vraifemblance pour le rendre intéreffant*."

" He had the letter in his hand," faid I ; " how can you doubt it ?"

" If he had twenty letters," replied the Frenchman, " I muft doubt it, becaufe a Pruffian corporal is generous in nothing but in *coups de batons* ; and it is not in the nature of a man who is diftributing thefe from morning to night, to have tender affections of any kind.—Such oppofite and difcordant qualities cannot inhabit the fame breaft."

The incredulity of my French acquaint-

* The tale is agreeable, and only needs probability to make it interefting.

ance

ance I think unreafonable ; and I will here infert an anecdote, although it is much more expofed to his criticifm, becaufe it comes from a quarter which leaves no doubt on my mind of its truth.

Monfieur de Bertrand, chevalier de Malte, and brother to Monfieur de Bertrand de Moleville late Minifter of the Marine, was arrefted and confined in the prifon of the Abbaye, foon after the 10th of Auguft. This gentleman was brought at midnight on the third of September before the dreadful tribunal in that prifon. He is a man of great coolnefs and firmnefs of mind, which was of infinite fervice to him in this emergency ; for although the fymptoms of fear ought not on fuch occafions to have been confidered as a prefumption of guilt, yet that conftruction was put on them by the judges, and, without any other prefumption, they fometimes proved fatal to the prifoner.

When Mr. Bertrand was queftioned, he
anfwered

answered with an undisturbed voice and countenance, " that he had not the least idea of what he had been arrested for, that those who arrested him could not inform him, that nobody had informed him since, and that he was convinced he had been taken up by mistake."

Struck with the cool and undaunted manner in which he addressed t h em, and having no particular accusation nor proof of any kind against him, the judges ordered him to be released.

Two men covered with blood, who had been employed in killing the prisoners, and attended in the expectation of the signal for dispatching Mr. Bertrand, seemed surprised but not displeased at the unusual order. They conducted him through the court of the Abbaye, and on the way asked if he had any relation to whose house he wished to go.

He answered, that he had a sister-in-law to whom he intended to go directly.

6

" How

" How very much furprifed a nd de-
lighted muft fhe be to fee you !" faid they.

" I am perfuaded fhe will," replied Mr.
Bertrand.

One of the men then afked the other if
he fhould not be glad to be prefent at this
meeting ; to which he eagerly faid he fhould :
and both declared they had a curiofity to be
witneffes to the joyful meeting between Mr.
Bertrand and his fifter-in-law.

The gentleman was aftonifhed and embar-
raffed : he reprefented, that his relation being
a delicate woman, their appearance might
very much alarm her, particularly at fuch an
unfeafonable hour ; that he could not think
of giving them fuch unneceffary trouble :"
and added whatever he thought would divert them from fo unexpected a propofal.

They urged that they would wait in the
parlour till he had advertifed the lady of
their being in the houfe, to prevent her
being alarmed : that fo far from being
a trouble,

a trouble, it would give them great pleafure to accompany him : that they wifhed to have a relaxation from the work in which they had been fo long employed, and they hoped he would not deny them the fatisfaction of feeing the meeting between him and his friends.

Mr. Bertrand did not think it prudent to refufe fuch petitioners any longer ; he therefore affented—they accompanied him to the houfe. He fent the fervant, who opened the door at the found of his voice, to advertife the lady that he was arrived, and well. He afterwards went himfelf and informed her of the ftrange fancy of the two men, who waited in another room. The lady had arifen and dreffed herfelf haftily on her firft hearing of his arrival : every body in the family had done the fame, and had flocked around him with expreffions of joy. The two men were admitted, and were witneffes to the happinefs that all manifefted : they feemed much gratified

tified and affected at the fight ; it formed the ftrongeft contraft with thofe they had fo lately feen. Mr. Bertrand offered them money, which they would on no account accept, declaring that they were already paid for accompanying him in the only way they defired. After remaining a confiderable time, they took their leave, wifhing the lady all happinefs, and thanking Mr. Bertrand for allowing them the pleafure of being witneffes to fo pleafing a meeting.

Nobody can be more aware than I am of the inconfiftency which from this narrative appears in the difpofitions of the fame individuals. That two men fo unfeeling as to be actively engaged in the remorfelefs fcenes at the prifon fhould have the fenfibility to wifh to be witneffes of the meeting between Mr. Bertrand and his friends, and behave on the whole as thofe two men did, is what no perfon, who has ftudied the ufual analogies and combinations of the human difpofitions,

I                                        would

would have expected. The firft turn of mind feems incompatible with the fecond : I know no theory by which they can be reconciled ; I attempt no explanation : I repeat the facts as I have them from authority to which I cannot refufe my belief, and becaufe they form a new inftance of the aftonifhing variety, and even oppofition of character to be found in that wonderful creature, MAN.

October 30.

Part of the equipage of the French Princes was feized during the retreat of the Duke of Brunfwick's army, amongft which was found a pocket-book belonging to *Monfieur* the King's brother. Several packets of letters, forming a confiderable correfpondence on various fubjects, between the emigrants and their friends, were alfo found at Verdun and Longwy by Kellermann's army. All thofe papers have been tranfmitted to the Convention, and by it fubmitted to the examination of a committee.

Moft

Moſt of the letters, I am told, are of a private nature, and no way relative to what concerns the ſtate or the public in general. It would be highly unbecoming therefore in the Convention to order thoſe to be publiſhed, which can have no other effect than to gratify the ſpirit of hatred, envy and ſlander, and create diſcord and jealouſy among families and acquaintance. It is likewiſe ſaid, that important diſcoveries have been made by ſome of theſe letters, and that they form a complete proof of an intelligence between the King and his brothers, for the ruin of the conſtitution*. In ſupport of this aſſertion, a letter was this day read in the Aſſembly, ſaid to have been found in the pocket book above mentioned. The letter is from the Marquis of Toulongeon,

* This *complete* proof, I make no doubt, will be of the nature of the proofs already publiſhed, which are alſo called complete, but to every candid mind muſt appear very deficient.

Lieutenant General in the French army of the King's brothers : it unfolds certain meafures he had taken for arranging the troops in fuch a manner as to facilitate their defertion to the Auftrians ; gives the reafon why he had not gone himfelf to join the Princes at Coblentz ; adds that he is of more ufe to their caufe by retaining a command in the French army ; that the motives of his conduct are known to the Emperor, and approved of by the King, &c.

A decree of accufation immediately paffed againft Toulongeon, who, fortunately for him, however, has already made his efcape : and after the paffing of this decree, a member expreffed his furprife, that among fo many decrees of accufation as had been paffed, they had not yet pronounced the moft important of all, namely one againft the King.

On which Maile, who is of the Committee of Legiflation, faid, that the procefs of

the

the King required the greateſt ſolemnity, not becauſe there was any difficulty in proving his guilt, nor to demonſtrate it to the French nation, who were already convinced, but to ſatisfy and give a great example to all Europe, and to avoid the errors which the Engliſh had committed in not obſerving all the neceſſary ſolemnities in the trial of Charles the Firſt, for which they were cenſured by many hiſtorians, and juſtified by none.

In anſwer to this, Ruhl obſerved, that the Engliſh nation had been juſtified for the ſentence paſſed on Charles Stuart by a writer of greater genius than all the hiſtorians who ever have written on the ſubject, namely, John Milton, author of Paradiſe Loſt.

Hitherto I had conſidered Ruhl in a favourable light; there is ſomething natural in his manner, and I thought him a man of

T 2                          humanity;

humanity; but one of that difpofition would hardly have made fuch an obfervation at this particular time in the Convention.

October 31.

The Trial of Charles the Firft of England, tranflated into French from the State Trials, is to be found of late on all the book-fellers tables around the hall of the Convention. An abridgement of the fame is cried by the hawkers of pamphlets in the Palais Royal and the various entries to the National Affembly: the converfation is now greatly turned to that fubject, and to the expected procefs of Lewis XVI. I never believed, however, that there was a ferious intention in the Convention to bring the King to trial, and ftill lefs did I think it probable that it would be in their contemplation to bring him to the fcaffold; an idea which I cannot entertain without horror. Befides, however

devoid

devoid of principle fome of them may be, I could not conceive that they would commit fuch an act of cruelty and injuftice, without any of the motives which incite wicked men to deeds of fuch atrocity. Their perfonal intereft evidently dictates the prefervation of the King's life, and it feemed unlikely that any member of the Convention, one only excepted, could be actuated by perfonal enmity : they are almoft all of the middle or inferior ranks of life ; none of them have ever had opportunities for that kind of intercourfe with the King, which ufually generates either perfonal friendfhip or hatred : they may like or diflike, refpect or defpife his general conduct and character ; but I could fee none of the ufual fources of perfonal hatred either good or bad, efpecially as, with refpect to the exercife of authority, the whole reign of Lewis XVI. has been a reign of moderation. He has always manifefted a defire to meet the wifhes of his fub-

jects ;

jects; and perhaps his averfion to every meafure which had the appearance of being violent, with too great a difpofition to *grant*, have deprived him of the power of *refufing*, and reduced him to the ftate he is in.——I am perfuaded that none of his anceftors had fo juft a claim to the epithets which the public and hiftorians have affixed to their names, as the unfortunate Lewis XVI. has to that of *Louis le trop bon.*

I have excepted one perfon, to whom the preceding reafoning does not fully apply, and who may be fuppofed to be inftigated by hatred or revenge ; but allowing this to be the cafe, from all I have obferved or heard fince I have been in this country, there is reafon to think that his influence is infinitely too fmall to engage either party in meafures of which they difapprove.

Thefe confidérations were fufficient hitherto to induce me to believe that there was no ferious intention in the Convention to

to bring the King to a trial.——But I now begin to fear that a procefs in fome fhape or
other will very foon be brought on, and
when once begun, there is no knowing
what may be the iffue in a town fo much in
the power of the populace, and of *fuch* a
populace as that which Paris contains at
prefent.

I am led to this alteration of opinion from
having very lately heard a number of citizens, whom I thought of a different opinion, declare their conviction that the King
was betraying the country. The rancorous
activity of his enemies has at length perfuaded them, that, inftead of another Henry
IV. between whom and Lewis XVI. they
formerly found a refemblance, they actually had another Lewis XI. or Charles
IX. on the throne.

Befides, whether the King ought or ought
not to be judged, is not merely confidered
as a matter of juftice or even of expediency,

T 4                                    but,

but, moſt unfortunately, it has become a party queſtion, in which paſſion may have more weight than either. Danton's party knows that the Girondiſts wiſh to ſave the King, which is reaſon ſufficient with the former to do every thing in their power to promote his trial and condemnation, and to repreſent the oppoſition of the other party as a proof of their being ariſtocrates and royaliſts in their hearts.

Marat, who is the great agent of Danton and Robeſpierre, declares that it is highly unjuſt, and would be a ſhameful deviation from the flattering tenet of egalité, after having condemned M. de la Porte and other inferior criminals, to paſs over the greateſt criminal of all.

Finally, I have been impreſſed with fears reſpecting the fate of the King from a variety of circumſtances, too minute to be mentioned, which have ſtruck me very lately. It is certainly horrid and diſgraceful to human

man nature, but I am afraid that the populace of this city have heard so much of a grand example that ought to be exhibited to Europe, and their imaginations have dwelt so long on the idea of a King being tried for his life, and afterwards led to execution, that they cannot with patience bear the thoughts of being disappointed of such an extraordinary spectacle.

November 1.

When Roland and his friends were attacked by so active and so virulent an opposition, it was not to be expected that they could escape an accusation so easy to make, and so difficult to refute, as that they were not actuated by the genuine principles of patriotism, but merely by selfish motives, and that they had no other object in view than to retain the lucrative offices of the state in their own hands.

To stifle the voice of slander at once, upon this subject, Genfonné surprised the Convention lately by a speech in which he lamented

lamented that a party-spirit had manifefted itfelf fo ftrongly among them. He
added that diffidence in each other, the natural effect of the numerous treafons which
had lately been difcovered, alfo prevailed to
an alarming degree; which, joined to the
envy which generates hatred, and produces divifion, might enable defpotifm to
arife again out of anarchy : he added, that
the prefent times required a great example
of felf-denial to dry up one great fource of
party fpirit, filence calumny, and prove to
the world that they had not made war on
royalty on purpofe to divide the regal fpoils
among themfelves, but to obtain freedom to
their country—He therefore moved that it
fhould be decreed that no member of the
Convention fhould be capable of enjoying
any office in the government for ten years
after the decree had paffed.

All the members, as if with one voice,
called out, Yes, yes : they fprung from their
feats,

feats, in a fit of enthufiafm, and demanded that the propofal of Genfonné fhould be inftantly decreed, which was done accordingly.

This practice of paffing decrees the inftant they are propofed, without reflection, may be attended with the worft confequences; as for this decree in particular, it ftrikes fo directly againft the views of the leading men of both parties, and is liable, in other refpects, to fo many weighty objections, that I fufpect it will not be long in force even in France; but if it fhould, it may afford comfort to the minds of Englifhmen at this awful period, when there is a juft dread of the prevalence of French manners and French opinions, to reflect that there is too much folid good fenfe in the Britifh Parliament to adopt fo foolifh a meafure

November 2.

A moſt unrelenting fpirit againſt the emigrants,

emigrants, appears as often as they are
mentioned in the Conventional Aſſembly—
I ſpoke of this to one of the deputies this
evening, expreſſing my ſurpriſe that no
member ever ſaid any thing in their favour,
although I could hardly imagine but that,
in ſo large an aſſembly, many of the members had relations or friends among them.

In anſwer to my obſervation the deputy
ſaid, that the greater part of the emigrants
were nobleſſe, of which claſs very few are
members of the Convention, ſo that there is
little or no connection by blood, and as little
by friendſhip, between the deputies and emigrants. I take it for granted, added he,
that you do not think any meaſure too ſevere for thoſe emigrants who have taken
arms againſt their country, and as for
thoſe who do not appear in arms, it is well
known that they are doing every thing in
their power to excite every nation in Europe,
particularly the Engliſh, againſt France, and

if

if they succeed, and produce a counter revolution, there is no doubt but these emigrants will exercise still greater cruelties against the patriots.

I replied, that the Assembly had saved the emigrants the trouble of exciting war, by declaring it first; for that no nation had declared war with France hitherto till France declared war with it; that with respect to England, I imagined that whether she should enter into a war with France or not, would depend on the conduct of the Convention, and not on any thing the emigrants could say or do; and, finally, that if men were to act cruelly towards those whose persons or property were in their power, on a supposition that, if the situations were reversed, those whom they oppress would oppress them, in that case there would be nothing but oppression and cruelty in the world.

I then mentioned the case of one person who

i

who had emigrated in very particular circumftances, and had returned to France foon
after, ftating the cafe in the ftrongeft and
moft favourable light, which I corroborated
with documents that I had in my poffeffion.

Other deputies joined us, to whom I
alfo mentioned this cafe, and one of them
taking me afide, affured me he faw it in the
fame point of view that I did, and that he
would do what he could to ferve the perfon in queftion, which, notwithftanding the
favourable circumftances, muft be attempted
with delicacy, becaufe fuch a hatred prevailed in the Convention againft all emigrants, and fuch a jealoufy of each other, that
whoever feemed active or zealous in their favour, had a greater probability of injuring
himfelf, than of ferving them. You will
readily believe, added he, how difficult it is to
procure any thing like favour to one who is
both a noble and an emigrant, at a period
when thofe nobles who never emigrated,

5

but

but on the contrary have taken an active part in the Revolution, are looked on with diftruftful and jealous eyes.—He then gave me directions how to proceed, and told me to whom, and in what manner to apply—I have followed his advice, and with the beft hopes of fuccefs.

In the gratification of this hatred to the emigrants, as in many other inftances, the Convention overfteps good policy.

General Cuftine has tranfmitted letters to the Convention, which have been addreffed to him from emigrants in foreign fervices, who now wifh to ferve their country, provided they may be allowed to return with fafety.

General Biron has likewife written to the Convention in favour of fome officers who have been in the army of the Prince of Condé, and now implore forgivenefs, and the General's mediation with the Affembly, that

that they may be permitted to return to France.

In both cafes the Convention paffed to the order of the day—yet as Biron is at prefent a very popular general, and as Cuftine has juft taken poffeffion of Frankfort, and has been always fuccefsful, it might have been expected that more attention would have been paid to their applications.

Befides, at this moment of fuccefs, lenient and conciliatory meafures towards thofe unfortunate people who left their country at a time when, affuredly, there were many reafons for leaving it, would appear generous to all Europe, it would pleafe the numerous relations and friends of the emigrants in every department of France, and go farther to attach the whole nation to the Revolution, than any of the decrees they have lately paffed, or perhaps than even the victories they have lately gained.

But

But there are men in this Convention, and unfortunately leading men too, who are ready to facrifice every confideration to the gratification of their paffions, and whofe ruling paffions feem to be hatred and revenge.

This day the Prefidency of Guadet ended, and Herault de Sechelles was elected to fucceed him.——Herault is a man of about thirty years of age, of an open engaging countenance, and genteel appearance, circumftances which diftinguifh him in this Affembly: it is alfo remarkable, that he is not confidered as fo much devoted to the Girondifts as any of the late Prefidents, which is confidered as a proof that they are rather lofing ground.

November 3.

As the General Council of the Municipality of Paris, which was formed at midnight on the ninth of Auguft, claim the whole glory of the Revolution, they thought they had the beft right to retain alfo the power of the ftate.

Without confulting the National Affembly, they iffued orders for fearching many hotels, under various pretexts; detachments of national guards, under leaders chofen by the Council, were alfo fent to particular churches and palaces in Paris and the neighbourhood, and confiderable quantities of plate and other valuable effects carried away, under the pretence of being for the public ufe, but of which a large portion has been embezzled.

Some members of the National Affembly began a fhort time after the tenth of Auguft to fpeak on the fubject of thefe embezzlements, and propofed to make an enquiry into that bufinefs : but the National Affembly had then loft all energy ; and, according to an expreffion of one of the deputies, it had become a mere engine for manufacturing

decrees

decrees at the requifition of the Council of the Commune. As often as any mention was made of eftablifhing a committee to examine into the extent of thefe embezzlements, and by whom they had been committed, the propofal was heard with evident marks of ill humour by all the members of the Affembly who were alfo members of the Commune, and by others intimately connected with them.—They who made fuch propofals, finding themfelves unfupported, dropped them ; it was not thought prudent to irritate the men who iffued thofe orders of arreft by which the prifons had been filled, and who, in the opinion of many, had alfo iffued the orders by which they had been emptied.

It was expected that the Convention would be able to effect what the late National Affembly attempted in vain, and to reftrain the power of the Municipality within its proper limits. An account of the ufurpa-

tions

tions of the General Council had been written to all the departments of France; many of the deputies to the Convention had come to Paris, prepoffeffed with the idea that Paris wifhed to govern the ftate independent of all the other departments—that the General Council governed Paris, and that Danton and Robefpierre governed the General Council.

Having heard that a debate of importance was expected, I went to the Conventional Affembly two days ago earlier than ufual.

Roland was to prefent a memorial refpecting the ftate of Paris. When he appeared, contrary to cuftom, they poftponed the bufinefs then tranfacting, to attend to him.—He began by faying, that if the ftrength of his voice was equal to that of his mind, he fhould himfelf read the addrefs which he held in his hand; but as his breaft was delicate, he begged that one of the fecretaries might be allowed to read it for him.—Lanjuinais afcended the tribune, and read.

In this memorial were ftated all the ufurpations and acts of defpotifm which had been committed by the Commune fince the tenth of Auguft, many of which were unknown to the generality of the deputies, and feemed to fill them with equal furprife and indignation.——Roland ftated that he had often required fome account of the money, plate, and effects which had been feized by commiffioners from the Commune at Senlis, Chantilly, l'Hotel de Coigny, and other hotels, without having had any fatisfactory anfwer : that he had alfo addreffed himfelf to them to know how Lewis XVI. and his family were treated in the Temple, but no notice had been taken of his demand. After having demonftrated how both public and private property had been violated, he demanded whether perfonal furety had been better protected. This led him to mention

the

the horrors of the beginning of September, which he pretty plainly insinuated were committed by the leaders of the Common Council, who, he asserted, were still meditating the most rapacious and bloody designs in support of their avarice and ambition.——With this memorial Roland presented a letter addressed to the Minister of Justice, in which information is given, "that expressions of the most alarming tendency had been used by certain persons of late; that it had been even insinuated that the business begun in September had not been completed; that the whole cabal of Roland and Briffot should be cut off; that there was a scheme for this purpose; that Vergniaud, Guadet, Buzot, La Source, and others displeased the real patriots; and that *Robespierre* was the properest person for conducting the government in the present emergency.

" Ah the villain !" one of the members
called

called aloud, as foon as this name was pronounced.

There was fuch an uproar in the Affembly for fome time after Roland's memorial had been read, that no perfon in particular could be diftinctly heard: the noife was moftly occafioned by expreffions of rage againft Robefpierre, and partly by a cry that the memorial fhould be printed, and fent to all the departments and all the municipalities in France.

Robefpierre afcended the tribune: the cry againft him was fo violent that his voice could not be diftinguifhed: he at laft was heard to fay, that he wifhed to juftify himfelf from the calumnies of the Minifter. He was interrupted by a new cry to clofe the difcuffion: he then faid he wifhed to fpeak againft the printing of the memorial.

This was alfo refufed by a pretty univerfal exclamation; but on its being obferved, that they could not decree a propofition

U 4 without

without hearing thofe who wifhed to fpeak againft it, he was allowed to proceed. He began with a few fentences concerning the printing the paper, and immediately deviated into an eulogium on his own conduct. Guadet, the Prefident, reminded him of the queftion.

"I have no need of your admonitions," faid Robefpierre; "I know very well on what I have to fpeak."

"He thinks himfelf already Dictator," exclaimed a member.

"Robefpierre, fpeak againft the printing," faid the Prefident.

Robefpierre then refumed, and declaimed on every thing except againft the printing.

His voice was again drowned by an outcry againft his wanderings. The Prefident ftrove to procure filence, that Robefpierre might be heard; which he no fooner was, than he accufed the Prefident of encouraging the clamour againft him.

No accufation could be more unjuft or more

more injudicious than this, becaufe it was
falfe, and becaufe every body prefent was
witnefs to its falfehood. The Prefident had
done all in his power that Robefpierre might
be heard, and had actually broken three bells
by ringing to procure him filence.

The Prefident then faid, " Robefpierre,
vous voyez les efforts que je fais pour ra-
mener le filence—mais je vous pardonne
une calomnie de plus *."

Robefpierre refumed, and continued to
fpeak of himfelf a confiderable time in the
moft flattering terms.

Many people prefer fpeaking of themfelves to any other topic of difcourfe, as well
as Robefpierre ; but in him this propenfity
is irrefiftible. Praife acts as a cordial on
the fpirits of moft people, but it is the praife
they receive from others which has that

* Robefpierre, you are yourfelf witnefs to the efforts
I have made to reftore filence ; but I forgive you that
additional calumny.

effect :

effect: what is peculiar to Robespierre is, that he seems as much enlivened by the eulogies he bestows on himself, as others are by the applause of their fellow-citizens.

The panegyric he pronounced on his own virtues evidently raised his spirits, and inspired him with a courage which at last precipitated him into rashness. "A system of calumny is established," said he with a lofty voice, "and against whom is it directed? against a zealous patriot. Yet who is there among you who dares rise and accuse me to my face?"

"Moi," exclaimed a voice from one end of the hall. There was a profound silence; in the midst of which, a thin, lank, pale-faced man stalked along the hall like a spectre; and being come directly opposite to the tribune, he fixed Robespierre, and said, *Oui, Robespierre, c'est moi qui t'accuse ＊*.

It was Jean-Baptiste Louvet.

＊ Yes, Robespierre, it is I who accuse you.

Robes—

Robefpierre was confounded : he ftood motionlefs, and turned pale ; he could not have feemed more alarmed had a bleeding head fpoken to him from a charger.

Louvet afcended, and appeared in the front of the tribune, while Robefpierre fhrunk to one fide.

Danton perceiving how very much his friend was difconcerted, called out, " Continue, Robefpierre, there are many good citizens here to hear you."

This feemed to be a hint to the people in the galleries, that they might fhew themfelves in fupport of the patriot—but they remained neuter.

The Affembly was in fuch confufion for fome time, that nothing diftinct could be heard. Robefpierre again attempted to fpeak —his difcourfe was as confufed as the Affembly—he quitted the tribune.

Danton went into it : his drift was to prevent Louvet from being heard, and to propofe a future day for taking into confideration

fideration Roland's memorial; and as Marat feemed at this time to be rather en mauvaife odeur with the Convention, Danton thought proper to make a declaration which had no connection with the debate, and which nobody thought fincere : " Je déclare à la Republique entière," he exclaimed, " que je n'aime point l'individu Marat. Je déclare avec franchife que j'ai fait l'expérience de fon temperament, et qu'il eft non-feulement volcanique et acariâtre—mais infociable *."

This conveys no favourable idea of Danton's eloquence. After finding the two firft qualities in Marat, it is furprifing that he could fearch for a third. It is as if a man were to give as his reafon for not keeping company with an old acquaintance, that he not only found him quite mad, and always ready to ftab thofe near him with a dagger,

---

* I declare to the whole Republic, that I do not love Marat. I frankly acknowledge that I have fome experience of the man ; and I find not only that he is boifterous and quarrelfome, but alfo unfociable.

but

but that, over and above, he was fometimes a-little too referved.

This did not divert Louvet from his purpofe : he perfevered, and the Affembly decreed that he fhould be heard.

November 4.

He began by requefting the Prefident's protection, that he might be heard without interruption, for he was going to mention things that would be mortally offenfive to fome prefent—who, he faid, were already fore, and would be apt to fcream when he came to touch the tender parts.—As he continued a little on fome preliminary topics, Danton exclaimed, " I defire that the accufer would put his finger into the wound."

" I intend it," replied Louvet; " but why does Danton fcream beforehand ?"

Louvet then proceeded to unfold the popular artifices by which Robefpierre acquired his influence in the Jacobin Society : " that he had introduced into it a number of men devoted

devoted to him, and, by an infolent exercife
of his power, had driven fome of the moſt
reſpectable members out of it; that after the
tenth of Auguſt he had been chofen of the
Council General of the Commune, and acquired equal influence there. Where he
was on that memorable day," faid Louvet,
" nobody can tell; all we know is, that,
like Sofia in the play, he did not appear till
after the battle. On the eleventh or twelfth
he prefented himfelf to the Commune, and
under *his* aufpices all the orders for arreſting
the citizens were iſſued;——that orders had
been given for arreſting Roland and Briſſot,
which, by the care of fome of their friends,
had not been executed;——that a band of
men had arrogated to themfelves the honour
of the Revolution of Auguſt, whereas the
maſſacres of September only belonged to
them."——Here Talien and fome others of
Robefpierre's faction, who were alfo of the
General Council, began to murmur; on

7                          which

which a member called out—Silence, les blessés! and Louvet resumed, with great animation—" Yes, barbarians ! to you belong the horrid massacres of September, which you now impute to the citizens of Paris. The citizens of Paris were all present at the Tuileries on the tenth of August, but who were witnesses to the murders in September? Two, or perhaps three hundred spectators, whom an incomprehensible curiosity had drawn before the prisons. But it is asked, Why then did not the citizens prevent them? Because they were struck with terror; the alarm guns had been fired, the tocsin had sounded; because their ears were imposed on by false rumours; because their eyes were astonished at the sight of municipal officers, dressed in scarfs, presiding at the executions; because Roland exclaimed in vain ; because Danton, the Minister of Justice, was silent ; and because Santerre, the Commander of the National Guards, remained inactive. Soon after

after these lamentable scenes," continued
Louvet, " the Legiflative Affembly was frequently calumniated, infulted, and even
threatened, by this infolent demagogue."

Here Louvet being interrupted by the
exclamations of Robefpierre's adherents,
La Croix went up to the tribune, and declared, that one evening, while he was Prefident of the Legiflative Affembly, but not
in the chair, Robefpierre, at the head of a
deputation of the General Council, came to
the bar with a particular petition, which
Lacroix oppofed, and the Affembly paffed
to the order of the day ; that having retired
to the extremity of the hall, Robefpierre
faid to him, that if the Legiflative Affembly
would not with good will do what he required, he would force them to do it by the
found of the tocfin ; on which Lacroix faid,
he had taken his feat as Prefident, and related to the Affembly what had paffed.

Other members bore teftimony of Robefpierre's

pierre's having pronounced the threat, and they confirmed the truth of all that Lacroix had related. One added, that Lacroix's friends had entreated him not to return to his own houfe that evening, by the Terrace of the Feuillans, becaufe affaffins were pofted there to murder him.

This interlude excited frefh indignation againft Robefpierre, who made fome efforts to be heard from the tribune. One of the members obferved, that a man accufed of fuch a crime ought not to place himfelf in the tribune, but at the bar.

Robefpierre perfifted ; but the Affembly decided, that he fhould not be heard till Louvet had finifhed.

" The Legiflative Affembly," faid Louvet, refuming the very fentence at which he had been interrupted, " was calumniated, infulted, and menaced by this infolent demagogue, who, with eternal profcriptions in his mouth, accufed fome of the moft de-

ferving reprefentatives of the people with
having fold the nation to Brunfwick, and
accufed them the day before the affaffinations began : in his bloody profcriptions all
the new minifters were included except one,
and that one always the fame. Will it be
in thy power, Danton," continued Louvet,
darting his eyes on the late Minifter of
Juftice, " to juftify thy character to pofterity
for that exception ? Do not expect to blind us
now by difavowing Marat, that *enfant perdu
de l'affaffinat* : it was through your influence,
by your harangues at the Electoral Affemblies, in which you blackened Prieftley, and
white-wafhed Marat, that he is now of this
Convention. Upon that occafion I demanded
leave to fpeak againft fuch a candidate : as
I retired, I was furrounded by thofe men,
with bludgeons and fabres, with whom the
future Dictator was always accompanied :
thofe body guards of Robefpierre, during
the period of the maffacres, often looked at
.me

me with threatening countenances, and one of them faid, *It will be your turn foon.*"

Louvet added, that he accufed Robefpierre of having calumniated fome of the moft meritorious citizens of the Republic; of having accufed them unjuftly, at a time when accufation was profcription; of having infulted and menaced the National Affembly; of having domineered over, and by intrigue and terror influenced, the elections of the Electoral Affemblies of Paris; and of having attempted the fupreme power. He demanded that a committee might be appointed to examine into his conduct.

He then faid that he accufed another man who had, to the aftonifhment of all France, been introduced among them by the former, of whom he was the tool. Several voices called out, Marat! Louvet concluded by faying, that he hoped they would alfo pronounce a decree againft all thofe monfters who inftigate to murder and affaffina-

X 2                              tion,

nation, againſt a faction which from perſonal ambition was tearing the Republic in pieces; and that they would alſo decree that the Executive Power, in caſes of commotion, might call upon all the military force in the department of Paris, and order it to act for the reſtoration of tranquillity in the manner it judged expedient.

Robeſpierre aſcended the tribune as ſoon as Louvet had finiſhed.

The Aſſembly ſeemed unwilling to hear him : ſome propoſed that the diſcuſſion ſhould be poſtponed till next day, and that then Robeſpierre ſhould be heard at the bar. Louvet moved that he ſhould be heard immediately. Robeſpierre declared that he did not intend to make his anſwer then, but deſired that the 5th of November might be appointed for that purpoſe.——This attack of Louvet, and the debate which followed, took place ſeveral days ago. Louvet was greatly admired for the firmneſs of his be-

3

haviour

haviour, and the acutenefs of fome of his remarks.

Robefpierre was thrown into fuch confufion, that he did not fully recover his fpirits and recollection afterwards. The effect of eloquence on an affembly of Frenchmen is violent and inftantaneous: the indignation which Louvet's fpeech raifed againft Robefpierre was prodigious; at fome particular parts I thought his perfon in danger. I fancy the demand of fo long an interval before he fhould make his defence, was fuggefted by Danton, or fome other of his friends; it was a prudent meafure, had he attempted to anfwer immediately, he muft have loft his caufe: all his eloquence and addrefs could not at that time have effaced the ftrong impreffion which Louvet had made.

Although he drew the attack on himfelf by his imprudent boafting, yet he was taken unprepared: the galleries in particular had been neglected on that day, for the audience

X 3

fhewed

shewed no partiality——a thing so unusual when he spoke, that it is believed to have helped greatly to disconcert him.

November 5.

Two or three days after the scene above described, Roland wrote to the Convention, that a late address of the Commune of Paris, which had *not* been ordered by the Convention to be printed, or transmitted to the departments, had nevertheless been inclosed in covers directed and franked by the Mayor of Paris, and put into the post-office : that he had ordered them to be stopped, because the Convention had disapproved of the address, and because he believed the name of Petion on the covers to be forged.

Petion immediately rose, and declared that he knew nothing of the intention of transmitting the address to the departments, and had franked none of the covers.

This letter from Roland produced a

warm

warm debate, which ferved only to animate the two parties more violently againft each other ; one accufing the Commune of a low and factious manœuvre, in endeavouring to circulate an addrefs difapproved of by the Convention, and which is of a pernicious tendency ; the other accufing the Minifter of a defpotic and illegal act in wounding public confidence, by arrefting the courfe of correfpondence.

Like all debates in a numerous affembly, where the paffions are inflamed, it foon deviated from the object on which it began, and extended to other fubjects of recrimination ; during which Barbaroux of Marfeilles, who had been prevented from fpeaking on the day on which Louvet accufed Robefpierre, made a very fpirited harangue againft the latter and his partifans. It was nearly to the fame purpofe with that of Louvet, but more correct and concife : its objects were to remove all jealoufy of the

X 4         Marfeillois,

Marfeillois, to urge the neceffity of an armed force to protect the Convention from the brutality. of the mob, and to increafe the fufpicions of the ambitious views of Robefpierre.

He began by afking " if the reprefentatives of twenty-five millions of men were to bend their heads to thirty factious perfons,"

" The inhabitants of the South are accufed of having projected a federal republic." continued Barbaroux ; " yet we, their reprefentatives, declare, that they have inftructed us to oppofe every project of that nature. I call on Marat to rife and prove that ever there was fuch a project, or to own himfelf to be a calumniator."

" The friends of Roland are accufed of wifhing to domineer by means of the armed force which is requifite to maintain the independence of the Convention : I undertake to prove, when that queftion comes regularly before us, that this is rendered impoffible by the very manner in in which that force is propofed to be eftablifhed. It is not to be formed of Swifs guards, but of French citizens from the eighty-three departments.

" Thofe agitators," continued Barbaroux, " who for villanous purpofes wifh to fpread anarchy over the nation, have the audacity to fay *they* brought on the revolution of Auguft, and by that falfehood try to make us forget their project of a Dictator, their numerous robberies and their horrid murders in September : but they never can be forgotten; nor fhall I ceafe to act againft that faction, till the murderers are punifhed, the effects reftored, and the dictators thrown from the rock.

" What," continued Barbaroux, " can more plainly demonftrate the ambitious projects of thofe men, than that which has already been mentioned in the Convention ; namely, that immediately before the 10th of Auguft, Robefpierre invited Rebecqui and

and me to his houfe ? He fpoke to us of the neceffity of our rallying all our force under fome man who enjoyed great popularity ; and Panis, as we took our leave, named Robefpierre as the propereft man for being Dictator. And Robefpierre himfelf propofed in the committee of twenty-one, that the Council General of the Commune fhould be authorifed to form itfelf at once into a jury of accufation, a jury of judgment, and a tribunal for applying the law. Let it be remembered that he himfelf had the chief influence in the General Council. And finally," faid Barbaroux, " this very man, on another occafion, eager to obtain a decree, came to the bar of the National Affembly, and threatened the reprefentatives of the nation to make the tocfin be founded, if they did not form one as he thought proper to dictate."

This difcourfe, while it increafed the indignation already kindled againft Robefpierre, muft alfo tend to make his adherents more

more zealous to defend him :—it is their own caufe :—when the murderers of the prifoners, and the embezzlers of goods are threatened, many members of the Convention, and more of the General Council, muft be in a ftate of fevere alarm. And feverely will this alarm be avenged if thefe men fhould ever obtain the afcendency in the Convention. On the 2d of September, they fhewed what is to be expected from them when in power.

November 6.

Great inconveniency was found in the Convention, from the petitions which formerly were allowed to be prefented at all times. By a late decree, all petitions are ordered to be referved for Sunday, when, unlefs fomething of great importance intervenes, the fole bufinefs is to attend to them.

This renders it the leaft interefting day for attending the Convention. I went laft Sunday, in company with an Englifh gentleman, to St. Cloud. This was the fummer

refidence

refidence of the Orleans family from the time that *Monfieur*, brother to Lewis XIV. built the chateau, till lately.

From the houfe itfelf, as well as from many parts of the delicious park, there is an extenfive view comprehending Paris, all the villas around it, a rich landfcape of hills, woods and meadows, through which the Seine flows in many graceful windings. The cafcade is greatly admired, and the park has been confidered as the happieft effort of the genius of Le Noftre, who has made a delightful ufe of all the variety of furface it contains, as well as of the Seine which flows by it.——St. Cloud, in the opinion of many, was preferable to any of the royal villas before it became one of them : it was purchafed by the Queen from the Duke of Orleans about five or fix years ago, fince which time, the apartments within the chateau have been altered at a great expence, and much improved. Nothing can

be

be conceived more commodious. Notwithftanding the richnefs and magnificence of
fome of the apartments, this palace, with all
its fplendid furniture, has remained hitherto
undefpoiled and unfullied.

The contraft between the magnificence
we were beholding, and the wretched apartment in which the perfon for whom that
magnificence was prepared is confined, naturally prefented itfelf to our minds. This idea,
with that of the various aggravating circumftances which attend her confinement, made
us contemplate the fplendour of St. Cloud
through a very gloomy medium. The whole
manner of the man who conducted us
through the apartments, fufficiently evinced
that his thoughts fprang from the fame
fource, and flowed in the fame channel with
ours.

Thofe who have had the curiofity to vifit
the houfes of princes and villas of nobility,
may have remarked with what oftentation
and

and pride the houfe-keeper and fervants conduct ftrangers through magnificent apartments : they enjoy the admiration of the vifitors, and fwell with felf-importance in proportion to the richnefs of the furniture. They are not, however, more grofsly miftaken than thofe proprietors, who, deriving all their importance from the fame quarter, think it amounts to a great deal.

Nothing of this kind, but all that is oppofite, appeared in the demeanour of the man who attended us through the palace of St. Cloud : his mind evidently borrowed no pride from the magnificence he had under his care, but feemed rather to be engroffed with the fad fate of the owners, and the folicitudes

—— —— laqueata circum tecta volantes.

The annals of the unfortunate do not record any fituation more dreadful than that of the unhappy Queen of France.

Any

Any woman in her fituation would be exceedingly miferable; but we cannot help thinking that fhe muft be more miferable than any other woman in the fame fituation.

The diftance at which her rank feemed to have placed her from the reach of the mifery which now furrounds and threatens to overwhelm her, renders her fufferings more acute. This circumftance, independent of any abfurd prejudice in favour of rank, muft increafe the fympathy of every feeling heart. Although fhe is the daughter of an Emprefs, the fifter of Emperors, and the wife of a King who was lately confidered the moft powerful in Europe, fhe feems now more pre-eminent in wretchednefs than ever fhe was in rank and fplendor.

She was not only a queen, but is a beautiful woman ; not only accuftomed to the interefted and oftentatious fubmiffion that attends power, but to that more pleafing attention

tion and obedience which are paid to beauty. Fortune accompanied her friendship, and happiness her smiles. She found her wishes anticipated, and saw her very looks obeyed.— How painful must now be the dreadful reverse! Shut up in a prison, surrounded with barbarians, wretches who rejoice in her calamity and insult her sorrow, with what affecting propriety might this unfortunate Queen adopt the pathetic complaint of Job! " He hath fenced up my way that I cannot pass, and he hath set darkness in my paths.

" He hath stripped me of my glory, and taken the crown from my head.

" He hath destroyed me on every side, and I am gone : and mine hope hath he removed like a tree.

" He hath put my brethren far from me.

" My kinsfolk have failed, and my friends have forgotten me."

What has this most unfortunate of women already suffered ? what is yet reserved

for

for her to endure? She has been shocked by
the cruel murder of many of her servants
and friends; some of them for no other reason than their fidelity to her. She now suf-
fers all the agonies of suspense—her heart
throbbing from recent wounds, and her
mind terrified, not for her own fate only,
but for those of her sister, her husband, and
her children.——No; the annals of the unfortunate do not record, nor has the imagination of the tragic poet invented, any thing
more dreadfully affecting than the misfortunes and sufferings of Marie Antoinette
queen of France; and for ages to come, her
name will never be pronounced unaccompa-
nied with execrations against the unmanly
and unrelenting wretches who have treated
her, and suffered her to be treated, in the
manner she has been.

November 7.

From St. Cloud we wished to drive to

Mont Calvaire, but found part of the road impaffable for a carriage, and were obliged to return and go directly to Paris.——It feems very ftrange, that a road between a royal palace and a neighbouring hill to which there is fo great a refort from other places fhould be in this ftate. The day was one of the fineft I ever faw. On coming to the barrier, immediately before we entered Paris, a waggon ftood acrofs the road, which ftopped our carriage: the coachman had fome words with the waggoner, who was drinking with fome fans-culottes. He feemed in no hurry to move his waggon out of the way, notwithftanding the repeated requefts of our coachman, who, after a little altercation, loft his temper fo far as to make ufe of the term *canaille*, which has fuch an ariftocratic found, that it alarmed me. I inftantly and very loudly rebuked the coachman; which pleafed the audience fo much, that they

they removed the waggon, and we paffed unmolefted to Paris.

I was the more alarmed at this expreffion, on account of a fcene which I had been witnefs to in the gallery of the National Affembly. A man dreffed like a gentleman had a difpute with two perfons of a poor appearance: he called them *canaille*, which drew the fevereft of all repartees from one of them, namely, that he was an ariftocrate. The people around took part againft the accufed perfon, who tried in vain to refute the charge; they would not liften, but obliged him to leave the gallery.

A gentleman who had entered with him was very near being reduced to the fame neceffity. One addreffed him in an angry tone, faying, " The people are not to be treated in the infolent manner your friend did, Sir."

To which the other anfwered with mildnefs, " Il n'eft pas probable, Monfieur, que

Y 2                              j'aie

j'aie la moindre intention d'infulter le peuple, puifque j'ai l'honneur d'en faire partie*."

November 8.

On the day on which Robefpierre made his defence, the galleries of the Conventional Affembly were crowded at an early hour; but having an order from the Prefident for the box of the Logographe, I was admitted at the ufual time.

There was not fo great a crowd of the populace at the entry to the Affembly, as I have fometimes feen; but thofe who were there expreffed their partiality for him, and diflike to his accufers. On the terrace of the Feuillans, the groups were moftly formed of his partifans: one fellow accompanied by two or three others carried tripe on a pole, which they fwore they would force thofe to eat, who fhould vote againft fo diftinguifhed a patriot.

* It is not probable that I fhould have any intention to infult the people, fince I have the honour to be one of them.

Imme-

Immediately before Robefpierre afcended
the tribune, a deputy complained that the
galleries were unfairly filled ; that certain
privileged perfons, chiefly women, had been
introduced for the purpofe of applaud-
ing, while all the impartial citizens were
kept out : " Des citoyennes," he exclaimed,
" font à la porte des tribunes, tandis que
d'autres porteufes de cartes privilégiées font
facilement entrées*."

This obfervation occafioned an univerfal
laugh, and every body turned their eyes to
the galleries, which were almoft entirely filled
with women. Robefpierre's eloquence is
faid to be peculiarly admired by the fex ; and
it has been remarked, that on the nights
when he was expected to fpeak at the Jacobins the proportion of females in the galleries was always greater than ufual.

* Some female citizens are kept at the door, while
other females with privileged tickets are feated in the
tribunes.

When

When Robefpierre appeared in the tribune, it was evident that he had entirely recovered his fpirits, and he certainly made a
much better figure than he did when he was
laft there.

"I am accufed," faid he, "of having aimed
at the fupreme power. If fuch a fcheme is
criminal, it muft be allowed to be ftill more
bold. To fucceed, I muft have been able not
only to overthrow the throne, but alfo to
annihilate the legiflature, and above all, to
prevent its being replaced by a National
Convention. But, in reality, I myfelf was
the firft who, in my public difcourfes and
writings, propofed a National Convention
as the only means of faving the country.
To arrive at the dictatorfhip, to render myfelf mafter of Paris, was not fufficient; I muft
alfo have been able to fubdue the other
eighty-two departments. Where were my
treafures? where were my armies? what
ftrongly fortified places had I fecured? All
the

the riches and power of the ſtate were in the
hands of my enemies. In ſuch circum-
ſtances, to make it credible that I had ſuch a
ſcheme, my accuſers muſt demonſtrate that
I am a complete madman."

" Ce n'eſt pas la l'embarras*," ſaid one of
the deputies near me to thoſe around him.

" And when they have made that point
clear," continued Robeſpierre, " I cannot
conceive what they will gain by it, for then
it will remain for them to prove that a madman can be dangerous in a ſtate."

" Bah!" ſaid the deputy who had already
ſpoken, " ils ſont les plus redoutables †."

Robeſpierre denied having ever had much
connection with Marat, and he explained by
what means he had been induced to have
the little which he avowed; and he aſſerted,
that Marat had not been choſen to the Convention from *his* recommendation, nor per-

---

* That would not be difficult.
† They are the moſt dangerous.

haps

haps from any high opinion which the electors had of that Deputy, but from their
hatred to the ariftocrates, whofe mortal
enemy they knew Marat to be.

"I am accufed," continued Robefpierre,
of having exercifed the defpotifm of opinion
in the Jacobin Society. That kind of defpotifm over the minds of a fociety of freemen
could only be acquired and obtained by reafoning. I find nothing therefore to blufh
for in this accufation. Nothing can be
more flattering to me than the good opinion
of the Jacobins, efpecially as Lewis XVI.
and Monf. de la Fayette have both found that
the opinion of the Jacobins is the opinion of
all France. But now, that fociety, as Louvet pretends, is not what it was, it has dege-
nerated ; and perhaps, after having accufed
me, his next ftep will be to demand the
profcription of the Jacobins. We fhall then
fee whether he will be more perfuafive and
more fuccefsful than Leopold and La Fayette.

"Louvet

" Louvet next tries to vilify the General Council of the Commune ; thofe men who, chofen by the fections, affembled in the Town Houfe on that awful night when the confpiracy of the Court was ready to burft forth ; thofe men who directed the movements of that infurrection which faved the ftate ; who difconcerted the meafures of the traitors in the Tuileries, by arrefting the Commander of the National Guards, who had given orders to the leaders of battalions to allow the people to pafs towards the Caroufel, and then attack them in the rear :. thofe patriots are of too much energy of character to be efteemed by the flaves of monarchy ; but it is not in the power of calumny and impofture to preclude the heroic fervice they were of to the Republic from the records of hiftory.

" They are accufed," continued he, " of arrefting men contrary to the forms of law, Was it expected, then, that we were to ac-
complifh

complish a revolution in the government with the code of the laws in our hands? Was it not becaufe the laws were impotent, that the Revolution was abfolutely neceffary? ——Why are we not accufed alfo of having difarmed fufpected citizens, and of excluding from the affemblies which deliberate on the public fafety, all known enemies of the Revolution? Why do you not bring accufations againft the Electoral Affemblies and the Primary Affemblies? they have all done acts, during this crifis, which are *illegal*, as illegal as the overthrowing of the Baftille, as illegal as Liberty itfelf.

" When the Roman conful had fuppreffed the confpiracy of Catiline, Clodius accufed him of having violated the laws. The Conful's defence was, that he had faved the Republic.

" We are accufed of fending Commiffioners to various departments.——What! is it imagined that the Revolution was to be com-

7

pleted

pleted by a simple coup de main, and seizing the Castle of the Tuileries? Was it not necessary to communicate to all France that salutary commotion which had electrified Paris?

" What species of persecution is this, which converts into crimes the very efforts by which we broke our chains? At this rate, what people will ever be able to shake off the yoke of despotism? The people of a large country cannot act together; the Tyrant can only be struck by those who are near him. How is it to be expected that they will venture to attack him, if those citizens who come from the distant parts of the nation shall, after the victory, make them responsible by law for the means they used to save their country? The friends of freedom, who assembled at Paris in the month of August, did their best for general liberty. You must approve or disavow their whole conduct taken together, and cannot, in candour, ex-

amine

amine into partial diforders, which have ever been infeparable from great revolutions. The people of France, who have chofen you as their delegates, have ratified all that happened in bringing about the Revolution. Your being now affembled here is a proof of this : you are not fent to this Convention as Juftices of the Peace, but as Legiflators : you are not delegated to look with inquifitorial eyes into every circumftance of that infurrection which has given liberty to France, but to cement by wife laws that fabric of freedom which France has obtained——Pofterity will pay attention to nothing in thofe events but their facred caufe, and their fublime effect."

Robefpierre denied however having any connection with the flaughter of the prifoners, which, he afferted, was entirely owing to the indignation of the public for M. Montmorin's being acquitted by the Criminal Tribunal, the efcape of the Prince de Poix, and

and other people of importance, joined to the emotion occafioned by the taking of Longwy. In this part of his defence he feems to have copied from a pamphlet written by Tallien, entitled, *La Verité fur les Evénemens du 2 S ptembre* \*, in which is hardly a word of truth.

Robefpierre then added (and it required a moft determined firmnefs of front to add this), " I am told that *one innocent* perfon perifhed among the prifoners, fome fay more ; but one is without doubt too much. Citizens, it is very natural to fhed tears on fuch an accident. I have wept bitterly my-felf for this fatal miftake. I am even forry that the other prifoners, though they all deferved death by the law, fhould have fallen facrifices to the irregular *juftice* of the people. But do not let us exhauft our tears on them; let us keep a few for ten thoufand patriots

---

\* The real Truth refpecting the Events of the 2d of September.

5

facrificed

facrificed by the tyrants around us ; weep for your fellow-citizens, expiring under their roofs, beat down by the cannon of thofe tyrants : let us referve a few tears for the children of our friends maffacred before their eyes, and their infants ftabbed in the arms of their mothers, by the mercenary barbarians who invade our country.——I acknowledge that I greatly fufpect that kind of fenfibility which is only fhewn in lamenting the death of the enemies of freedom. On hearing thofe pathetic lamentations for Lamballe and Montmorin, I think I hear the manifefto of Brunfwick. Ceafe to unfold the bloody robe of the tyrant before the eyes of the people, otherwife I fhall believe you wifh to throw Rome back again into flavery. Admirable humanity ! which tends to enflave the nation, and manifefts a barbarous defire of fhedding the blood of the beft patriots !"

Robefpierre, having finifhed his fpeech, came

came down from the tribune, amidſt the applauſe of the galleries, and of part of the Convention.

Louvet took his place, and declared, that he was ready to refute every argument, or ſhadow of argument, that had been urged in his defence. The uproar prevented his proceeding: ſome called for the printing of Robeſpierre's ſpeech — others declaimed againſt it—there was a great confuſion for ſome time—the queſtion was at laſt put, and the printing decreed.

Merlin of Thionville ſaid, that Roland had diſperſed 15,000 copies of Louvet's accuſation: he therefore moved, that the ſame number of the defence ſhould be printed.

When a great debate is expected, thoſe members who intend to ſpeak give their names to the Secretaries, and the Preſident calls them in the order in which the names have been given. Thirteen members gave their names on this occaſion: three declared they

they intended to speak in defence of Robespierre, five against him, and five on the subject in general. This formidable number of speakers, and the known tediousness of some of them, appeared so awful, that the Assembly became disposed to preclude the discussion. Barrere proposed to close it immediately. Barbaroux was so eager to be heard, that, when refused as a member, he presented himself at the bar as an accuser. Couthon and other friends of Robespierre exclaimed against this, and insisted on the business being stifled, by passing to the order of the day.

.Barbaroux retired from the bar, and Louvet attempted to speak—he could not be heard.

One member remarked that, if Robespierre felt himself innocent, he would desire that his adversaries should be heard.

Barrere at last ascended the tribune, and immediately there appeared a disposition in the

the Affembly to hear him, he was confidered as an impartial man, who belonged to neither party. His fpeech feemed to have been prepared : the tendency of it was to fhew that accufations and recriminations only ferved to irritate individuals, and injure the intereft of the public ; that the time of the Convention was due to the nation, and ought not to be engroffed by deliberations on the crimes or virtues of one or two perfons. " It is time," faid he, " to eftimate thofe little undertakers of revolutions at their juft value ; it is time to give over thinking of them and their manœuvres : for my part, I can fee neither Syllas nor Cromwells in men of fuch moderate capacities ; and inftead of beftowing any more time on them and their intrigues, we ought to turn our attention to the great queftions which intereft the Republic."

He then moved to pafs to the order of the day ; which, after fome further debate,

was agreed to ; feveral members who had
fhewn great eagernefs to proceed with feverity againft Robefpierre immediately after
Louvet's accufation, having, during the interval, either been gained by his friends, or
influenced by their own reflections, that it
was beft to give up a meafure, which, however proper in itfelf, feemed inexpedient
in the prefent ftate of men's minds. Some
of them think that, if Robefpierre were ordered to be arrefted, it would occafion an
infurrection, and that an attempt to punifh
the authors of the maffacres would occafion
their renewal.

Thus this bufinefs ended in a kind of
drawn battle, which is perhaps the worft end
it could have for the intereft of the Republic ; for the parties remain too nearly
equal in force, and likely to ruin the common
intereft by their mutual animofity.

November 9.

An account of Louvet's fpeech againft

Robef-

Robefpierre was given the fame night at the Jacobin Society; it excited great indignation. What is fuppofed to have provoked fome of the members moft, was the propofal to examine into the fource of the maffacres, and to punifh the authors. This, however, could not be avowed; they affected therefore to feel only for the attack on Robefpierre, which was denominated by various fpeakers a confpiracy againft patriotifm itfelf, by a fet of men of ariftocratic principles, who were in the pay of Roland.

The names of Louvet, Rebecqui, and Barbaroux, were ftill on their lifts as members of this Society: it was propofed to expel them, and the vote was carried.

Robefpierre himfelf was not in the Society, but his brother was. He made a fpeech on the occafion, in which he declared, that he had been often afraid, during Louvet's fpeech, that fome members of the Convention would have ftabbed his brother; that

Z 2

he

he had heard one of them fwear that he was determined on it. There was an outcry immediately that he fhould name the horrid wretch; but the brother of Robefpierre ac-knowledged that *he aid not* know his name.

The Convention's having paffed to the order of the day after hearing Robefpierre's defence, is confidered by his friends as a victory: their triumph on that account is as great as their rage was at his accufation, and they leave no means untried to infpire the citizens with hatred to his enemies. Legendre and Tallien afferted lately in the Convention, that a party of the Marfeillois, with fome dragoons of the Republic, had appeared with drawn fwords in the ftreets, crying, "Off with the head of Marat!" A bas la tête de Marat! and finging a fong, the burden of which is,

Robefpierre, Marat, Danton, et tous ceux
Qui s'en mêleront, à la guillotine, ô gué, &c.

Tallien

Tallien added, that thefe fame *fédérés* had curfed thefe Deputies in a coffee-houfe on the Boulevards, and had cried, " Vive Roland ! point de procès au Roi !"

It is true that fome *fédérés* and dragoons, being in liquor, fung the words above mentioned in the ftreets : but the other article is without foundation, and added on purpofe to throw odium on the Minifter ; for the moft dangerous afperfion that can be thrown out againft any perfon at prefent, is, that he wifhes to prevent the condemnation of the King.——In the mean time, Marat thinks proper to keep himfelf concealed ; and an uncommon number of patrols have been remarked in the ftreets, particularly near the dwellings of Robefpierre and Danton, ever fince Louvet's accufation. Some people affert, that Santerre has given orders for this, merely to convey the notion that the lives of thofe great patriots are in danger from the Marfeillois. Whether this is the cafe or not, I

cannot

cannot tell; but I do obferve, that thofe who fay they are in danger with them to live, and thofe who infift upon it that they are quite fafe would be very happy to hear of their death.

As for Santerre, whatever his motive may be for ordering thofe patrols, it was well obferved in one of the late journals, that if he had paid half the attention to protect the poor prifoners, that he now fhews to guard Robefpierre, there would have been no maffacres in September.

November 10.

The Girondifts affect to turn the triumph of Robefpierre's friends into ridicule: they infift upon it, that paffing to the order of the day on an accufation of the nature of that brought by Louvet againft Robefpierre, would be the moft fevere and humiliating of all mortifications to a man of good character and common feeling. Whatever truth there may be in that, it is evident that his

party

party are in higher fpirits, and have gained
ftrength fince he made his defence. The
friends of Roland certainly expected that
Louvet's accufation would have thrown fuch
an odium on Robefpierre and all his adherents, as would have gone far to annihilate their influence in the Convention;
inftead of which, thofe members who fpoke
with horror of his conduct before, mention
it with caution and moderation now.——
Barrere, by alluding to him with contempt
as a dictator, has removed part of the indignation that prevailed againft him; and in
moving the order of the day he rendered
a very important fervice to Robefpierre,
and did what was highly agreeable to Danton, who had done every thing he could,
from the beginning, to prevent any fcrutiny
from being made relative either to the conduct of Robefpierre, or the murder of the
prifoners. I am perfuaded, therefore, that
Barrere thinks Roland's party, notwith-

ftanding

standing the majority which on some questions they may still have in the Convention, is on the whole the weaker of the two, and that he means to attach himself to that of Danton.

Condorcet, however, judges otherwise; for his conduct, which some time since was thought doubtful, now plainly indicates a decided preference of the Girondists.

M. Condorcet very seldom speaks in the Conventional Assembly: in a public paper under his direction he delivers his political sentiments with more effect than he could by speaking: in this he has of late directed such strokes of ridicule against Robespierre, as no man would do who wished to keep on good terms with him.

In the Chronique de Paris of yesterday is the following curious article, which I shall insert, because it shews M. Condorcet's idea of a man who has made so much noise in this country, particularly of late.

"	II

" Il y a, dans la Révolution Française, des hommes et des événemens qui n'y font un certain bruit paſſager, que parceque la turbulence nationale groſſit et gonfle tout, et qu'il y a peu d'obſervateurs tranquilles. Ces petits hommes et ces petits faits ne tiendront que quatre lignes dans l'hiſtoire.

" Une de ces circonſtances de huit jours, c'eſt l'accuſation intentée contre Robeſpierre, par un homme de beaucoup d'eſprit et de talent, mais qui a beaucoup plus d'imagination encore. L'accuſateur et l'accuſé ont été tous les deux entendus, et tous les deux ont prouvé qu'il étoit impoſſible de faire de Robeſpierre un Dictateur.

" Tout le monde a remarqué que l'on avoit amené beaucoup de femmes à la ſéance : les tribunes en contenoient ſept ou huit cents, et deux cents hommes tout au plus, et les paſſages étoient obſtrués de femmes.

" On demande quelquefois pourquoi tant de femmes à la ſuite de Robeſpierre, chez lui,

à la

à la tribune des Jacobins, aux Cordeliers, à la Convention ? C'est que la Révolution Française est une religion, et que Robespierre y fait une secte : c'est un prêtre qui a des dévôtes ; mais il est évident que toute sa puissance est en quenouille. Robespierre prêche, Robespierre censure ; il est furieux, grave, mélancholique, exalté à froid, suivi dans ses pensées et dans sa conduite ; il tonne contre les riches et les grands ; il vit de peu, et ne connoît pas les besoins physiques ; il n'a qu'une seule mission, c'est de parler, et il parle presque toujours.——Il refuse les places où il pourroit servir le peuple, et choisit les postes où il croit pouvoir le gouverner ; il paroit quand il peut faire sensation, il disparoit quand la scéne est remplie par d'autres ; il a tous les caracteres, non pas d'un chef de religion, mais d'un chef de secte ; il se fait une réputation d'austérité qui vise à la sainteté ; il monte sur des bancs ; il parle de Dieu et de la Providence ;

il

il fe dit l'ami des pauvres et des foibles ; il fe fait fuivre par les femmes ; il reçoit gravement leurs adorations et leurs hommages ; il difparoit avant le danger, et l'on ne voit que lui quand le danger eft paffé. Robefpierre eft un prêtre, et ne fera jamais que cela*."

Bazire,

* In the French Revolution certain men and certain events have made a temporary noife, only becaufe national turbulence fwells and enlarges every thing, and becaufe there are but few cool obfervers. Thofe little men, and thofe unimportant events will not employ four lines of hiftory.

One of thofe incidents of a week is the accufation of Robefpierre, by a man of great underftanding and talents, but whofe imagination is more extenfive than either. The accufer and the accufed have both been heard, and both have proved that it is impoffible to make a Dictator of Robefpierre.

Every body remarked that a great many women had been brought to the galleries of the National Affembly when Robefpierre made his defence ; among feven or eight hundred which the galleries contain, there were at the moft.two hundred men, and all the paffages were filled with women.

November 11.

Bazire, one of the deputies for the department of the Côte d'Or, and ftrongly attached to the party of Robefpierre, made a report

lately

It is fometimes afked, how it happens that fuch numbers of women are continually attending Robefpierre wherever he is, at his own houfe, at the galleries of the Jacobins, of the Cordeliers, and of the Convention?

It is becaufe the French Revolution is confidered as a religion, of which Robefpierre is the leader of a fect. He is a prieft who has devotees, but it is evident that all his power is *en quenouille\**. Robefpierre preaches, Robefpierre cenfures; he is furious, grave, melancholic, affectedly exalted, followed in his opinions, and in his conduct; he thunders againft the rich and the great; he lives on little, is moderate in his natural appetites; his chief miffion is to fpeak, and he fpeaks continually. He refufes thofe offices in which he might be of fervice to the people, and choofes thofe in which he expects to govern them; he appears where he can make a figure, and difappears when the fcene is occupied by

* This expreffion is ufed in the ancient French chronicles relative to the fucceffion of the crown, to declare that women are excluded, *la couronne en France ne tombe jamais en quenouille.* It is now applied in other cafes, and here implies that Robefpierre's power is chiefly over women.

others;

lately from the Committee of General Safety on the prefent ftate of the city of Paris.

In this he reprefented Paris as in great tranquillity—with a view, no doubt, to prove that the armed force which has been fo often required for the fecurity of the Convention is not neceffary.

He endeavoured to juftify in a great meafure the maffacres of the prifoners in September, and afterwards made one of the moft improbable affertions that ever was imagined, namely, that fome fervants of a lady of the court (it was imagined he meant Madame

---

others; he has all the characteriftics, not of the leader of a religion, but of the leader of a fect; he attempts to eftablifh a reputation of aufterity which points to fanctity; he mounts on forms, and talks of God and of Providence; he calls himfelf the friend of the poor and of the weak; he makes himfelf be followed by women, and gravely accepts of their homage and admiration; he retires before danger, and nobody is fo confpicuous as he when the danger is over. Robefpierre is a prieft, and never can be any thing more.

de

de Lamballe) began the affaffinations, with a view to fave their miftrefs. His words are : " Je dois dire cependant, qu'il eft prouvé que les domeftiques d'une femme célébre à la cour fe déguifèrent en fans-culottes, s'armèrent de piques et de tranchans, fe portèrent aux prifons, et les premiers égorgèrent des prifonniers avec des marques de fureur affez atroces, et des propos affez violens, pour acquérir quelque crédit dans la foule, et fauver par ce moyen leur maitreffe.

" Voilà quels furent les premiers auteurs de ces maffacres !

" Celui des prifonniers d'Orléans s'eft fait particulièrement par des gens attachés au fervice de la Reine, reconnus à la tête de l'attroupement de Verfailles *."

And he added, that as he was in the Committee of Surveillance during thefe fcenes,

* I muft declare, however, that it has been proved that

fcenes, he knew fome important facts relating to them, which it would be improper to reveal at prefent, but which he would publifh perhaps at fome futur eperiod†.

Bazire terminated his difcourfe by blaming

that the fervants of a lady of the court difguifed themfelves like fans-culottes, and, being armed with pikes and other deadly weapons, went to the prifons, and joined in the maffacres of the prifoners with fuch fury as they imagined would gain credit with the populace, and enable them to fave their miftrefs.

Thofe men were the firft authors of the maffacres.

As for the maffacre of the Orleans prifoners, that was chiefly executed by men in the fervice of the Queen, who are known to have put themfelves at the head of the band of affaffins at Verfailles.

† When I heard Bazire pronounce this, I confidered it as entirely falfe ; but I have been fince affured, from good authority, that fome fervants of Madame de Lamballe and of the Princeffe de Tarente, particularly the valet-de-chambre of the latter, actually joined the mob that furrounded the prifon of La Force, and, by adopting the furious language of the mob, endeavoured to gain fo much credit as would enable them to fave their miftreffes. But thefe fervants in no other way joined with the affaffins ; and the plan, which certainly was

ing the conduct of thofe who were continually mentioning thefe fcenes in September, which, he infinuated, had been of more
fervice to the confolidating of the Revolution
than at firft fight might appear; and he advifed all parties to forget their former diffe-
rences, wave all idea of accufations on the
account of the fcenes in September, and unite
in mutual confidence and friendfhip for the
public welfare.

While Bazire was in this manner preaching peace and tranquillity, the Affembly was
in an uproar, and the actions and exclamations of the members indicated fury and
deadly hatred.

Some called out for printing and difperfing the report, others oppofed it.

At laft St. André, formerly a calvinift

was formed on the moft generous motives, did fucceed
with regard to Madame de Tarente.

The affertion refpecting the Queen's fervants at Verfailles is without any foundation.

minifter,

minifter, now a deputy for the department
du Lot, one of the moft violent partifans of
Robefpierre, made a fpeech, the tendency of
which was to prove the utility of printing
and difperfing the report ; which would fhew
the good people how unanimous the Convention was ; that all former feeds of diffen-
fion were now blafted ; that there was no appearance of diftruft or accufation ; and would
remove the error in which the departments
were in believing there was any need of a
guard for the Convention, where mutual
confidence, freedom of opinion, and tranquillity reigned.

The falfehood of thefe reprefentations,
which were delivered in a canting hypocritical tone, were fo well known to the Affembly, that they produced a laugh ; after which
Buzot faid, " I fhould be glad to fee real union
founded on mutual efteem eftablifhed among
us ; but there can be neither efteem nor
union between the heroes of the 10th of Au-

guft and the affaffins of September; there can be no union between virtue and vice."

At this phrafe, murmurs were heard.

" I defpife thefe murmurs," refumed Buzot; " I am as little enriched by the maffacres as by the civil lift. I confider Bazire's report as an apology for the maffacres, and entirely falfe, and I oppofe its being printed."

Buzot's fpeech prevented Bazire's report from being printed; but the debate on this occafion augmented that hatred and animofity which before was too violent between the two parties. The Girondifts in general have expreffed fuch a determination of profecuting the authors of the maffacres, and have fhewn fuch contempt for the underftanding of their opponents, as feem to have kindled mortal hatred, and an implacable thirft of revenge in the breafts of the latter.

November 12.

An event has taken place which has raifed the

the spirits of the Convention, before too lofty, to the higheſt pitch of exaltation.

I was in the Aſſembly when letters were received from Dumourier with an account of a victory obtained by him at Jemmappe, which was followed by the ſurrender of Mons to the French troops. An aid-de-camp of the General ſtood at the bar. After the letters had been read, he addreſſed the Convention to this effect :

" Citizens Repreſentatives,

" I am a ſoldier, and no orator; but I will inform you of one memorable thing of which I was witneſs on that day. Baptiſte, valet-de-chambre to General Dumourier, rallied ſome ſquadrons in the midſt of the battle, put himſelf at their head, led them again to the enemy, and ſeized, ſword in hand, a poſt of importance."

One of the ſecretaries then read a paſſage from a letter of the General to the War Miniſter, in which he recommends Baptiſte,

confirms

confirms the account which the aid-de-camp had given of his gallant behaviour in the action, with this additional circumftance——that when Dumourier offered a pecuniary recompenfe to Baptifte, the latter declared that he defired no other reward than that of being permitted to wear the national uniform.

Baptifte was brought to the bar, and in the midft of loud and repeated applaufe it was decreed, " That the citizen Baptifte, who had rallied a regiment of dragoons, and four battalions of volunteers, at the battle near Mons, fhould receive the fraternal kifs of the Prefident of the Convention; that he fhould be clothed and armed at the expence of the Republic; and that the Minifter at War fhould authorife General Dumourier to give him a commiffion in his army."

A variety of letters were then read relative to Dumourier's operations before the battle, and until his making himfelf mafter of Mons; in which the officers who had

most

moſt diſtinguiſhed themſelves were mentioned, many of whom were ſeverely wounded; one officer in particular of the Gendarmerie Nationale, received one-and-forty wounds with ſabres, after having killed ſeven of the enemy with his own hand. Dumourier alſo highly praiſes young General Egalité for his intrepid and ſkilful conduct, and Lieutenant-colonel Larue his aid-de-camp, with whom he ſends the diſpatches.

Monſieur Egalité himſelf, who had never before ventured to ſpeak in the Aſſembly, thought this a favourable moment for him to appear in the tribune: he ſaid that he wiſhed to communicate to the Convention what General Dumourier's modeſty had prevented him from mentioning; namely, that he had perſonally led on the troops who had taken ſeveral redoubts ſword in hand.

Cambon ſaid, " As many citizens may be

near death in the various provinces of France, I require, that extraordinary couriers may be immediately sent to all the departments, that our dying countrymen may enjoy the comfort of being acquainted with the triumph of the Republic before they expire."

Jean Debry proposed that the sixth of November, on which the victory of Jemmappe was gained, should be appointed as a day of annual rejoicing.

Lafource opposed this. " Let us wait," said he, " until the triumph of Liberty is complete, by the defeat of all the tyrants at war with us ; let us not by partial distinctions create jealousy in the other armies of the Republic : remember the success of Custine, and the 20th of September, which does so much honour to Kellermann."

" Let us decree no national rejoicing," said Barrere, " when so many men have perished. The ancients, after their victories, appointed

appointed funeral ceremonies only. Tyrants order rejoicings, although their subjects have perished. Shall republicans imitate the unfeeling joy of tyrants? You ordained with propriety a public rejoicing for the conquest of Savoy, because it cost no blood. Here 4000 men have perished; the Austrians are men; 300* French have likewise perished, and yet you talk of rejoicing !"

But Vergniaud, with a discernment superior to such unnatural and affected sentiments, said, " Undoubtedly men have perished, but the cause of freedom is triumphant. Let us beware of metaphysical abstractions; the love of glory, of our country and of liberty is natural to man; and we, as legislators, ought to cherish those generous sentiments in the hearts of our countrymen.

* It cannot be believed that this account of the killed and wounded is just. Private letters from the army state a much greater number of the French among the slain.

Wretched

Wretched is the philofophy which damps them! If fuch fentiments had not glowed in the breafts of Frenchmen, where fhould we now have been? where our armies? where our victories? One way to keep this facred fire alive, is public rejoicings on fuch occafions as the prefent. Let a national feaft, therefore, be decreed for the fuccefs of all our armies. To a funeral oration's being pronounced on the fame occafion I give my confent; but that a national feaft be decreed, I demand."

The feaft was decreed.

Baptifte, who had withdrawn immediately after the decree had paffed in his favour, now appeared again at the bar, dreffed in the uniform of the National Guards: he is a handfome and genteel young man. The aid-de-camp, who had remained at the bar while the other was withdrawn, threw his arms around his neck and embraced him

the

the inftant he appeared. The hall refounded with reiterated applaufe.

" Brave citizen," faid the Prefident, " enter within the fanctuary of law ; the legiflators are impatient to have one who deferves fo well of his country, feated among them ; they are impatient till you receive the recompenfe due to your intrepidity."

Baptifte and Lieutenant-colonel Larue entered into the Affembly ; the former was led up to the tribune, where the Prefident faluted him, and prefented him with a fword as the gift of his country. How exquifite muft have been the fenfations of this young man at that moment ! the mere idea of them was delightfully affecting. When a gentleman diftinguifhes himfelf by any noble action, he attracts praife and admiration, although we prefume that he has had honourable fentiments inculcated into his mind from his infancy ; but when one born in the loweft rank, who has not received the advantage of education, and whofe chief con-

cern

cern for a confiderable part of his life, probably, was to ward off the mifery of want,
and fecure daily bread, difplays a mind fuperior to every fordid confideration, and
capable of the moſt generous effort——fuch a
man affuredly is an object of ftill greater admiration.

November 13.

The battalion of Marfeillois and fome
fédérés from other departments, now at Paris, give uneafinefs to the party of Danton
and Robefpierre, in fpite of their influence
in the General Council and in the fuburbs :
they find that Roland is fupported by a majority in the Convention : they fear that this
will continue to be the cafe as long as the
Marfeillois and fédérés remain in the capital.
Their prefence damps the energy of the patriots of St. Antoine, and prevents Danton
from reaping the full benefit of their attachment. Great pains have been taken to render the Marfeillois odious, and excite a jealoufy

loufy of them in the minds of the fuburb fans-culottes. It was expected that, confiding in their numbers, the latter would have driven the ftrangers out of Paris ; but the very name of Marfeillois keeps the fuburb patriots in check ; and although the courage of the former has not been put to the proof fince their arrival at Paris, that of their townfmen, to which the fans-culottes were witneffes on the 10th of Auguft, impreffes their minds with an awful refpect for the fmall band from the fame town, now at the capital.

As it was found difficult to drive them out of Paris by force, a plan was formed to get rid of them by policy.

Pache has been War Minifter ever fince Servan was appointed to the command of the army on the frontiers next to Spain. He owed his fituation entirely to the recommendation of Roland ; but Danton and Robefpierre have had the addrefs to convince him that he will have the beft chance of retaining

ing

ing it, by attaching himself to them; and Pache, like many others, being more influenced by the favours he expects than by those he has already received, is supposed to have entered into their views.

Custine lately made a requisition of reinforcements for his army: Pache informed the Military Committee of this, and at the same time hinted that it would be proper to send all the fédérés now at Paris, as part of the reinforcement. This plan had the better chance of succeeding, as the first suggestion came from Pache, a man supposed to be the friend of Roland, and as none of the principal members of Danton's party seemed to interest themselves in it.

It was no sooner mentioned in the Convention, however, than Buzot saw through the whole scheme, and unfolded it at full length, as an intrigue to expose the Convention to the most mortifying of all situations, and subject them to the insolence of a faction

faction which had the direction of the inhabitants of two of the suburbs.

Barbaroux also represented it as an abominable conspiracy, which if carried into execution, might expose the lives of many of the Deputies, and end in the pillage of Paris: he insisted that the *fédérés* could not be of so much service to their country any where as at the capital, where they were ever ready to join with the most respectable citizens in defence of the legislative body, and for the protection of property.

Cambon being struck with the observations made by Buzot and Barbaroux, and with the recollection of some scenes that had been acted immediately after the tenth of August, ascended the tribune with a precipitation, and raised his voice to a pitch that surprised the Assembly, and commanded their attention. He put them in mind of the tyrannical manner in which the last

6                                        Assembly

Affembly had been treated by thofe men who had the direction of the Fauxbourgs, and by that General Council who on the tenth of Auguft had feized the government, and infulted the Reprefentatives of the Nation. He afked if they had forgotten that thofe ufurpers had ordered the barriers to be fhut, the tocfin to be founded ; that they had threatened the members; and that when the Swifs who had refigned their arms were placed within the walls of the Affembly, and under the fafeguard of the public faith, a gang of blood-thirfty ruffians had come to the doors of the Affembly-hall, and demanded that they fhould be delivered up to their favage rage ; that thofe furious men were on the point of burfting into the Affembly, and dragging them out to be flaughtered ; and that they were not turned from their purpofe till Lacroix and fome other deputies begged of them *upon*

*their*

*their knees* not to proceed to so horrid an outrage * !

" Would you be again subjected to the same tyranny ?" continued Cambon. " If so, order the *fédérés* to leave Paris before an armed force is decreed and established for the protection of the Convention ; put yourselves again in the power of those whose despotism you have experienced——the very tyrants who enslaved the Legiflative Assembly ; and foon, in the midst of anarchy and civil war, the French Cromwell will appear, and tell you that he will be your Protector, and give you peace ; that you stand in need of his popularity and despotism to render you happy. But no ; we will have no Protector, no King, no Triumvirs, no Tribunes, we will be free ; for which purpose, let us secure the independency of the National

* Although I was in the National Assembly when this happened, I was ignorant of it at that time, and therefore it is not inserted in the Journal ; but Lacroix, on the present occasion, confirmed the truth of Cambon's assertion.

I                    Assembly,

Affembly, and on no pretext allow the *fédérés* to be removed from Paris till an organized force is formed from all the departments of the Republic, which can prevent the Reprefentatives from being under the influence of one department only."

Cambon pronounced this with great fire and energy, which feemed to proceed entirely from the ftrong conviction he felt of the importance of his fubject; and which had the greater effect, as his ufual ftyle of fpeaking is uncommonly cold and uninterefting. His manner is awkward, and his countenance dull. He is of a methodical, calculating turn of mind, and confidered as their beft financier. I have frequently heard him fpeak before; and generally when he began, I heard it obferved—" Now we fhall have fomething worth hearing; this is a man of admirable good fenfe:" but I always found his good fenfe fo exceffively tirefome, that I never could

liften

liften to it long. But on this occafion he commanded all my attention, and his difcourfe made a ftrong impreffion on the Affembly; it is believed to have contributed more than all that had been previoufly faid, to the failure of the plan which had been very artfully arranged for fending away the *fédérés.*

The importance put on fuch a queftion as this, fhews how very loofe and unfettled the affairs of this country are; and that in whofe hands the government is to remain, depends more on the fans-culottes of two or three of the fuburbs of Paris, and a handful of determined fellows from Marfeilles, than on the unbiaffed will of the Conventional Affembly.

Roland and the Girondifts feem to be in fomething of the fame fituation that the Court was in a little before the tenth of Auguft. The party of Danton and Robefpierre are as earneft for the deftruction of the firſt, as ever they were for that of the ſecond; and they ſeem preparing to attempt it by the ſame means.

The Court a little before that epoch had the majority of the National Aſſembly with them—Roland's party have the majority of the Convention with them at preſent.

The Court had a battalion of Swiſs and a band of gentlemen to protect them. The Girondiſts have a battalion of men from Marſeilles and ſome *fédérés* from other departments for their guards: whether theſe laſt will prove more ſucceſsful than the Swiſs is yet to be tried. In the mean time it is evident that each party is more afraid of the other, than either is of all their external enemies.

November 14.

Some days ago I ſaw the following article in the Chronique de Paris:

" Lorſque Louis a été conduit au Temple,

il

il n'avoit pas le fols ; le citoyen Pétion lui a prêté deux mille livres. Voici fon billet :

"Le Roi reconnoit avoir reçu de M. Pétion la fomme de 2526 liv. y compris 526 liv. que MM. les Commiſſaires de la Municipalité fe font chargés de remettre à M. Hue, qui les avoit avancés pour le fervice du Roi.

*Paris, ce 3 Septembre* 1792. (Signé) LOUIS *."

I had the curiofity to fhew this to a perfon whom I knew to be of Petion's acquaintance, afking him, at the fame time, if he believed it.

---

* When Lewis was conducted to the Temple, he had not a penny; Citizen Petion lent him two thoufand livres——here follows his receipt :

The King acknowledges having received from M. Petion the fum of 2526 livres, 526 livres of which the Commiffioners of the Municipality are to pay to M. Hue, who had advanced them for the fervice of the King.

Paris, this 3d of Sept. 1792. (Signed) LOUIS.

He

He faid he could not tell whether it was true or not, but that he would inform me of fomething to the fame purpofe, which I might depend upon was true. He then told me, that, having fome bufinefs with the Mayor, he had waited on him on the 31ft of Auguft; that while he was with him a letter was delivered to the Mayor, which having read he threw carelefsly on the table, and faid to the fervant, *Very well.* He then turned to my acquaintance, and converfed with him on the bufinefs which had brought him there; and afterwards, as he happened to have his eyes fixed on the letter, which lay open on the table, the Mayor faid, You may read it, if you pleafe. ——It was from the King, and what follows is a literal tranflation :

" The King would be glad that Mr. Petion gave an anfwer to the letter written to him five days ago--this is the laft day of the month, and he has received no money to defray his ex-
pences :

pences : the King will be obliged to Mr. Petion, if he will let him know what he is to receive, and fend him an anfwer to-day.

(Signed)       LOUIS."

Counterfigned by two other names.

The patience with which the King has endured every hardfhip which preffed on himfelf alone, gives reafon to believe that he has been prevailed on to write on this fubject from a confideration for others ; it is probable that the firft letter was written by fome attendant, and that this not having been anfwered, the King has been under the neceffity of writing the fecond himfelf.

That either was neceffary is abominable, and betrays real meannefs of fpirit in thofe who are affecting grandeur of mind and a manner of thinking fuperior to vulgar prejudices.

November 15.

It is difficult to be informed of the treat-

B b 3

ment

ment which the Royal Family are fubjected to in the Temple. Many circumftances of a public nature, however, indicate, that it is indelicate and harfh in the higheft degree.

A Committee appointed by the General Council of the Commune of Paris fit there conftantly, and, accordingto directions given, regulate every thing refpecting the Royal Family.

As they have been more clofely confined of late, and not feen by the Guards which do duty at the Temple, a report was fpread that the King had efcaped, although the fame number of men as ufual continued to mount guard: it was faid, that this was done merely to deceive the people, till fome ex- cufe could be thought of to avert the public indignation from the Committee for their negligence or treachery. Full of this idea, a body of men from the Sections of Paris, who were on guard at the Temple, infifted upon feeing the King and Royal Family,

that

that they might be satisfied themselves, and enabled to satisfy their fellow citizens, that the King actually was in the Temple, and that they were not guarding empty apartments, as was strongly suspected.

The Municipal Officers refused to comply with this demand; the guard insisted, and threatened to force their way into the apartments. Santerre was sent for: he expostulated with those mutineers, and assured them, that all the family were safe in the prison. This at length satisfied the volunteers from the Sections; but the cannoniers persisted in their demand, and Santerre was under the necessity of appealing to the multitude assembled at the gates of the Temple, who in character of Peuple Souverain decided against the cannoniers, and they were obliged to give up the point.

The Municipal Committee, to whose care the Royal Family are peculiarly entrusted, have made frequent reports to the General Council,

B b 4

Council, in which they pretend, that there seems to be a plan of delivering them from the Temple—and the smallest accidental circumstances which occur are considered as signals from without, which are fully understood by the prisoners within.——Mention has been made in those returns to the General Council, of a man's being heard playing on a flute at midnight, of the songs that are sung in the street, the expressions used by the common criers that pass; and it is insinuated that by all these, more is meant than meets the ear. Some time since, the Committee represented, that when the family walked in the garden, or appeared on the balcony, a number of persons came to the windows of the adjacent houses, and made signals, which seemed to be understood by the prisoners.——One Member of the Council proposed, that, to prevent this last, the King and Royal Family should never be permitted to come into the open air, till it

was

was fo dark that they could not to be feen; another propofed to raife the walls in the garden, and make fuch alterations in the Temple as would effectually prevent the prifoners from being feen by any perfon without.

Both thefe ingenious propofals were rendered unneceffary by an order from the Council, that all the family fhould be prevented from walking in the garden, or even appearing at the windows of their apartments; and when they affemble at the hour of dinner, which is always in the prefence of one or two Municipal Officers, every look, word, or gefture of the unhappy prifoners is obferved, interpreted, and frequently reported to the Council General as having a myfterious meaning.

Among other circumftances equally unimportant, it was mentioned in one of the memorials of the Committee, made a confiderable time ago, that the King continued to wear his ftar and ribbons, which raifed the

petulance

petulance of the author of a daily journal, who, on the subject of this memorial, expresses himself in the following indecent terms : " Si Louis avoit le sens commun, il auroit quitté lui-même toutes ces chamarrures féodales : il seroit aujourd'hui Republicain, c'est à-dire, plus qu'un Roi ; car un Roi n'est que le premier esclave de son empire*."——He then adds, that, so far from stripping him of them, it would be better, provided the nation allows him to live, to condemn him to wear those shameful emblems for life ; and proposes that all who should be convicted of certain crimes should be sentenced to the same punishment——and concludes : " Qu'on les exposât aux regards du peuple bardés de cordons, et l'habit garni d'aigles, de pigeons, d'éléphans, de moutons : les Romains ne

---

* If Lewis had common sense, he would of his own accord have thrown aside all those feudal trappings ; he would by this time have become a Republican, which is being greater than a King ; for a King is only the highest slave in his own dominions.

dépouilloien t

dépouilloient pas les rois vaincus des attribut de la royauté; ils les en revêtoient au contraire avec grand foin, et cela pour cracher deſſus*."

The Council General however faw this in a different point of view. Eager to diſplay a contempt for ariſtocracy, and conſtantly aſſerting that the people in general deteſt monarchy, they cannot help often betraying a dread of the firſt, and a fuſpicion that the nation ſtill retains its old affection for the fecond—they feem afraid of every thing that puts them in mind of either. Manuel was ordered to go to the Temple, and announce to the King, that as royalty was abolifhed, there was no propriety in his wearing his former ornaments any longer. The dialogue which paſſed between the

* Let them be expofed to the view of the people covered with ribbons, and their clothes trimmed with pigeons, elephants, eagles and fheep ; the Romans did not ſtrip the vanquifhed Kings of the emblems of royalty. On the contrary, they carefully dreſſed them in them for the purpofe of fpitting on them.

King

King and Manuel on this occasion, has been published in some of the Journals, probably by Manuel himself : even from this account it appears, that the King received this message with that manly indifference, and undisturbed resignation, which he has shewn since the beginning of his misfortunes. I have always heard that Lewis XVI. never was much affected by the magnificence of royalty, even when he possessed it in its highest splendour; he seems now to be as little affected by the loss of it ; and the malice of his enemies, displayed in these paltry instances, instead of throwing disgrace on the Monarch, renders his good qualities more conspicuous.

November 16.

In a work published some years ago*, I endeavoured to give an idea of that enthusiastic attachment and affection, which the

* View of Society and Manners in France, &c.

French

French of thofe days had, or pretended to have, for their Monarchs.

They fpoke of loyalty as a quality of the mind, like generofity or courage : they feemed proud to think that they poffeffed this quality, if not exclufively, at leaft in a higher degree than any other people ; and every Frenchman wifhed to be thought loyal, as every man wifhes to be thought generous or brave. They feemed even to confider it as a virtue, which ought to be cherifhed in the breaft of the fubject, independent of the good qualities, and in fpite of the bad qualities, of the Sovereign; and they were vain to point out to ftrangers how far their countrymen furpaffed all others in the exercife of it.

An Englifh officer, after having paffed fome days at Verfailles during the reign of Lewis XV. fupped in company with feveral French Gentlemen on the evening that he returned to Paris. The converfation turned

5

on

on the great attachment and affection of the French nation to their monarchs; and one of the company underſtanding that the court had been greatly crowded, and that many people of diſtinction from Paris had been at Verſailles during the officer's reſidence there, aſked him if he had not been ſurpriſed at ſeeing ſuch marks of loyalty.

" No," replied the officer, " I ſhould have been ſurpriſed if I had not ſeen them."

" To be ſure," reſumed the Frenchman, " the King is the moſt amiable man in the world, and it is quite natural that all the world ſhould love him."

" That is indiſputable," ſaid the officer ; " but I was thinking of other reaſons which thoſe I ſaw ſo aſſiduouſly paying their court to the King might have, and which are ſufficient to account for all the zeal and attachment they diſplayed."

The other affected not to underſtand him,

2

him, and afked with great politenefs what other reafons they could have.

" Why," replied the officer, " has not the King governments, and regiments, and bifhopricks, and many other very beneficial things to beftow ? I fhould imagine that this confideration might render the King an ob- jeĉt of great attention, and produce many marks of zealous attachment to his perfon, even although he were not quite the moft amiable man in the world, as all the world allow him to be."

" Be affured, Sir," rejoined the French- man, " that there is no people on earth who have fuch a veneration for their Kings, and fo much difinterefted loyalty as the French."

" Forgive me," faid the officer, " I know a people who can difpute thofe qualifica- tions with them, and whofe courtiers give ftronger proofs of veneration and loyalty to their Prince than even thofe of Verfailles."

" What people ?"

" The

" The fubjects of the Emperor of Morocco," replied the officer : " there is a monarch for you, gentlemen, who hardly ever fpeaks to his fubjects *qu'à coup de fabre*, and yet they venerate him in the moft aftonifhing manner. When I was in garrifon at Gibraltar, I paffed over to his dominions, and had the honour of fpending fome time at his court at Fez : one of this beloved monarch's morning amufements, is fhooting arrows at his fubjects ; when he chances to mifs, which feldom happens, for by frequent practice he is an excellent markfman, the perfon at whom it is directed takes up the arrow, and with all the zeal of the moft devoted courtier prefents it on his knee to the Emperor.

" On fome occafions, he does his fubjects the honour of cutting off their heads with his own hands, and is much praifed by the courtiers around for his dexterity ; in fhort, they difplay every mark of attachment to his

perfon

perfon, and may be faid with truth to love their fovereign to diftraction.——This is, gentlemen, what I call difinterefted loyalty." But now the French, at leaft all of them who remain in France, are as folicitous to declare that they never poffeffed this enthufiaftic loyalty, as formerly they were anxious to have it thought they did ; and as they began to difavow this principle during the reign of the moft mild and moft equitable monarch they ever had, as foon as his power began to be abridged, and continued to profefs the moft ardent loyalty towards the moft oppreffive and tyrannical of his predeceffors while they retained their power, it is pretty clear on what that boafted loyalty was founded.

But as the men fhew an abject and flavifh difpofition, who affect attachment and veneration for a foolifh or wicked prince, fo thofe on the other hand betray a malevolent and odious character, who are deficient in refpect and gratitude to a mild and equitable monarch, who through the whole of his reign has manifefted a love of juftice, and an equal regard for the rights of his fubjects and for his own prerogative.

The loyalty of a man of fenfe and fpirit arifes from a due refpect for the firft magif-trate in the ftate, whofe lawful authority he is ready to fupport for the good of the com-munity, independent of every other confide-ration. To this fentiment of loyalty to the monarch as firft magiftrate, efteem for per-fonal good qualities, if they exift, and gra-titude for favours received, will be added in every well formed mind. But thefe fenti-ments do not exclufively belong to loyalty, but are felt for every perfon of our ac-quaintance who poffeffes great or amiable qualities, and from whom we have received favours. But the oftentatious indications of loyalty which are fometimes exhibited, in the vulgar, generally proceed from a mere love of noife; in fome of fuperior rank, from

the

the defire of being looked on as the particular friends of the royal family, unconnected with any idea of their good qualities; and in many it is founded on a lucrative office in poffeffion or in expectation.

November 17.

At the beginning of the revolution, when a veneration for the chriftian religion was ftill pretty general in the minds of the people, a democratic abbé, with a view to infpire his audience with a deteftation for ariftocrates, affured them in his fermon that Jefus Chrift was crucified by the ariftocrates of Jerufalem.

Some people imagine that the fame affertion made in a fermon now, would not produce the fame horror in the minds of a French audience that it did three years ago, being of opinion that religious impreffions are much weaker now than they were then.

One diftinguifhing doctrine of chriftianity, namely, the forgivenefs of injuries, feems to be greatly exploded, and confidered rather as the effect of weaknefs than magnanimity: revenge, on the contrary, is applauded as a virtue, and proclaimed as a duty, and the people are ftimulated to vengeance, on every real or fuppofed injury.

Thofe who excite the populace againft the King, tell them, that his execution is neceffary, to *avenge* the murder of their brethren in the Caroufel on the 10th of Auguft; and that the affairs of the nation cannot profper, until their flaughter is amply *revenged.*

It was mentioned in the National Affembly, that fome of thofe patriots, while they lay expiring on the ground, had had the confolation of feeing the Swifs cut in pieces, before their eyes were entirely clofed.

The new levies are affured by way of encouragement, that in cafe they fhould be killed in battle, they may make themfelves perfectly

perfectly eafy, for that their deaths fhall be fully revenged.

A poor woman was weeping bitterly for the death of her fon, killed at the battle of Valmy: the foldier who had brought her the news endeavoured to comfort her, faying, " Confolez-vous, Marguerite, je vous reponds qu'il a été bien vengé *."

At the civic feaft, which took place on account of the conqueft of Savoy, a new ftanza was added to the hymn of the Marfeillois, and was fung by a company of young boys on that occafion:

Nous entrerons dans la carrière,
Quand nos aînés n'y feront plus :
Nous y trouverons leur pouffière
Et la trace de leurs vertus.
Bien moins jaloux de leur furvivre,
Que de partager leur cercueil,
Nous aurons le fublime orgueil
De les *venger* ou de les fuivre.
Aux armes, Citoyens!——Formez vos bataillons !
Marchez !——Qu'un fang impur abreuve nos fillons.

* Comfort yourfelf, Margaret, for I can affure you that he was well avenged.

C c 3

I was

I was at the Convention lately, when a young officer belonging to the regiment of Beaurepaire appeared at the bar.

He had been at Verdun when the Colonel fhot himfelf: he fpoke highly of that officer, by whom, he faid, the garrifon had been animated to fuch a pitch of enthufiafm, that they had refolved to be buried in the ruins of the town, rather than furrender: he gave an affecting account of the indignation and grief of the foldiers, when they found that the Magiftrates had capitulated, and were told of the cataftrophe of their Colonel : he faid, he was deputed from his regiment, to demand vengeance on the traitors who had betrayed Verdun to the enemy, and driven their Commander to defpair. He read the names of thofe he accufed, confifting of the Magiftrates of Verdun, and fome of the Field Officers of the National Guards.

This young officer was handfome, and of a genteel figure : he fpoke with fluency and grace;

grace; and what interefted the audience greatly in his favour, was, that a letter from Dumourier was read, which informed the Convention, that the regiment to which he belonged had behaved remarkably well againft the Pruffians; and that the officer who brought the accufation had diftinguifhed himfelf in a very gallant manner.

Some of the Members began to talk of avenging the death of Beaurepaire on the heads of the perfons accufed by the officer; and the Affembly feemed fo much enraged againft them, that I was afraid of their decreeing fomething very violent inftantly — but one Deputy, who had preferved coolnefs in the midft of all this emotion, fhewed the impropriety of coming to any refolution againft the accufed citizens, in the prefent ftate of their minds, and begged that the accufation might be referred to the confideration of a Committee.

This meafure was at laft adopted.

November

November 18.

There are eight or ten theatres for dramatic entertainments of one kind or other at prefent in Paris: moft of them are open four times a week. The pieces reprefented are generally new, and adapted to the fpirit of the times, and to fortify the minds of the audience in fentiments favourable to the Revolution. Kings and Princes are reprefented as rapacious, voluptuous, and tyrannical; Nobility as frivolous and unfeeling, fawning to the fovereign, and infolent to their fellow fubjects; Priefts as hypocritical, artful, and wicked. To infpire a hatred to monarchical government, and a love of republicanifm, is one great object of almoft every new piece —even in thofe comic pieces whofe plots turn on an amorous intrigue, or fome object equally remote from politics or forms of government, fentiments of the fame tendency occur, and however awkwardly introduced

duced they are fure of being received with applaufe. A ftrict adherence to the unities of time and place, and other critical rules, for which the French theatre was formerly diftinguifhed, is now little attended to.

The dramatic writers hate fetters, as much as the Sans Culottes, and fometimes defpife decorum as much.

I was lately at the Theatre de la Variété: the piece was entitled *La Mort de Beaurepaire.*

The hero, on hearing that the Magiftrates of Verdun have delivered a gate of the town to the Pruffians, fhoots himfelf on the ftage. The Duke of Brunfwick, furrounded by his guards, enters, and finds a French foldier lamenting over the body of his commander: while the Duke is queftioning him, another French foldier is brought in, who has juft fhot a Pruffian officer in the ftreet. The Duke afks, who bribed him to commit this affaffination? The foldier replies, " That

3

" That he needed no bribe to determine him to deftroy the enemies of his country; that he had no part in the infamous capitulation, by which the Pruffians were permitted to enter Verdun; that he had miftaken the officer he had killed, for the Duke himfelf, and highly regrets the miftake."—— The foldier in his turn demands of the Duke, " who had bribed *him* to invade a country which had renounced conqueft, and to make war on a people, who wifhed only to be governed by laws of their own making, under a form agreeable to their own tafte ?" The Duke makes fome reply to this, and the difpute becomes warm : but although the foldier is reprefented as having by much the beft of the argument, he is ordered to immediate execution. It appears foon after, that on his way he has leaped over a bridge, and by that means efcaped a more painful death. The firft foldier concludes the piece, by affuring the Duke, that he will make nothing

of

of his prefent enterprife, which he had beft relinquifh in time; for *the fhorteft follies are the fooneft remedied.*

Many little dramas are daily exhibited on the Boulevards, to the fame tendency, and ballads are fung in the ftreets and public walks: one is entitled, Comparaifon du Régime Ancien avec le Nouveau ; the laft ftanza is as follows :

> Jadis, quand pour l'armée un fils partoit,
> Sa bonne mere tout auffi-tot pleuroit,
> Et le retirer elle ne pouvoit ;
>     C'étoit régime defpote.
>
> Aujourd'hui, l'on voit toutes les mamans
> Faire le paquet, armer leurs enfans,
> Et les envoyer fervir dans les camps ;
>     Vive un régime patriote.

The two following ftanzas are from another, which is much relifhed by the people :

> Savez-vous la belle hiftoire
> De ces fameux Pruffiens ?
> Ils marchoient à la victoire
> Avec les Autrichiens ;
> Au lieu de palme de gloire
> Ils ont cueilli des—raifins.

Le

Le Grand Frédéric s'échappe,
Prenant le plus court chemin ;
Mais Dumourier le ratrappe,
Et lui chante ce refrain :
N'allez plus mordre à la grappe
Dans la vigne du voisin.

A writer in one of the Journals observes, that small springs are capable of moving great machines; and that popular ballads have had considerable influence in the revolutions of nations;—he adds, " La chanson des Marseillois éclaire, inspire, et réjouit à la fois. Je conclus à ce que l'on attache quatre chanteurs à chacune de nos armées. Faire notre Révolution en chantant, est un moyen presque sûr de l'empêcher de finir par de chansons *."

What truth is in this observation, is not worth examining; but, if the termina-

* The Song of the Marseillois at once enlightens, inspires, and rejoices. I therefore move, that four good Singers shall be appointed to each of our armies. To accomplish our Revolution with gaiety and good humour, is one sure way to prevent its ending in a song.

tion

tion of the French Revolution depends on the good humour and humanity with which it has of late been carried on, it will have a difmal ending.

November 19.

Marat has kept himfelf concealed for fome time, but his Journal is continued as ufual. He dates it from a fubterraneous habitation (d'un Souterrain); in which, he fays, he is obliged to bury himfelf alive, that he may be fafe from the daggers of affaffins. And why am I obliged to hide myfelf? he afks of the people, to whom his Journal is addreffed—" O peuple, que je chéris, que je porte dans mon cœur, pour avoir pris votre défence, pour avoir été votre ami, &c. &c.*"

It feems extraordinary, to addrefs the mob of Paris in the ftyle of a lover to his mif-trefs; but it is ftill more extraordinary, that a mob, who have given fuch proofs of fe-

* O people, whom I love, who are always neareft my heart, for having always been your friend and ad-vocate.

rocity,

rocity, fhould be deluded by the language which feduces a fond girl.

The general turn of his Journal, however, is not in the fame tender ftrain, even fince he dated from below ground. The manner in which he vindicates himfelf from the accufation of being fanguinary, will be thought curious.

" Le grand cheval de bataille de mes détracteurs eft de me peindre comme un homme fanguinaire, qui eft fans ceffe à prêcher le meurtre et l'affaffinat. Mais je les défie de faire voir autre chofe dans mes écrits, fi ce n'eft pas que j'ai demontré la néceffité d'abatre quelques centaines de têtes criminelles pour conferver trois cent mille têtes innocentes*."

In his Journal of this day, is the following paragraph: " Je ne croirai pas à la Re-

---

* The great aim of my detractors is to paint me as a fanguinary man, who is always preaching murder and affaffination. But I defy them to point out any thing in my writings, unlefs that I have demonftrated the neceffity of cutting off a few hundred criminal heads to preferve three hundred thoufand innocent ones.

publique

publique, que lorfque la tête de Louis Capet
ne fera plus fur fes épaules, et que les foldats
de la liberté ne feront plus menés à la
boucherie par des géneraux courtifans *."

In the midft of all the fuccefs of Dumourier, this man exclaims againft him for
having permitted the Pruffians to efcape out
of France ; and he writes in the fame ftyle
of the other Generals, whom he defcribes
as men of ariftocratic principles, and enemies of the people; and adds whatever
he thinks moft likely to excite the populace
againft Louvet, Barbaroux, Genfonnet,
Guadet, Buzot, Vergniaud, Kerfaint, and
all the faction Rol-Briffotine, as he deno-
minates them. But what may lead to more
extenfive mifchief than all the reft is the
drift of the motto of his Journal: " Ut re-
deat miferis, abeat fortuna fuperbis:" that
is to fay, " Take the money from the rich,

---

* I fhall never think the Republic eftablifhed, until
the head of Lewis Capet is no longer on his fhoulders,
and until the foldiers of Liberty fhall be no longer led
to flaughter by generals who are courtiers.

that

that it may be reftored to the poor." This plainly prompts to univerfal pillage : and perhaps the wickednefs of faction never was pufhed farther than in the protection given to fuch an incendiary as this Marat; for, notwithftanding all the public difavowals that have been made, that he is powerfully protected feems to me evident. —He dates from a cellar, but every body believes he is now living at his eafe in very good quarters, above ground ; and nobody can doubt, but that it would be a very eafy matter to difcover them, if it were thought fafe and prudent to feize the man. But they cannot even fupprefs his Journal ; it is cried every night in the Palais Royal: a little boy came bawling after me with it, as I returned home a few nights ago, " Journal par Marat, l'Ami du Peuple !—combien voulez-vous, Citoyen Anglais? Journal par l'Ami du Peuple!—Ah, c'eft bien intéreffant aujourd'hui—vous prendrez deux ou trois, n'eft-il pas vrai, mon cher Milor ?"

November

November 20.

It is moſt unpleaſant to obſerve how little ſenſation the cruel ſtate in which the Royal Family is occaſions in Paris, and how ſmall a part of general converſation it occupies: as for the loweſt mob, they never mention them but with ſome foul epithet of abuſe: this does not ſurpriſe me, becauſe they are either hired for the purpoſe, or, like all mobs, join in the cry that is ſuggeſted, and preſs blindly on, according to the impulſe given by others; I ſpeak not therefore of them, but of the other ranks of ſociety.

Whatever people's ſentiments are with regard to the Revolution, whether they are what is here called Ariſtocrates, or Democrates, one ſhould think that ſo ſevere a reverſe of fortune, and one ſo unexampled in the political ſtate in which Europe has ſo long been, would occaſion more general ſympathy. That this ſympathy ſhould not

VOL. II.  D d  be

be difplayed in public, is eafily accounted for: but even in private and confidential converfations, where no referve is ufed on topics equally dangerous, the misfortunes of the Royal Family feem to be felt in a very flight manner, by fome who might have been expected to feel them moft feverely.

What an affecting contraft does this indifference and neglect make with the obfequious attention, almoft to adoration, which was paid to this family by the whole French nation ; with the emulation and unwearied affiduity of all ranks to captivate their notice and gratify their wifhes ; with the proteftations of efteem, refpect, and affection they have been àccuftomed to hear from their childhood !

All thofe external marks of veneration were accompanied, no doubt, with the ftrongeft affurances of their being the offspring of genuine fentimental preference, beftowed on per-

fonal

ſonal virtues, uninfluenced by any expectation from their power, and purified from
all ſelfiſh conſiderations.

  The cannon of St. Antoine, and the ſabres of the Marſeillois, exterminated the
virtues of the King on the 10th of Auguſt;
and every day of his impriſonment in the
Temple ſeems to have added ſome new article to a liſt of vices of which he is now
accuſed, and which were never heard of before.——I never ſee a man in the Conventional Aſſembly, or elſewhere, eager to dif-
tinguiſh himſelf by violent ſallies againſt
the King and his unfortunate family, but
I imagine I behold a wretch who would be
the moſt abject of his courtiers, if, by an
unexpected turn of affairs, the Monarch
were re-eſtabliſhed on the throne. Nor
did I ever know any men, who were dif-
tinguiſhed for adopting the prejudices,
abetting the caprices, and affecting wonderful attachment to the perſons of Princes in

the

the fulnefs of power, without fufpecting
that they would be the moft turbulent demagogues, and the bittereft enemies of thofe
very Princes, if by any accident they
fhould ever be in the fame fituation with
the Royal Family of France.

November 21.

When a man, who, from his fituation in
life, or from the commiffion he enjoys, is
guarded from retaliation, treats another, who
is in his power, with infolence or cruelty,
it naturally excites feelings of indignation
and contempt. When an inferior behaves
with infolence to his fuperior, a blackguard,
for example, to a gentleman in the ftreets
of London, it raifes difguft, but not contempt as in the former inftance, becaufe the
blackguard *may* run fome rifk——he is not
abfolutely fure of impunity.

It was natural to fuppofe, that the imprudent introduction of the term *égalité* would
produce

produce an univerſal inſolence among the lower claſſes of people in France towards their ſuperiors: and I am ſtill convinced it will in proceſs of time be the caſe; but I confeſs I have not hitherto remarked any diſagreeable inſtance of this nature. No perſon, indeed, of whatever rank, is allowed to dreſs his footmen in livery, but every one is allowed to have as many footmen as he pleaſes; and when L. L's carriage was driving, a day or two ſince, in at the gate of the Louvre, it was ſtopped by the ſentinel, who had obſerved that the hammercloth had fringes of a different colour; and informed his Lordſhip, that ſuch a kind of diſtinction was no longer permitted in France, being contrary to that égalité which every Frenchman had ſworn to. The coachman had been ordered never to uſe any but a plain cloth; but, having a fringed one in his poſſeſſion of which he was very vain, he had ventured to

D d 3

adorn

adorn his coach-box with it on this unfortunate day. As the poor fellow was taking it
off with a very mortified air, the valet de
place reproached him for having put it on;
which the fentinel overhearing, faid angrily
to the coachman, "Il fied bien à un gueux
comme toi d'être ariftocrate *."

A few days fince I faw a man dreffed in
the uniform of a General Officer come up
to a poor fellow, who, with a pike in his
hand, ftood fentinel at a gate, and, addreffing
him by the name of " *Citoyen Soldat*," afked
him the way to a particular ftreet.

The pike-men were formerly confidered
as of a rank inferior to the National Guards,
who are armed with mufkets: but of late
they are put on a footing, and do duty
together; but ftill it might have been expected, that this gentleman's rank in the
army would have commanded the ftrongeft
marks of refpect from a common foldier,

---

* It well becomes a beggar like you to give yourfelf the airs of an ariftocrate.

if

if his laced coat failed to produce them in a poor fellow almoſt in rags.

" Tenez, mon camarade," ſaid the pikeman: " you will firſt turn to the right, and then walk ſtraight on until, &c."

The Officer having heard the directions returned thanks to the Citoyen Soldat, and, moving his hat, walked away.

November 22.

Some time ſince I was walking with a man, who has the rank of Lieutenant Colonel in the National Guards :—ſeven or eight men belonging to his battalion came up to him with a complaint; they pretended that injuſtice had been done to their company, in the arrangements reſpecting the duty; and they alſo complained of ſome other grievances :—the perſon they had choſen to ſpeak for them ſeemed to be of rather a fiery temper; and he ſtated the grievances with more heat and leſs ceremony than I had been accuſtomed to ſee ſoldiers uſe when

D d 4                addreſſing

addreffing their officers.——The Lieutenant Colonel on his part heard the complaints with attention and coolnefs; only faying, from time to time, as the orator proceeded, " Tu as raifon, tu as raifon, mon ami"——and gave no other interruption or anfwer, till he had quite finifhed. The officer then began with the phrafe he had already ufed fo frequently, " Tu as raifon, mon ami, cela eft clair; but there is one point in which you are a little miftaken."

This one point turned out to be the whole affair in queftion. The officer proceeded to put the bufinefs in a very different light; fometimes addreffing himfelf to the orator, and fometimes to others of the circle; and in a fhort time convinced the whole, that what they afked was unreafonable, and difmiffed them fatisfied, and repeating " *Le Colonel a raifon.*"

When they were gone, he faid to me fmiling, " This is my conftant method, when

they

they come with an unreasonable requeft : I hear them with patience; and after I have acknowledged two or three times that they are in the right, they allow me quietly to convince them that they are in the wrong :—whereas, were I to tell them at once they were in the wrong, they would think me unjuft ; but not that they themfelves were unreafonable.

"When their complaint is well founded," continued the officer, "and in my power to remedy, there is no need of reafoning ; I get the grievance redreffed as foon as poffible, and am happy it is in my power."

"All this," faid I, "will do very well in civil life ; but I fhould hardly think it would anfwer in the military, where fubordination and implicit obedience are fo neceffary."

To this the officer anfwered, "That men who clothe themfelves and ferve without pay,

pay, cannot be treated with the fame feverity as foldiers who are paid and clothed
by the public: it is rather to be wondered
at, that fo many poor tradefmen and day-
labourers all over France fubmit to lofe the
profit of their work for one day, and fometimes two, in a week, bear fo much fatigue,
and perform the military duty required of
them, fo cheerfully as they do. When
thofe men are ordered to the frontiers, and
obliged to perform the duty of foldiers
every day, they then receive pay, and are
fubjected to a feverer difcipline."

" I cannot help thinking," refumed I,
" that a General, who commands foldiers
who are taught to obey without thinking,
has a great advantage over one whofe army
muft be reafoned with. The Duke of Brunfwick has only to iffue his orders, and he is
as fure of being obeyed, as I am certain this
watch will ftrike when I prefs the fpring,"
continued I, making the watch, which I
held

held in my hand, repeat the hour; " whereas I underſtand, that Dumourier is often
obliged to convince his ſoldiers *qu'il a
raiſon*, before they will execute his orders."

" The temper and national character of
the ſoldiers muſt be conſidered by the General who commands them," reſumed the
officer: " Frenchmen would be diſpirited,
rendered good for nothing, or would deſert,
if they were treated with as much ſeverity
as German and Ruſſian ſoldiers.  I am of
opinion, that the introduction of the puniſhment of the cane (coups des batons)
was one reaſon of the defection of the army
at the beginning of the revolution.  I know
that many regiments were quite diſguſted
with that practice.  The French and Germans are as different animals as greyhounds
and fox-hounds; they accompliſh the deſtruction of their enemy by different en-
dowments, and require a very different
treatment."

" I do

" I do not wifh to depreciate the merit of
Dumourier," continued the officer; " but I
muft obferve, that the difadvantage you
mention might be compenfated by that enthufiafm, which in the prefent emergency
acts on the minds of French foldiers with
an energy beyond the force of any mecha-
nical fpring. Befides, you muft recollect,
that it has always been the cuftom in France,
to enlift foldiers for three or four years only;
for which reafon, great numbers of young
tradefmen and labourers choofe to go and
ferve during that time in the army; after
which, they return to their trades and villages, where their adventures in the army are
a fource of converfation to themfelves, and
of admiration to their wives and children
for the reft of their lives: and when the
whole country is called forth as on the prefent occafion, there are among the recruits
of every department a confiderable number of old foldiers, who not only inftruct
the

the new men in the effential parts of the exercife, but alfo give them an example of regularity and obedience; fo that the hafty levies with which Dumourier was reinforced at St. Menehould were not entirely raw recruits.

November 23.

In keeping this journal, my object was not to confine myfelf to the public events which take place in this country at this critical period, but to give alfo fome idea of the effect which thefe events have on the manners and fentiments of the people, which I imagine is better done by relating facts and incidents, than by general defcription. With this view, I mention the following which occurred to an Englifh gentleman and lady of my acquaintance: Hearing there was to be a debate on an important fubject in the Convention, the gentleman hired two perfons to go early and keep places for them in the front of the gallery

lery oppofite to the Prefident. The gentleman and lady went themfelves an hour after. A fentinel who was placed within the
gallery, told them there was no room. They
faid that two perfons in the front would
yield them their places, and the two perfons
rofe accordingly and offered to withdraw;
but the people in the gallery objected to the
new comers taking their places, which, they
faid, naturally belonged to thofe who fat
neareft. The Englifhman appealed to the
fentinel : "Ma foi, citoyen," faid the fentinel, " l'affaire eft un peu épineufe ; you muft
let it be judged by the company."

This is the ufual way on all difputes in
the galleries ; a jury is immediately formed
of the people neareft, who decide by the
plurality of votes, and their verdict is always
obeyed.

The Englifhman then afked of the company, whether the two perfons whom he
had fent to the gallery had not a right to
keep

keep their places. It was unanimoufly agreed that they had ; but that, if they retired, the two who fat neareft them had a right to the places they left ; and fo every couple might advance in fucceffion, but thofe who came laft muft be content with the worft places, till new vacancies occurred. "But," refumed the Englifhman, "I have paid thofe two men for keeping places for this lady and me, and that we fhould have them is founded on juftice."——" Mais non pas fur *l'égalité*," faid one of the jury ; to which opinion all the reft adhered.

" You fee, citizen," refumed the fentinel, " that the caufe is given againft you, and there is no more to be faid."

It is not furprifing that this idea of equality is very favourably received by the loweft order of fociety, particularly according to the fenfe in which many of them underftand it; and I make no manner of doubt but that there are men of acknowledged dulnefs, and women decidedly ugly, who

who would rejoice in a decree for an equality of genius and beauty, and who, to that variety in which nature delights, would prefer an infipid monotony of talents and looks all over the world.——But until Nature fhall iffue fuch a decree, the decrees of all the National Conventions on earth to eftablifh égalité will be vain. Were equality decreed by the univerfal confent of mankind this year, there would be inequality of riches and importance all over the earth the next.

November 24.

As I walked to-day on the terrace of the Feuillans, which is contiguous to the hall of the National Affembly, I obferved a young man ftanding on a chair: at his fide, there was a pike thruft into the ground, on the upper end of which a fmall board was fixed with this infcription : *L'Apôtre de la Liberté.* A crowd furrounded him, to whom he harangued in praife of the glorious revolution of the 10th of Auguft, and of the patriots to

whom

whom France owed its liberty, which he afferted to be thofe determined men who were on the preceding night appointed to be of the General Council of the Commune, and not the Briffots, Vergniauds, Guadets, Buzots, and ftill lefs Louvet the calumniator of Robefpierre. He faid that all thefe men, with Roland at their head, were doing every thing they could to fave the life of Louis Capet, the various inftances of whofe perjury he attempted to prove, as well as his ingratitude to the Nation, which had behaved fo generoufly to him. " But," he added, " Lewis the traitor has now filled up the meafure of his treachery fo high, that even his friends in the affembly could not deny his guilt, though they were ftriving with all their cunning to fave his life."

This fellow was evidently hired to animate the populace againft Roland and his friends, and make them confider every attempt to poftpone or evade the condemna-

tion of the King as a proof of their ariſtocracy and treachery. No ſovereign that
ever reigned has had more pains taken to
miſlead and impoſe upon his judgment,
than the Peuple Souverain who at preſent
governs France; and being naturally of a
thoughtleſs and giddy character, it is no
wonder he falls into the ſnares which are ſo
artfully laid for him.

November 25.

That ſpirit of hatred and accuſation which
prevails in the Convention, has extended to
the Generals of the armies, and ſeems to aug-
ment daily in this place.

Some weeks ago, Cuſtine, in a letter which
was read in the aſſembly, accuſed Kellermann
of negligence, or ſomething worſe, in having permitted the Pruſſians and Heſſians to
eſcape out of France, and reach Coblentz.

He aſſerted, that if Kellermann had paſſed
the Mozelle and the Sarre, he would have

made

made himfelf mafter of Treves and Coblentz with little difficulty ; and he referred to ftatements which he fent at the fame time, to prove the truth of his accufation.

The Commiffioners who had been in Kellermann's army, and had feen the correfpondence between him and Cuftine, declared that it would have been highly imprudent in the former, to have joined Cuftine with his cavalry at Treves at the time it was demanded.

When Cuftine fent this letter to the Convention, he wrote at the fame time to Kellermann informing him of it. Kellermann alfo wrote to the Convention, and has this expreffion in his letter : *Les inculpations de Cuftine n'ont pu être écrites que dans le vin* *.

On this occafion, it happens fortunately that thofe Generals are particularly attached to neither party. If they were, their military fkill, as well as their patriotifm, would be eftimated, as is the cafe in other coun-

* The accufations of Cuftine muft have been made in his cups.

tries,

tries, according to the political party to which they belonged ; and he, who was efteemed a good General by one fet of men becaufe he was of their party, would have been called a bad one by another for that very reafon.

But as in this inftance the fpirit of party has not interfered, both are fpoken of as good officers and faithful fervants to the public, and their mifunderftanding is univerfally regretted.

A member in the Convention having fpoken highly of the recent fucceffes of Cuftine, another immediately obferved, that if the fucceffes of Cuftine, which were immediately before their eyes, had enlarged their external dominions, Kellermann's victory on the 20th of September had faved the interior parts of France.——This was equally applauded by both parties.

In confequence of Cuftine's accufation, Kellermann was called from his army, and

has

has been for some time in Paris. He is by birth a German, and served for many years in the German armies. I have been several times in company with him. Once, when several Deputies were present, he could not abstain from speaking with indignation of the accusation of Custine, which gave him no otherwise uneasiness, he said, than as it obliged him to remain inactive at Paris, while the brave army he had commanded were in the field. Kellermann is a man of plain manners conveying the idea of sincerity, and whose talents are calculated to render him much more brilliant at the head of an army than in conversation. There is no doubt of his being soon restored to his command.

November 26.

In a company of bourgeois, a person was lamenting yesterday the fatal effects which might happen from discord; but added, he

understood

underſtood that the two political parties were on the point of uniting.

On which a chemiſt who was preſent, ſhaking his head, ſaid, he queſtioned it very much: " becauſe," continued he, " ſince fear did not compreſs them together when the Pruſſian and Auſtrian armies were advancing into the heart of the country, there is little probability that ſuch heterogeneous ſub-ſtances will unite by elective attraction."

However pedantic the chemiſt's language may be thought, his argument ſeems juſt.— Every day, I am more and more confirmed in the opinion, that the animoſity between the two parties will never end but in the deſtruction of one of them ; and ſome people think that Roland and his party would have been overſet before now, had it not been for the fédérés, particularly thoſe from Mar-ſeilles, who are now at Paris.

The effect which their name has on the minds of the ſuburb ſans-culottes is won-derful

derful—this greatly vexes Marat. In one of his Journals, he infinuates that Dumourier expofed the Parifian battalions at the battle of Jemmappe, more than the reft of the army, on purpofe to have them deftroyed ; and that this was done in compliance with the directions he received from Roland, Briffot, and that party. His words are : " Pour affurer le fuccès de leurs projets ambitieux, ces tyrans ont enlevés notre bouillante jeuneffe, toujours la premiere à marcher contre les fuppôts du defpotifme, et à former une barriere autour des défenfeurs du peuple." He afterwards mentions what this bouillante jeuneffe confifted of : " nos forts-de-la-halle, continues he, " nos charbonniers, nos cochers de place."

Thofe who have feen Marat, and are acquainted with the manners and fentiments of Chabot, Legendre, Merlin de Thionville, and fome other of his coadjutors, will not be furprifed at their having fome partiality to

hackney

hackney coachmen, colliers, and whatever is rough and vulgar.

A writer of great ingenuity and eminence regrets, that " we fhall never more behold that generous loyalty to rank and fex, that proud fubmiffion, that dignified obedience, that fubordination of the heart, which kept alive, even in fervitude itfelf, the fpirit of an exalted freedom ;" and adds, that with thefe are alfo fled " that fenfibility of principle, that chaftity of honour, which felt a ftain like a wound, which infpired courage while it mitigated ferocity, which ennobled whatever it touched, and under which *vice itself loft half its evil, by lofing all its groffnefs.*"

Notwithftanding the fplendid elegance and force of this paffage, the concluding fentiment has been cenfured. No man however can with lefs reafon than the honourable gentleman above alluded to, be fuppofed to mean this as a palliative for vice of any kind; and it is moft certain, that

in

in general fociety, politenefs is a convenient fubftitute for benevolence, and that when rude and polifhed men are equally vicious, the latter are always lefs difgufting and fometimes lefs mifchievous than the former. A favage, when he hates a man, or has violent defire for a woman, will murder the one and ravifh the other; in polifhed fociety, a man with the fame paffions will do neither. It is equally true, that a great deal of the groffnefs of vice may be removed, without a grain of its intrinfic wickednefs being removed with it. The courtier, who, in elegant terms, profeffes friendfhip to the man he is endeavouring to fupplant, and politely careffes thofe he means to betray, exhibits as much genuine vice as the moft vulgar footpad that ever knocked a man down, or informed againft his accomplice.

All the refinement of Courts cannot alter the nature of falfehood, ingratitude, or treachery; nor can all the perfumes of the

Eaft

East sweeten the corruption of vice. On the whole, though polish in some cases renders vice less mischievous than it would otherwise be, in other cases it may make it more dangerous by being more attractive; like furbishing the knife of a child, which does least harm when rusty, and is most dangerous when brilliant.

The Deputies above mentioned, and others of the Convention, cannot have this laid to their charge; their nauseous manners and debasing sentiments exhibit vice in its native deformity.

November 27.

Assertions frequently and boldly repeated seldom fail to make an impression on the minds of the populace, and at length to gain belief, in spite of the most clear and rational evidence of their falsehood.

Marat has been exciting the people to mutual rancour, to pillaging, and cutting

each

each other's throats, fince the beginning of the Revolution; but he affures them in all his fpeeches, and he tells them every morning in his Journal, that he is l'Ami du Peuple!——and the populace believe them.

It is univerfally known, that the Girondifts exculpate the citizens of Paris from the horrid crimes of September; whereas Robefpierre, St. André, Tallien, Chabot, Bazire, and all that party, affert, that the maffacres were committed by the people. But as, at the fame time, St. André always calls them " le bon peuple," Marat fays " he carries them in his heart," and Robefpierre declares " he would willingly facrifice his life for them," the populace confider this faction as their friends, and look on Roland and the Girondifts as their calumniators.

It is alfo notorious, that Roland, Claviere, Genfonnet, Guadet, and the other leaders of that party are republicans; that
they

they made open attempts to establish that form of government, at the time the King was brought back from Varennes; that Robespierre, Danton, and many of their friends opposed it, and declaimed in the Jacobin Society against it, and in favour of monarchy. Yet, as the favouring of monarchy is now confidered as the greatest of all crimes, those very persons accuse the Girondists of that crime, and of being determined enemies to the Republic; which affertions, by dint of repetition, begin to be believed; and Roland, Briffot, Guadet, and the whole of that party, are of courfe becoming daily lefs popular.

In a fmall company, a few days fince, a perfon remarked, " That the great fondnefs which Robespierre, Danton, and fome others, fhewed for a republican form of government, was of a very late date; and that although they displayed fuch deadly rancour against Lewis XVI, by whom they

thought

thought they never could be forgiven, yet they had no hatred to monarchy, provided they could have a King of their own choofing."

Another of the company obferved, " That he could not believe that fo fierce and infolent a fpirit as Danton would bear to fee any King eftablifhed in France."

" I am convinced, however," faid a third, " that he would like well enough to fee M. Egalité on the throne."

" Remember," refumed the firft fpeaker, " what Benferade faid, when he was told that a certain lady was fond of the Duc de la Vantadour, who was the uglieft man in France: " Parbleu, fi elle aime celuila, elle en aimera bien un autre*."

November 28.

It is not furprifing, that a people of great

* If fhe can love him, fhe will foon love another.

fenfibility,

fenfibility, and naturally verfatile, fhould fly from one extreme to another; yet one would hardly have expected that Republican manners would have been much to the tafte of the French nation.

There is however in Paris at prefent, a great affectation of that plainnefs in drefs, and fimplicity of expreffion, which are fuppofed to belong to Republicans. I have fometimes been in company, fince I came laft to Paris, with a young man, of one of the firft families in France, who, contrary to the wifhes and example of his relations, is a violent democrate. He came into the box where I was laft night at the playhoufe; he was in boots, his hair cropt, and his whole drefs flovenly: on this being taken notice of, he faid, " That he was accuftoming himfelf to appear like a Republican." It reminded me of a lady, who being reproached with having a very ugly man for her
lover,

lover, said, *C'est pour m'accoutumer à la laideur de mon mari\**.

They begin to *tutoyer* each other, that is, to use in conversation the singular pronoun *tu*, instead of the plural *vous*, as the Romans did, and the Quakers do. They have substituted the name Citoyen, for Monsieur, when talking to or of any person; but more frequently, particularly in the National Assembly, they pronounce the name simply, as Buzot, Guadet, Vergniaud. It has even been proposed in some of the Journals, that the custom of taking off the hat and bowing the head should be abolished, as remains of the ancient slavery, and unbecoming the independent spirit of free men ; instead of which they are desired, on meeting their acquaintance in the street, to place their right hand to their heart as a sign of cordiality.

* It is to accustom myself to the ugliness of my husband.

All

All this appears a little premature. If the Republic is permanent, new manners will gradually be introduced, and a new national character will of courfe be formed ; but fo very fudden a change of decoration is too much in the ftyle of a harlequin entertainment to be durable. The example of the Greeks and Romans is, in my opinion, too often held out ; and when I hear the names of Lycurgus and Brutus and Cato repeated in the Convention, it raifes recollections which are not favourable to thofe legiflators and patriots to whofe debates I am liftening. One of the beft obfervations I have feen in any of Marat's Journals, is the following: After fneering at fome of the Deputies, on account of their high pretenfions to patriotifm, he adds, " Thefe are the men, who are on every flight occafion telling us, ' Souvenez-vous que nous fommes Républicains, que tout ce qui n'eft pas grand et fublime n'eft pas digne de nous.'——

5                                        Meffieurs,

Meſſieurs, ſoyez d'abord honnêtes gens: après cela, vous ferez des Camille, des Regulus, des Catons, ſi vous le pouvez*."

. David, the eelebrated painter, who is a Member of the Convention and a zealous Republican, has ſketched ſome deſigns for a republican dreſs, which he ſeems eager to have introduced ; it reſembles the old Spaniſh dreſs, conſiſting of a jacket with tight trowſers, a coat without ſleeves above the jacket, a ſhort cloak, which may either hang looſe from the left ſhoulder or be drawn over both: a belt to which two piſtols and a ſword may be attached, a round hat and feather, are alſo part of this dreſs, according to the ſketches of David ; in which full as much attention is paid to picturesque effect as to conveniency. This artiſt is uſing all

* Remember that we are Republicans, that nothing but what is great and ſublime is worthy of us.——Pray, gentlemen, try in the firſt place to be honeſt men : after that, each of you may become a Camillus, a Regulus, or a Cato, if he can.

F f     his

his influence, I underftand, to engage his friends to adopt it, and is in hopes that the Municipality of Paris will appear in it at a public feaft, or rejoicing, which is expected foon. I faid to the perfon who gave me this account, " that I was furprifed that David, who was fo great a patriot, fhould be fo anxious about an object of this kind."

He anfwered, " that David had been a painter before he was a patriot."

Part of this drefs is already adopted by many; but I have only feen one perfon in public completely equipped with the whole; and as he had managed it, his appearance was rather fantaftical. His jacket and trow-fers were blue; his coat, through which the blue fleeves appeared, was white with a fcar-let cape; his round hat was amply fupplied with plumage; he had two piftols ftuck in his belt, and a very formidable fabre at his fide: he is a tall man, and of a very warlike figure; I took him for a Major of Dragoons

8

at

at leaſt : on enquiry I find he is a miniature painter.

November 29.

General Kellermann is reſtored to his com-mand, and is to ſet out for the army in a few days : having heard that he was to be at the Jacobin Society laſt night, I went there.

The General made a ſhort ſpeech, im-porting that he had come to take his leave of the friends of the people previous to his leaving Paris. The General is no orator, nor did he attempt eloquence ; what he ſaid, however, was applauded. One of his friends roſe, and demanded that he might be re-ceived as a member into the Society : this propoſal occaſioned a murmur, which ſur-priſed me after the applauſe with which the General himſelf had been heard.

I ſoon underſtood from thoſe around me, that this manner of propoſing a member was contrary to the rules of the Society ;

that

that if he wifhed to be admitted, he ought
to have made the propofal himfelf, fince he
was prefent, and not by deputation. One
of the Members whifpered ·the General,
who immediately rofe, and afked the favour
of being received as a member of the Society.

✓ Still there was a demur and whifpering
through the hall. I heard fome who were
near me fay, that the ufual formalities ought
not to be difpenfed with, it was a bad prece-
dent; others might expect to be admitted in
the fame manner: it was unworthy of Republicans to pay any regard to his rank in
the army, &c. &c.

The General rofe again, and declared, that
he had not been acquainted with the particular forms of the Jacobin Society of Paris,
otherwife he would have ftrictly obferved
them in the application he made; that perhaps it was too late, as he fhould be obliged
fo foon to fet out for the army; that he

2                                                    had

had imagined they might be the leſs neceſſary in his cafe, as he was already a member of the Jacobin Society of Straſbourg, and had been ſometimes honoured with the name of the Jacobin General. Cicero could have ſaid nothing more perſuaſive than this. Kellermann was declared a member amidſt the applauſe of all preſent.

The Preſident gave him the kiſs of fraternity, and made him a ſhort addreſs, the tendency of which was to wiſh him victory, and that he might ſpread the ſentiments of liberty and equality among the ſuperſtitious ſlaves of Italy, and inſpire the ſubjects of the Pope with the ſentiments of the Roman Republic: he finiſhed by exhorting the General not to allow his mind to be elated by the victories which he had already obtained, or thoſe which the army of the Republic might hereafter obtain under his command; but remember, that after them all, he muſt return to the condition of a private citizen, and be

reſpected,

respected, not according to the rank he was raised to in the army, but according to his virtues, and the service he had rendered to his country.

Kellermann heard this admonition with the grave and respectful air of a timid student receiving instructions from a Professor.

After this, a member of the Society, whose face I had never seen, and whose name I do not remember, ascended the tribune, and made a tedious and disgusting harangue, to prove the right the Nation has to try and condemn the King; representing all the arguments in favour of his inviolability as sophistical, and hinting that those who used them were traitors to their country : the orator added every thing that malice could suggest, to inflame the audience against the unfortunate Monarch. Among other assertions, unsupported by probability or proof, he said, " that the King had gone from the Tuileries to the Assembly Hall
partly

partly from fear of being wounded or killed during the attack which he had ordered to be made on the people, and partly with a view to point out the members he wifhed to be murdered by the Swifs, and by the Chevaliers du Poignard, whom he expected every moment to fee enter the hall, reeking from the flaughter of the citizens. He reprefented the Queen in the fame light ; and concluded, that both merited an immediate and ignominious death :'' at which fome woman in the galleries, who had fhewn much fatisfaction during the difcourfe, exclaimed, " *Oui, oui.*''

November 30.

When I returned from the Jacobins laft night, I expreffed to the perfon who had procured me admiffion, my furprife at the hefitation in receiving Kellermann as a member. " I fhould have thought," faid I, " that they would have been eager to admit a victorious General."

F f 4 " In

"" In my opinion they were in the right to hefitate," he replied: "" no fet of men are fo apt to over-value themfelves as thofe who are at the head of armies :—they talk of their victories as if they had been gained, like that of Samfon, by the ftrength of one arm ; whereas nothing is more certain, than that victories are often obtained by the valour of the troops, in fpite of the blunders of their Generals. Kellermann," continued he, "" did his duty at Valmy ; fo did every foldier of his army, in which it cannot be doubted there are at leaft an hundred who are as fit to command as he, and fome of them, in all probability, more fo ;—and are thofe gentry to expect to be admitted into a fociety like that of the Jacobins, without obferving the fame forms with others ? No, no, fuch diftinctions are dangerous to liberty, particularly when beftowed on the General of an army. Who was it," continued he, "" that overturned the Roman Republic ?

Julius

Julius Cæfar, the General of an army. Who difmiffed the Parliament of England, and eftablifhed military defpotifm ? Oliver Cromwell, the General of an army. Who reftored royalty in the fame country ? Monk, the General of an army."

" Do you imagine," faid I, " that little mortifications of this kind will prevent fimilar events from happening in France? All thofe who are at the head of your armies may not have the moderation of Wafhington."

" We do not rely on the moderation of our Generals," anfwered he, " but on the fpirit of freedom which pervades the French armies, and will prove a check to the ambitious or treacherous views of their leaders. This fpirit did not exift in any of the armies above mentioned. The army of Cæfar looked up to him, and to him only ; at his order they marched with as little reluctance againſt the Senate, as againſt the Gauls : the armies of Cromwell and Monk were ſo deceived and modelled, as to become the blind inſtruments of the will of their Generals : the armies of France are more enlightened, and are organiſed in a different manner ; they will follow their leaders againſt the foreign enemy, but not againſt their country. No General was ever more popular than La Fayette; yet he would have been arreſted in the midſt of his own army, if he had not fled ; and if the Convention thought proper, they could arreſt Dumourier to-morrow in the middle of his, notwithſtanding all his victories. But civil honours and diſtinctions would render the Generals of armies more dangerous ; and therefore, in civil ſociety, they ſhould be made to feel themſelves on a level with their fellow citizens, and obliged to ſubmit to the ſame regulations in public ſocieties with the other members. Every kind of

particular

particular diftinction fhewn to profeffional rank, or to birth, is unworthy of the inde-pendent fpirit of Republicans; "and you might obferve," continued he, " that when citoyen Egalité entered and feated himfelf by you, his appearance produced no fenfa-tion :—no, notice was taken of him."

" Forgive me," anfwered I, " his en-trance did-produce a fenfation; and if I had not before been acquainted with his perfon, I fhould have gueffed it to be him, by an affectation which I remarked in thofe around, not to take notice of him."

December 1.

Few things fhock a ftranger more on his firft arrival in this country, than the unre-lenting and indelicate ftyle in which the Queen is fpoken of; and nothing feems more contrary to what was formerly con-fidered as characteriftic of the French na-tion. They have been often accufed of

paying

paying fo great an attention to politenefs, that they neglected morality ; they are now in danger of neglecting the firft, without paying more attention to the fecond, and of lofing every attribute 'of courtiers, except that of abandoning the unfortunate.

The report in the name of the Committee of Legiflation, on the mode of conducting the King's trial, was read lately in the Convention by Mailhe:——after which, he faid, " We have faid nothing of Marie Antoinette; what right has fhe to have her cafe confounded with that of Lewis XVI ? The lives of thofe women who have had the titles of Queen of France were never confidered as more inviolable or more facred than thofe of other rebels or confpirators; therefore, in cafe you think proper to bring a decree of accufation againft her, fhe will of courfe be tried by fome of the ordinary criminal courts."

As the mode of trying the King was the

fole

fole object fubmitted to the confideration of the Committee, I was reflecting what could be this man's motive for departing from the fubject of the report, on purpofe to make this brutal attack on the Queen; but when he had finifhed, and I heard the galleries refound with applaufe, I was no longer at a lofs. As foon as the noife was over, I heard one of the Deputies fay to his neighbour, " I fhould not be furprifed, that fhe were condemned to occupy Madame de la Motte's vacant place at the Bicêtre *."

But what furprifed me more than any thing I have had occafion to obferve on this fubject, was a converfation I had at a coffee-houfe, in the Palais Royal, with a perfon I have fometimes accidentally met there: he is a man of a grave and refpect-

* The perfon's name who made this harfh and indecent fpeech, is in my original Journal; I omit it here, becaufe I afterwards knew of a very effential fervice which he rendered to an unfortunate Emigrant.

able

able appearance, of about forty-five or fifty years of age, well dreſſed, but rather in the ſtyle that was faſhionable before, than ſince the Revolution. He is not a member of the Convention, but I had ſeen him there often, and had ſometimes converſed with him : I took him for a man of moderation and humanity, he now convinced me how much I had been miſtaken.——I aſked him a queſtion concerning the intended trial of the King—there was nothing remarkable in his anſwer. I then ſaid ſomething expreſſive of ſympathy for the deplorable ſituation of the Queen: his eyes kindled, and his countenance altered at the name; the mention of the Queen affected him as that of chivalry did Don Quixote; his diſcourſe, from that of a man of ſenſe, became the ravings of a madman ; he poured out the moſt illiberal torrent of rancorous abuſe againſt her that I ever heard; and concluded the whole with this horrid ſentiment, which I tranſlate literally:

terally : " I hope *that* woman will be obliged to drink the full draught of mifery which is poured out for her, to the very dregs."

The rancour which in this country is manifefted againft the Queen, is more violent and more unaccountable than even that which appeared in Scotland againft Mary Queen of Scots, though many circumftances concurred to create a jealoufy in the minds of the people of Scotland, againft their Sovereign, which do not exift in the other inftance. Endowed with unrivalled beauty, and adorned with every elegant accomplifhment, Mary had been accuftomed to the fplendor of a licentious Court, over which prefided an unprincipled woman, of whofe politics, gallantry was a principal engine. She returned to her native country at a time when it was fo overfhadowed with fanatical gloom, that the inhabitants con-

fidered

fidered gaiety as finful, and pleafure as a profanation.

Mary was of a religion which the Scottifh nation held in abhorrence: how could a people endure the varied ornamented robes of Popery, in whofe eyes the decent furplice of the Church of England was detefted, as a rag of the ftrumpet of Babylon, whofe worfhip they fufpected their young Queen wifhed to introduce into her native country?

The manners of the Court of Vienna were very different from thofe of the Louvre; and the character of Maria Therefa was the reverfe of that of Catherine of Medicis. —That their Queen was beautiful, and elegant, and gay; that fhe loved fplendor, and was a Roman Catholic, were circumftances of a nature to gain, and not to alienate a people like the French.

Befides, the crimes imputed to Mary, whether

ther true or false, were of a much deeper dye than any which calumny has ever laid to the charge of the Queen of France. And although the fate of the former was moft affecting and deplorable, yet the caufes which brought it on are not uncommon. Mary fell the victim of hypocrify, female jealoufy, and political fear; whereas the fufferings of the Queen of France are as contrary to policy as to humanity, and proceed from a people, who, before they could behave to her in the barbarous manner they did, muft have renounced every amiable quality imputed to them by their friends, and adopted the difpofition of which they are accufed by their bittereft enemies.

December 2.

The moft deplorable circumftance which diftinguifhes this Revolution from others, is, that when its original object was in a great meafure obtained, order, tranquillity,

VOL. II.          G g                    and

and fubmiffion to law did not return. One
revolution has been grafted on another;
new alterations have been imagined, and
executed by men more violent, and means
more bloody, than the former; the populace, ftimulated by unprincipled leaders, have
committed all the exceffes of revolted ne-
groes, or of flaves who have burft from the
galleys. At this moment, four years after
the firft infurrection, inftead of the bleffings
of freedom, the unhappy people of France
are, under the name of a Republic, fuffering
more intolerable oppreffion than they ever
did under the moft defpotic of their monarchs; and are at the fame time expofed to
the attacks of external enemies, whofe number is daily increafing by the imprudent
conduct of their new governors.

Of all the evils which have attended this
extraordinary Revolution, the moft important to mankind in general, perhaps, is, that
it weakens the indignation which every
liberal

liberal mind naturally feels for defpotifm, and inclines them to fubmit to the awful tranquillity of methodifed oppreffion, rather than rifk fuch fcenes of anarchy and carnage as have been of late exhibited in this country.

Yet it ought to be remembered, that defpotifm, though lefs favage, is more hopelefs than anarchy, which contains within itfelf the feeds of its own deftruction; whereas, the pillars of defpotifm, being artfully arranged for the fupport of each other, as well as of that of the general fabric, may ftand for ages. Were it not for this circumftance, and if there were no choice but to live under arbitrary government, or to be expofed to the unreftrained ravages and cruelties of a frantic populace, perhaps the former would be preferred as the leffer evil. —For, in fpite of the vitiating tendency of unlimited power on the human heart, hiftory affords inftances of perhaps one in a

dozen

dozen of Princes whofe power was unlimited, and who yet preferved the virtues
of humanity ; whereas a mob is always furious, brutal, and cruel.'

But Heaven has not confined mankind
to this miferable alternative; nor is every
nation poffeffed of the impetuofity of the
French, which, at the firft fenfation of freedom, has hurried them headlong into exceffes without any rational object—like the
lunatic, who having fpoken the language of
moderation, and announced a peaceable difpofition, makes ufe of his liberty in attacking every body around, and fighting furi-
oufly, till, his ftrength being exhaufted, he
is again brought back to his fetters.

The emigration of the Nobleffe was moft
unfortunate; I fpeak of that which took
place at the beginning of the Revolution,
when it was ftill fafe for them to remain in
their country; and not of thofe which have
happened fince, and were abfolutely neceffary

fary for felf-prefervation : but it is more than probable that the neceffity for thefe laft emigrations arofe from the unneceffary one which took place at firft. Had all the Nobleffe remained, it cannot be imagined but that a body of men of the moft extenfive property muft, in fpite of the torrent of the times, have retained great influence, and prevented many of the diforders which have diftracted this unhappy country. Numbers of the Nobleffe would have been elected into the Affemblies, and thus have precluded fome Deputies who perhaps have been the caufe of great mifchief: by accommodating themfelves in fome degree to the prevailing opinions, they would have gradually rendered them more mild and conciliatory, and prevented that degree of acrimonious prejudice which at prefent prevails againft the whole body of Nobility. The earlieft emigrants being confidered as the inftigators of a combination of foreign

powers

powers againſt France, as determined to re-eſtabliſh the ancient government, and as filled with the moſt implacable deſire of vengeance; the odium againſt them became ſtronger every day, and was by the populace, ever incapable of diſcrimination, extended to the whole claſs. The Nobleſſe who remained in the country were daily provoked by new injuries from their countrymen within, and piqued by letters from thoſe without, accuſing them of meanneſs in ſubmitting to the new order of things, and of cowardice for not joining the armies of the Princes. It is not to be wondered at, therefore, that many of them left their country. After the tenth of Auguſt, it became dangerous for any of them who had ſhewn themſelves the friends of limited Monarchy, and eager to ſupport the Conſtitution, to remain in France.

As for that party which is known by the name

name of Girondiſte, and to which Roland, Briſſot, Buzot, Condorcet, and many other deputies who do not come from the Gironde, belong, they are certainly free from the dreadful guilt of the maſſacre of the priſoners; I am perſuaded alſo, that they not only wiſhed to ſave the life of the King, but that ſome of them have riſked their own lives in the various meaſures they have uſed for that purpoſe: yet being acquitted of theſe, other charges of a highly criminal nature remain againſt them.

After the Conſtitution was accepted by the King, and after they themſelves had ſworn to maintain it, they continued their efforts to overthrow it.

Judging of the King from what they thought muſt be his ſecret wiſh, and what, it is probable, they were conſcious would have been their own conduct in his ſituation, they could never believe that he would remain faithful to the Conſtitu-

G g 4                        tion;

tion; they were convinced that in his heart he abhorred it, and would seize the first opportunity to overturn it, to punish all who had any hand in establishing it, and to restore the ancient system with renewed force and augmented terror. They were convinced that the freedom of France could have no sure foundation but in a Republic; and on this conviction, they scrupled not to use the most perfidious means to introduce that form of government.

They endeavoured to vilify the character of the King, with a view to render royalty odious and contemptible; they gave circulation to innumerable stories, to the prejudice of others of the Royal family, which they either knew to be false, or had no proof of their being true.

On mere conjecture, they accused the King and Queen of undermining the Constitution to restore despotism, while they were conscious of undermining it themselves, on purpose

purpose to rear a Republic. They involved their country in a war with the Emperor, on pretexts which they knew to be
groundless, and solely in the expectation
that it would increase that jealousy of the
King which already existed, and give rise
to incidents and circumstances on which
plausible accusations against him and his
Ministers might be founded.

By those means, they rendered a bene-
volent Prince, who was anxious for the
welfare of his subjects, unpopular; by those
means they produced the insurrection of
the 20th of June, and prepared the minds
of the populace for that of the 10th of August; and by making it be believed, that a
Prince of such a quiet, unambitious character as Lewis XVI. could not remain satisfied with the power granted by the Constitution, but was secretly conspiring to restore
despotism, conveying the idea, that every
one who could be placed on the throne
would

would do the fame, the French nation were tricked into a republican form of government, when there is great reaſon to believe that a vaſt majority would have preferred a limited monarchy.

December 3.

That ficklenefs of difpoſition which has been conſidered as the general characteriſtic of the populace of every nation, certainly belongs in a ſtronger degree, and more peculiarly to the French than to any other, and has appeared more perſpicuouſly ſince the preſent Revolution than it perhaps ever did before.

Nothing could ſurpaſs the popularity of Necker at one period. Although a ſtranger and a proteſtant, the whole nation, fixing their eyes on him, ſeemed to exclaim, *Tu maximus ille es*—and to conſider him as the only perſon who could ſave the country from ruin, and reſtore their affairs. A ſhort time

time after he had been recalled by the united voice of the people, he began to be neglected, and is now almoſt forgotten.

La Fayette, who was adored, is now detested.

The popularity of Petion, which was in its meridian when we arrived in France, begins already to decline.

Orleans and others have had their moments of popularity, which, as a genuine poet beautifully obſerves of pleaſures, has had the fate

Of ſnow that falls upon the river,
A moment white—then melts for ever ;
Or like the borealis race,
That flit ere you can point their place ;
Or like the rainbow's lovely form
Evaniſhing amid the ſtorm *.

The ſame fickleneſs which the French have diſplayed in a manner ſo ſtriking, with reſpect to their favourites, at various pe-

* Burns's Poems,

riods of the Revolution, is also conspicuous
with regard to their taste in government.
When the attempt was made to introduce
a republican form, after the King's return
from Varennes, it was rejected.

In the month of July last, a member of
the National Assembly declared, that he was
as much against a Republic being established
in France, as a despotic Monarchy; and he
invited all who were of the same opinion,
to avow it by standing up.

All the members instantly stood up.

This happened in the month of July, and
the National Convention decreed the abolition of monarchy on the 21st of September.

I stated this to a Member of the Convention yesterday, as a proof that his countrymen were free from that stubbornness of
which some people are accused.

He answered, " that although he did not
believe the change of opinion to be so uni-

4                                    versal

'verfal as fome wifhed to have it thought, yet he *did* believe, that there was a confiderable change fince the 10th of Auguft, which he imagined was in a great meafure owing to two caufes: Firft, the idea that prevailed, that the papers found in the King's cabinet on that day, and thofe lately difcovered in the iron cheft, in the wall of the palace, formed a convincing proof of the King's having confpired with the foreign enemy to betray the country. " This," he faid, " had raifed a general indignation, and had reconciled many minds to the idea of a Republic, who formerly thought that form of government very unfuitable to France.

" A fecond caufe which contributed to the fame effect," he faid, " was the prodigious fuccefs of their arms; which was in a great meafure imputed to the energy which the idea of being republicans and freemen imprefled on the minds of the French."

I ob-

I obferved, " that if this laft confideration had any weight, it muft entirely proceed from the infpiriting fentiment of freedom, and the French might have been free without being Republicans."

The perfon with whom I was converfing, being himfelf a Republican, fhook his head at this obfervation ;—on which I added, " It is equally certain, that they may be Republicans without being free *."

Accounts of towns taken, battles gained, and fuccefs of every kind, are announced in the Convention almoft daily. Four ftandards taken from the Piedmontefe were prefented to them yefterday, by an aid-de-camp of General Anfelme, fent from his army for that purpofe; the colours were unrolled and difplayed in the middle of the hall; the applaufe and fhouting were of

---

* This perfon, who was attached to the party of Roland and Briffot, has had fevere experience of the truth of this remark.

courfe

courſe loud and perſevering.——In his addreſs to the Aſſembly, the officer made uſe of ſome expreſſions which indicate pretty juſtly to what a height national vanity is mounted in this country: I tranſlate them literally.

" Legiſlators, our enemies had the audacity to appear: Anſelme ſhewed himſelf, and they fled as uſual. Our army ardently deſires to enter into the heart of Italy. Naples inſults you, Rome excommunicates you, the King of Sardinia does not acknowledge you his conquerors: only give us the order, and all the crowns of the South ſhall be brought to your bar. Our ſoldiers declare, that each of them has a heart to bleſs your decrees, and two hands to execute them. The Romans in their degeneracy called out for bread, and public ſpectacles; the French, being regenerated, demand bread and the proſperity of the Republic."

The Imperial Eagle, which formerly ſtood on the top of the ſteeple of Namur, has been

removed

removed to Paris : it was placed on an open carriage, and drawn in the moſt oſtentatious manner from the gate of the city to the door of the Aſſembly hall, eſcorted by a party of dragoons, one of whom rode immediately before the carrriage, holding a chain, the other end of which was around the Eagle's neck.

I was at the Convention when the commander of the party came to the bar, and addreſſing the Aſſembly ſaid : " Legiſlateurs, Monſeignieur l'Aigle Imperiale attend vos ordres."

One Deputy moved, that it ſhould be placed, with the claws and beak cut off, on the top of the obeliſk now erecting in the Place de Victoire. Merlin of Thionville propoſed that it ſhould rather be hung by the legs from the ſame monument. Another deſired that the Eagle ſhould be permitted to ſtand in his uſual poſture, but with the cap of Liberty on his head.

Theſe

These witticisms, such as they are, afforded great entertainment.

The prodigious torrent of success which has flowed on the Republic of late, might have intoxicated a nation of soberer brains than the French. Had this produced no other effects than huzzas and processions in the streets, allusions to their victories, and self-praise in songs and declamations at the theatres, or the rhodomontades of a few orators in the Convention, there would have been no great harm ; but most unfortunately the intoxication has affected the judgment of a majority of the deputies, as evidently appears by the decision of the Executive Council of the 16th of November, sent to the French Generals commanding the expedition to Brabant, to use every measure in their power to open the navigation of the Scheldt ; and by the inconsiderate and rash decree of the 19th of November, by which the Convention declares, " au nom de la Nation Françoise, qu'elle accordera fraternité et secours à tous les peuples qui voudront recouvrir leur liberté * ;" and likewise by charging the Executive Power to give the commanders of the French armies orders to protect the citizens of every country who may be disturbed or vexed for the cause of liberty.

Which is in effect telling the inhabitants of every country, that whenever they choose to rise in insurrection against their government, they will be assisted by the French.

So far from adhering to their former professions of a love of peace with all their neighbours, it is proclaiming a challenge to all Europe, and laying the foundation of everlasting war; for what country exists, or ever did exist, in which part of the inhabitants did not think that they laboured un-

---

* In the name of the French nation, that they will assist the people of every country who wish to recover their liberty.

der

der inconveniences, which they might call vexations or infringements of their liberty? This decree therefore announces to all the people of Europe, that as often as any part of them chooses to rebel against their government, it will be supported by France. By a decree of the 27th of November, Savoy is declared an eighty-fourth department, under the name of the department of Mont Blanc; which, contrary to their former declarations, renouncing every idea of conquest, is to all intents and purposes making a conquest, and evincing as great an ambition for extent of dominion as Lewis XIV, or any French monarch ever displayed; and of course the Republic will rouse the jealousy of Europe as much as he did.

December 4.

A Committee had been appointed to examine certain papers, lately discovered in an iron chest, concealed in a cavity of the wall of the palace.

As

As a report was this day to be made to the Convention concerning thofe papers, we went to the Affembly to hear it, although we had previoufly determined to leave Paris early in the morning.

Some very important difcoveries were expected from thofe papers. When Rhul, of Strafburgh, who was Prefident of the Committee, afcended the tribune to make the report, a moft profound and awful filence took place; it was underftood, that there were a number of letters to the King, and his Minifters, among thofe papers. Every Member of the Convention muft therefore have been in a ftate of anxiety, either on his own account or on account of fome of his friends: an imprudent expreffion in a letter to a Minifter might, in the prefent ftate of men's minds, expofe the writer to great danger. The papers however proved to be of very little importance. Barrere, who at prefent is Prefident of the Convention,

tion, is mentioned in some of these papers; so are Dumourier, Claviere, Kerfaint, all as having had some connection or intercourse with the Court, but not in a way that can be considered as criminal.——But, although no suspicion of treason could be inferred from them, one particular letter does afford one of the strongest proofs of self-sufficiency and presumption that has been recorded in history or fable since the days of Phaeton. It is from Rouyer, a member of the Convention, who had also been of the former Assembly.

The man had frequently drawn my attention before: he is remarkably noisy and bustling; but as his importance seemed to be founded on his own single opinion, and what he said, although pronounced with great force, had little weight, I had never inquired his name.

The letter is dated in March, and is addressed to the King himself.

The following are extracts from it:

" Pre-

" Profondement occupé dés maux qui dechirent ma patrie, j'ai dû compter auffi fes innombrables reffources ; j'ai fondé fes bleffures et calculé fes forces ; j'ai tout comparé, tout aprofondi, tout prévu \*." He then declares, that he has a fecret which will within two months reftore the health of the empire, " cicatrifer fes plaies, diffiper fes alarmes, annihiler fes périls, rendre à la France le repos qui la fuit, la dignité qui lui convient, et au trône l'amour qui l'affermit avec l'éclat qui le décore †." He at laft reveals his fecret, which is, only that the King would place the whole power of the State in his hands; and he continues, " Sire,

---

\* —Deeply concerned for the misfortunes of my country, I have alfo reflected on her innumerable refources ; I have founded her wounds and calculated her force ; I have compared them, I have fathomed them, I have forefeen every thing——

† That will heal her wounds, diffipate her alarms, annihilate her dangers, and reftore to France the tranquillity which has fled from her, and the dignity which becomes her; and to the Crown the public love which renders it fecure, and the fplendor which adorns it ——

je le repète encore à votre Majesté, je m'engage à rétablir dans deux mois la paix mi dedans, la consideration au dehors, la félicité publique et l'autorité royale ——— J'irai vous révéler ce que vos Ministres vous cachent, ou vous apprendre ce qu'ils ignorent———Pour moi, Sire, je connois si bien nos forces et nos moyens, qu'en jetant les yeux sur les ennemis qui nous menacent, j'ai peine à me defendre d'un sentiment de pitié.——J'ai porté mes regards sur toutes les Cours de l'Europe, et je suis bien sûr de les forcer à la paix.———Je jouirai, dans le silence, du fruit de més conseils——Heureux du bonheur de tous, je dirigerai vers vous seul la reconnoissance publique *."

This

---

* Sire, I again repeat to your Majesty, that I engage to re-establish, within the space of two months, peace within, importance from without, general felicity, and the royal authority ——

I will reveal to you what your Ministers conceal, and I will instruct you in what they are ignorant. ——As for my own part, Sire, I am so intimately acquainted

with

This letter had, it is probable, been kept as a curiofity of its kind, and thrown into the cheft with the other papers found there.

Barrere's name having been mentioned in one of them, namely, in a letter from M. de la Porte to the King, he thought proper to demand leave to be heard before any other perfon; as the Prefident of the National Convention ought not to remain a moment under fufpicion.——He defired Guadet to occupy his place as Prefident, while he himfelf went to the tribune, to explain how he came to be mentioned in De la Porte's letter.

Before he began, Charlier fuddenly ftood up, and faid, that the fame delicacy which had prompted Barrere to quit his place as

with our force, that on contemplating the enemies who threaten us, I can fcarcely fupprefs a fentiment of pity. I have thrown my eyes on all the Courts of Europe, and I am certain of being able to force them into peace.——I fhall enjoy in filence the fruit of my counfel.——Satisfied with the general profperity, I fhall direct the public gratitude to your Majefty.

President,

Prefident, ought to have prevented Guadet from taking it.

Many voices exclaimed, that Guadet was not mentioned in any of the papers.

Charlier infifted, that although his name had not been read to the Convention, yet he was pofitively included in the defcription given by the Member who had made the report.

The way in which he attempted to make out this, is fingular enough : " For," continued Charlier, " in one of the papers addreffed to the King, it is faid, that thirteen or fourteen of the moft eloquent Members of the Convention were *dans les bonnes difpofitions* ; and although none of them are named, yet it is evident that Guadet muft be one of them ; for every body knows, that there are not thirteen members of the Convention more eloquent than he."

Rhul, who was the organ of the Committee in making the report, was fo much offended at hearing this, that he declared

8                                      with

with great heat, that if his expreffions were to be twifted into accufations, he would refign his place as a Member of the Committee.

Charlier's conftruction was condemned; Rhul was appeafed; Guadet was allowed to perform the function of Prefident, until Barrere made his defence, which was eafily done; after which he refumed his office.

Guadet then quitting the Prefident's chair, afcended the tribune, and, in reply to Charlier's infinuation, declared, that he had never been connected with the Court—"But if I had, and if I were confcious of guilt, I know how I could obtain my pardon: I know," continued he with animation, and looking to that part of the hall which the party of the Mountain occupied, " I know under whofe ftandard *thofe place themfelves, who have need of forgivenefs for the moft horrid crimes.*" This apoftrophe threw the Mountain into convulfions, in the midft of which I left the Convention, and foon after we fet out from Paris.

7                                    Lille,

Lille, December 7.

As it was late in the afternoon before we left Paris, we got no farther than the small town of Louvre that night, to which, a little after our arrival, a party of National Guards brought about sixty prisoners. The guards sung the hymn of the Marseillois as they marched through the town; the prisoners had their hair entirely cut from their head; they were tied two and two together, the right arm of one being bound to the left of another. Those men had behaved ill at Jemappe, and Dumourier had ordered them to be carried in this disgraceful manner to Paris, to be disposed of as the Convention should ordain. The National Guards of each town through which they passed, guarded them to the next. They were to be marched to St. Denis the following morning by a party from Louvre, and the National Guards of St. Denis would the day after conduct them to Paris.

The

The punishment seems well imagined, and must make a strong impression on the troops on the whole route from Mons to Paris.

At Pont St. Maxence, a Courier from the Cabinet, with dispatches for Dumourier, overtook us ; he travelled in a cabriolet adorned with the Cap of Liberty and other insignia of the Republic. This man, understanding that our road and his was the same as far as Cambray, made a proposal to take one of the servants into his carriage on certain conditions, informing us at the same time, that it would be advantageous to have him with us, because he being a messenger from the Cabinet, the gates of all the towns through which we were to pass, would be opened to us at whatever hour of the night we might arrive.

We agreed to his proposal, and proceeded to Peronne, where we arrived an hour after it was dark : there we should have remained that

that night, but as the gates were to be opened
at any hour for the Courier, we were perfuaded by him, to go on, for he affured
us, "that we were within three pofts of
one of the beft inns in France, which was
protected by General Dumourier, and where
he always lodged when he travelled on that
road, for the landlord and landlady were the
moft hofpitable and obliging people in the
world." The Courier gave fuch an inviting
defcription of this inn, that in fpite of the
exceffive rain and darknefs of the night we
left Peronne, travelled three pofts farther,
and arrived at the gate of this famous
inn about midnight. After a great deal of
knocking, a fervant looked out of a window, and having in a very angry tone faid,
" *On ne loge pas ici,*" fhut the window
with a great deal more force than was requifite: this was rather difagreeable news
to people who had been travelling fince five
in the morning, and flattering their imagination

nation during the laft four hours, with the hopes of refreſhment and reſt.

Our Courier was a good deal confuſed at this ; but on farther inquiry, he was informed that the landlord and landlady were both ill of a malignant fever, which had proved fatal to one of the principal ſervants, and many other perſons in the neighbourhood.

It is fortunate for men, when the beſt meaſure they could adopt is the only one which is left in their power. Our not paſſing the night at this inn, in ſpite of the malignant fever, did not depend entirely on our prudence. We were under the neceſſity of proceeding in the midſt of the rain to Cambray ; the Courier renewing his aſſurances, that as he was un Courier du Cabinet, the gates would be opened as ſoon as he ſhould be announced.

At about two or three in the morning, we ſtopped at a moſt miſerable hovel, immediately without the gates of Cambray.

Had

Had we been ever so much disposed to complain of hardship or fatigue, every expression of that kind would have been suppressed by the behaviour of a young dragoon, who jumped from behind our carriage as soon as it stopped. His arm was in a scarf: he informed us, " that his thumb and two of his fingers had been shot off at the action near Menehould; that he had been at Paris to solicit a small pension, to prevent him from starving, because," added he, holding up his wounded hand, " avec cette b—— de main, I can neither fire a musket, nor work:—the Secretary of the Minister told me, that I could not obtain a pension without a recommendation from my Colonel; I saw very well, qu'il se —— de moi *, for he knew that my Colonel was with the army. I immediately determined to set out for it myself, being sure of getting

---

* That he made a jest of me.

a rea recommendation from the Colonel, who is un brave garçon; and I fhould have been obliged to have made the whole journey on foot, had it not been for the politenefs of Monfieur le Courrier, who iuvited me to go behind your chaife, where I have fat as happy as a king all the way from Peronne, for I always have been very fortunate."

This poor fellow had a little dog in his arms, which he endeavoured to dry with the fkirts* of his coat. He was defired to come near a furnace with fome embers in it, which ftood in the middle of the room, and we lamented to fee him quite drenched with rain. " Ce n'eft rien, Citoyen Anglais," faid he, " j'y fuis accoutumé—mais je crois bien que mon pauvre chien a froid—viens, viens, mon ami," continued he, careffing the dog, " viens te chauffer *. My wife got

* It is nothing to me, Citizen — I am ufed to it; but I fear my poor dog may be cold; come, come hither, poor fellow, and warm yourfelf.

this

this little dog when he was quite a puppy, and it will prove the moft fortunate thing in the world, for I intend him as a prefent to my Colonel, who is diftractedly fond of dogs, and will in return give me a very ftrong recommendation ; but I have all my life been a very fortunate fellow ; viens, mon petit Azor, baife ton maitre : Oh, il eft im-payable *!"

" You fay you have two children," faid I. " Yes, citizen," replied he, " and both by my wife."

" I do not underftand," refumed I, " how you could maintain a wife and two children on the pay of a dragoon." "Ce qui eft impoffible n'eft pas aifé à comprendre, Ci-toyen †," anfwered he ; " but the truth is, it was my wife who maintained me and the

* Come, my little Azor—kifs your mafter.  O, he is a treafure !

† What is abfolutely impoffible, is not eafily under-ftood.

children : fhe is a very induftrious woman, and ufed to get three livres ten fols for making a fhirt, when fhe made for people of quality ; but at prefent, when there are no people of quality, fhe receives only forty fols for each fhirt. Je ne me plains pas, parce que je fuis bon Patriote moi——mais il y a une grande difference entre 40 f. et trois livres dix. Malgré cela j'ai toujours eu du bonheur."

" Eh votre main," faid the Courier.

" Ma main——ma main," anfwered the dragoon ;—" ça pouvoit être mon bras : un de mes camarades à deux pas de moi a eu la cuiffe emportée—eft-ce que le General Kellermann n'a pas eu auffi un cheval tué fous lui?——c'eft une plus grande perte que mes f— doigts pour le General. Ainfi vous voyez, Citoyen, combien j'ai toujours été heureux *."

We

* I do not complain—becaufe I am a good Patriot —but

We were indebted to the high fpirits and gaiety of this young fellow, for keeping us in tolerable good humour during two hours that we remained in this wretched place; the horfes being all the time expofed to the rain, for there was no ftable.

Our Courier of the Cabinet mean while was bluftering and fwearing at the fentinel on the rampart, who could not immediately find any body to fend to the Magiftrates for an order to open the gates—for there was no regular garrifon at this time in Cambray; and when the order was obtained, a good deal of time was loft before the man who kept the keys could be roufed.

—but there is a great difference between 40 fols and three livres ten. In fpite of that, however, I have always been fortunate.

What fay you to the wound in your hand?

. My hand—why, I fay, it might have been my whole arm : one of my comrades, within two fteps of me, had his thigh carried off; and had not General Kellermann a horfe killed under him? and that was a greater lofs to the General than my fhabby fingers.—So you perceive that I have always been fortunate.

Three

Three men armed with muſkets, but without uniforms, came at laſt, and informed us, that the gates were open. The Courier recommenced his bluſtering, and threatened the whole Municipality of Cambray with the vengeance of Dumourier. He alſo expreſſed a fear that the General would blame him for the delay.

The dragoon, who was of the happy diſpoſition to view every thing in the moſt favourable light, endeavoured to conſole him, ſaying, " Non ; Dumourier ne vous blamera pas : il eſt trop bon ſoldat pour ne pas ſavoir, que quand on ne peut pas prendre une ville d'aſſaut, il faut attendre qu'elle ſe rende *."

On entering Cambray, the Courier went directly to the town-houſe, and got a formal atteſtation of the time he had been de-

* Dumourier will not blame you : he is too good a ſoldier not to know, that when a town cannot be taken by aſſault, it is neceſſary to wait till it ſurrenders.

tained

tained at the gate, to fhew to Dumourier, as an excufe for his delay—and immediately proceeded on his journey, accompanied by the dragoon.

As no gate was allowed to be opened except that at which they went out, we were detained two or three hours longer, till the ufual time of throwing open all the gates.

We paffed through Douay, and arrived the fame evening at this town.

We have vifited the quarter where the Auftrians formed their entrenchments and batteries, from which the town was bombarded: a large village, near which the entrenchments were formed, was, before the main body of the Auftrian army advanced, unexpectedly furrounded by their light troops; and, as we are told, the wretched inhabitants, with many more peafants driven there by the body of the army, were forced to work in the trenches, fo that the fire from the ramparts deftroyed a much greater num-

ber

ber of the country people than of the foldiers.

The anfwer returned by the municipality to the fummons of Prince Albert of Saxony, was firm and laconic.

" Nous venons de renouveller notre ferment, d'être fideles à la nation, de maintenir la liberté et l'égalité, ou de mourir à notre pofte. Nous ne fommes point des periures*.

    " Fait à la Maifon Commune, le 29 Septembre 1792, l'an 1. de la République Francaife.

    " Le Confeil permanent de la Commune de Lille.

(Signé)   ANDRE, Maire.

         ROHART, Secretaire-Greffier."

  * We have juft renewed our oath of fidelity to the nation, that we are determined to maintain liberty and equality, or to die at our poft.

We are refolved not to be perjured.

                               The

The bombs and red hot bullets were particularly directed againſt that part of the town where the poorer inhabitants lived, with the double purpoſe of ſparing the moſt valuable buildings in a city, which, as was expected, was ſoon to belong to the Emperor, and alſo to excite the moſt numerous claſs of the inhabitants againſt the rich, and make them force the commander to deliver up the town. It had no ſuch effect, however, and the enthuſiaſm of the inhabitants increaſed every hour. The courage and alacrity of the inhabitants in ſeizing and removing the hot bullets before they had time to kindle the wood was ſurpriſing. They had iron inſtruments contrived for that purpoſe; and the towns of Armentiers, Bethune, Arras, Dunkirk, Caſſel, Cambray and others ſent their engines for extinguiſhing fire, to Lille, and volunteers from all thoſe cities preſented themſelves in great

numbers

numbers for the defence of the place ; which obliged the Auſtrians to retreat from the town, after having beaten down by the bombardment three complete ſtreets in the quarter of St. Sauveur, and many other houſes in different parts of the town, which ſtill remain in ruins. There are few houſes into which ſome bullets have not entered, and they are kept as precious relicks by the inhabitants.

In the hotel de Bourbon, twenty bullets entered during the ſiege ; and the mark of the burning on the floor, occaſioned by one of them in the room where I now write, is very evident : but no perſon was killed belonging to the family, except the chief waiter, as he was croſſing the ſquare to put a letter into the poſt-office.

A poor fellow who is decrotteur to the hotel, told me that it was owing to the watchful care and mercy of Providence, that he happened to be out of the way when that

letter

letter was fent ; for otherwife, as he ufually carried the letters to the poft-office, he *him-felf* might have been killed inftead of the waiter.

I do not know whether it will be confidered as a fign that a fenfe of religion is declining among the French, that the beggars in afking charity no longer add *pour l'amour de Dieu*, but inftead of that, generally cry *Vive la nation* ; but that religious fentiments are becoming every day weaker on the minds of the common people of this country, is moft apparent ; but it never occurred to me, that one order of fociety was gaining in that article, what another was lofing. A friend of mine told me, however, that he was this forenoon in a bookfeller's fhop ; that having obferved the fhelves of one fide entirely filled with books of devotion, he had afked of the bookfeller, if books of that kind were in much requeft at prefent.

" A good

"A good deal," replied the bookſeller, "with the ariſtocrates : as for the patriots, they hardly ever look into them."

"The reaſon of that," reſumed my friend, "perhaps is, that the patriots being the poorer have not money to lay out on books."

"They uſed to purchaſe them formerly," ſaid the bookſeller ; "and it is only ſince the ariſtocrates became poor, that many of them began to purchaſe them at all."

How far the bookſeller's account of this matter is to be depended on I know not ; but it is a lamentable truth that a great proportion of mankind think very little of the next world, till the preſent becomes inſupportable to them. And with regard to the inhabitants of this country, it muſt be acknowledged that the revolution has been hitherto ſo wretchedly managed, as to render the higher orders of ſociety miſerable, without making the lower happy.

Although

Although my Journal is continued until the 14th of December, when I returned to England, I omit the remainder, that I may infert what will be thought more interefting.

Some of the following particulars relative to the King's procefs, and the treatment which he and his family met with in the Temple, I learnt while I was in France; others I have been informed of fince my return in England. I imagine the whole may be placed with propriety at this place, with an account of the King's death.

With whatever irregularity, precipitation and injuftice the procefs againft the King will be thought to have been carried on, it was with much difficulty and perfonal danger, to one party of the Convention, that it was fo long protracted. I have reafon to believe that fome of the Convention regretted

gretted exceedingly the precipitate decree which abolifhed royalty, and were convinced that it would have equally tended to the happinefs and lafting freedom of France, if the Convention had reftored the King and re-eftablifhed the conftitution, with fuch alterations as might have been thought expedient.

I have reafon to believe that there was a ftill greater number of the members who were of opinion, that after the republican form of government was decreed, the moft equitable and moft politic meafure which the Convention could adopt, was to declare that they would make no inquiry whether the King had been in correfpondence with the enemy or not ; becaufe, at any rate, the nation was determined on a republican form of government, and therefore fhould order the whole Royal family to be efcorted to the frontiers, and permitted to go wherever they judged proper, with an

annual penſion of at leaſt one hundred thouſand louis, to be regularly paid as long as
they ſhould live in tranquillity, without exciting war againſt France, or a civil war in
it for their reſtoration ; revoking at the ſame
time the decree againſt Savoy, and renewing their original declaration, againſt extending their dominions and offenſive war
of any kind.

That part of the Convention who were
of either of thoſe opinions, with all who
were deſirous of ſaving the King, finding
it dangerous to avow their ſentiments,
endeavoured by various means to prevent a
trial, until the public mind ſhould be ſo
much ſoftened as to admit of a fair trial, or
till the idea of trial ſhould diſſipate altogether. When this failed, they attempted to
carry the ſentence of confinement during
the war, and exile after it : when that failed,
they tried the appeal to the primary aſſemblies ; and finally, they endeavoured to ſave
him

him by voting to poftpone the execution of the fentence.

Inftead of thofe evafive meafures, the no-bler part would have been, no doubt, to have voted him not guilty at the firft nomi-nal appeal.

I do not know that this was the opinion of any of them ; but I have heard feveral of them declare, that they thought the King's life fully protected by the Conftitution, and that he could not be juftly condemned to death, although all were proved which was laid to his charge, which in their opinion was not the cafe.

The violent party againft the King, on the other hand, took great pains and ufed many arts, both within and without the Affembly, to have all forms of procefs cut fhort by a bloody and fudden cataftrophe.

Legendre propofed that all thofe who had publifhed their opinions, or put them in writing, fhould lay them on the table of the

Affembly ;

Affembly; and that after the intervention of one day, the Convention fhould pronounce fentence witnout hearing the King.

Robefpierre was for ending the whole in twenty-four hours without feparating.

St. André declared that the King had been judged and condemned by the people on the 10th of Auguft, and that the Convention had nothing to do but to order his execution.

It was dreaded by fome who wifhed the death of the monarch, that his appearance at the bar of the Convention would foften the people, and perhaps move them in his favour; and when they found that others of their own party, who were equally the enemies of the King, were determined that he fhould be heard, they imagined means of the moft profligate nature to prevent it.

Papers were cried through the ftreets to inflame the minds of the populace to fuch a degree, that they fhould infift on his immediate execution; and if

3

that

that was delayed, to execute him themselves, either in prison or when he should be carried to the Assembly. It was asserted that the country never could be happy while he lived; that all the misfortunes of the country, all the distress the people suffered, and the still greater with which they were threatened, proceeded from the King's being suffered to live; that a party in the Convention, namely, the Gironde and the friends of Roland and Briſſot, were bribed by the Powers at war with France, to save the King, and prolong the distreſſes of France; and that although they durſt not openly in the Convention deny that he was criminal, and deferved death, yet they were endeavouring, under various pretexts, to prolong his procefs, and delay his execution, till an opportunity occurred to re-eſtablish him on the throne.

The moſt abfurd aſſertions were made in the Convention itſelf to this tendency. At one time, a little before I left Paris, when there

there was a difcuffion concerning the fcarcity of grain, which by different members was imputed to different caufes, I heard a voice pronounce, *La véritable caufe eft dans le Temple.* I was informed that this wife obfervation came from Legendre.

Hand-bills were diftributed with thefe words : " Républicains, guillotinez moi Louis XVI. et l'Autrichienne fi vous voulez avoir du pain." And the printed opinion of Marat was fold at the fame time.

When the Royal Family were firft lodged in the Temple, they were treated with fome degree of refpect, and they were allowed the comfort of each other's company, and the liberty of walking in the garden of the Temple ; but the appearance of refpect gradually diminifhed, and at laft the treatment they received was in many inftances brutal.

A perfon who was admitted into the Temple by the means of a near relation on duty there about the beginning of December, affured me, that at the hour at which, by a ftanding order from the Council, the prifoners were to be confined to their apartments, he faw the keeper go to the King, who was ftill walking in the garden, and addrefs him in thefe words : " *Allons, monfieur Veto, il faut monter.*"

When the Royal Family dined, a Commiffioner from the Commune of Paris was always prefent. The Queen happened at one time to raife the hand in which fhe held her knife a little fuddenly towards her breaft.——The Commiffioner feemed alarmed, and made a movement as if he dreaded that fhe had an intention againft her life ; which the Queen obferving, faid with emphafis : " Non, Monfieur, je réferve cet honneur aux Francois*."

From the time that the King's procefs was refolved upon, the Royal Family were

---

* I referve that honour to the Convention.

confined

confined more clofely, and watched more ftrictly than ever. The Council ordered that in future two Commiffioners fhould pafs the night in his bed-chamber, inftead of one, which had been the cafe before. All perfons who were admitted into the prefence of any of the Royal Family were previoufly fearched. Orders were given that the razors with which the King was in the ufe of fhaving himfelf fhould be removed: this was done from a fear that he might prefer fuicide to the humiliation of a public trial before the Convention.

Such an idea was remote from the King's way of thinking. When his razors and penknife were demanded from him, " Do you think me fuch a coward as to kill myfelf?" faid he.

The order not only comprehended knives and razors, but alfo fciffars, and all inftruments contondant, tranchant et *piquant*, and it was extended to all the Royal Family.

K k 2 " It

"Il faudroit auffi nous enlever nos aiguilles," faid the Queen when it was read to her.

When the King, afterwards, repeatedly applied for a razor, it was at laft granted by the Council, who directed, however, that he fhould fhave himfelf under the infpection of the Commiffioners: and the Queen and Princefs Elizabeth were allowed fciffars to pare their nails with the fame reftriction. This laft feems ridiculous, and the former abfurd; for if the King had had any intention of ufing a razor in the manner they fufpected, he could have put it in execution as effectually while the Commiffioners were prefent as at any other time.

After a long and warm debate, it was decreed by the Convention, that the King fhould be brought to their bar; that the act of accufation fhould be read to him; that the Prefident fhould put certain queftions to him, which were previoufly drawn up by the committee,

committee, and approved of by the Affembly; and that after his anfwers had been taken down, a day fhould be appointed for hearing him finally, and pronouncing judgment. It was alfo decreed that the opinions of the Deputies fhould be taken by the appel nominal.

This mode was violently infifted on by the faction of the Mountain, in the hopes that fome, whofe confciences acquitted him, might, from a terror of the mob, be induced to pronounce againft him.

Had the opinion of the Convention been taken in the ufual way, it would have been lefs under the influence of fear; but the moft certain method of getting the unbiaffed judgment of the deputies, would have been by ballot : had that been adopted, there would probably have been a majority in favour of the King, even on the firft general queftion of guilty or not ; and there is no doubt but it would have been carried by a

great

great majority aga'nft the pains of death, if the firſt queſtion had been loſt.

In the mean time, the King knew nothing of its being decreed that he ſhould appear at the bar of the Convention. In an extract from the report of the Commiſſioners that were on ſervice at the Temple on that day, the following particulars are mentioned :——

The King roſe as uſual at ſeven ; he ſpent only a few minutes in dreſſing, and about three quarters of an hour in prayer. At eight the drums were heard ; he enquired of the Commiſſioners what was the meaning of it, as he had not before heard them ſo early.

The Commiſſioners pretended ignorance. "Do you not think," rejoined the King, "that they beat the general ?" The Commiſſioners replied, they could not diſtinguiſh. The King walked muſing through the room, and ſometimes ſtood liſtening attentively. " I think

think I hear the sound of horses' feet in the court," said he. The Commissioners gave no explanation.

The Royal Family breakfasted together that morning; they were full of alarm and disquietude at the noise, which increased every moment, and of which they plainly perceived the cause was carefully concealed from them.

Uncertainty in such circumstances agitates the mind more than a full assurance of the worst; the Queen and Princesses went to their own apartments after breakfast, and left the Prince Royal with the King. The Commissioners at last informed him, that he was about to receive a visit from the Mayor of Paris.——" So much the better," said the King. " But I must inform you," resumed the Commissioner, " that he cannot speak to you in the presence of your son." The King then, after pressing the child to his breast, desired him to go and embrace

K k 4

his

his mother in his name. Clery, the valet who attended the King, withdrew with the Prince.

The King afked the Commiffioner, " if he knew what the Mayor's bufinefs with him was," and was anfwered in the negative. He walked about the room for fome time, flopping at intervals to afk queftions refpecting the perfon and character of the Mayor. The Commiffioner anfwered, " that he was not particularly acquainted with him, but that he was of a good character, and, to the beft of his recollection, of a middle age, thin, and rather tall. The King feated himfelf in a chair, and continued abforbed in meditation. Meanwhile the Commiffioner had moved behind the chair on which the King was feated. When he awaked from his reverie, not feeing any body, he turned fuddenly round, and perceiving the Commiffioner clofe behind him, faid with quicknefs, " What do you want, Sir ?"

Sir?" " Nothing," replied the other; "but fearing you were indifpofed, I approached to know what ailed you*."

Monfieur Chambon, the Mayor, entered foon after, and informed the King, that he came to conduct him to the National Convention: the King accompanied him without making any objection. When he came to the court, which was full of troops, horfe as well as foot, he feemed furprifed at feeing fome of them in uniforms with which he was unacquainted.

Before he ftepped into the Mayor's coach, he threw up his eyes to the window of the apartment in which his family were confined, and the tears were obferved to trickle down his cheeks,

* Thefe particulars, which fome may think of a nature too trifling and minute, ftrongly paint the ftate of agitation and fufpicion, in which the mind of the unhappy Monarch was at this time.

5

The

The coach then proceeded to the Convention, attended by the troops.

The Commissioner ascended to the Queen's apartment, and found the whole family overwhelmed with fear and sorrow. He acquainted them that the Mayor had been with the King: the young Prince had already informed them: " We know that," said the Queen ; " but now—where have they carried the King now ?" " To the Convention," replied the Commissioner. " You would have saved us much uneasiness," said the Princess Elizabeth, " if you had informed us of this sooner."

What dreadful apprehensions must this Princess have been under, to find any relief in hearing that her brother was carried before an Assembly of men so prejudiced against him as she knew the Convention to be!

The King was conducted to the Convention

vention by the Boulevards, la rue neuve des Capucines, la place Vendôme, et la cour des Feuillans. All the streets which open to the Boulevards had guards stationed in them, with orders to prevent a multitude from affembling; and cannon were placed at the entrance of all thofe ftreets; patrols were ordered to prevent any kind of obftruction by groups, or carriages, along the whole of the way that the King was to be conducted. Strong guards were placed at different pofts near the Tuileries and Hall of the Affembly. It is faid there were near 100,000 men in arms that day in Paris.

The glaffes of the coach were down during the whole way, and there was no difturbance. Great numbers however were waiting, in all the paffages leading to the Affembly, and the tribunes had been filled from fix in the morning. It was remarked, that Marat was dreffed in a new fuit; and that

that his features announced fatisfaction and good humour, which was confidered as ftill a greater rarity.

The act of Accufation having been read, fome of the Deputies mentioned circumftances, which they thought of importance, that had been omitted. Drouet, the poftmafter, who was the caufe of the King's being ftopped at Varennes, had been elected a Deputy to the Convention for that fervice. He thought this a good opportunity to diftinguifh himfelf as an orator—" Lewis," faid he, " is a *cheat* (fourbe), and wifhed to impofe upon the nation, in faying that he intended to go to Montmedi, for the villain (fcelerat) was expected at the Abbaye d'Orvalle; and the traitor knew that a detachment of huffars were waiting for him a few leagues from Varennes : *the monfter* then had the intention, &c. &c. &c."

This was more than his audience, prejudiced as it was againft the King, could bear; the

poft-mafter

poſt-maſter was obliged to ſtop in the middle of his abuſive career, his voice being
ſtifled by an univerſal murmur *.

It was announced by the Preſident, that
from the moment that Lewis ſhould appear
at the bar, no petition ſhould be heard, no
motion of any kind made, no ſign of approbation or diſapprobation given, but a
profound ſilence maintained. When Lewis
appears, exclaimed Legendre, " *il faut qu'il
regne ici le ſilence des tombeaux.*" This brutal
inſinuation had no better ſucceſs than the
eloquence of Drouet.

Marat, however, had the fairneſs to declare, that, in his opinion, the King ought
not to be queſtioned about any thing
previous to his acceptance of the Conſtitution: this is ſo evident, that it is won-

* When Drouet was in the middle of his harangue,
a gentleman aſked one of the Deputies, who he was :
" Monſieur," replied the Deputy, " c'eſt un Maître de
Poſte, qui a voulu faire claquer ſon fouet bien mal-
à-propos."

derful

derful it was left to Marat to make the obfervation, and more fo that it was difregarded when made.

Other propofals were made by other members, and fome adopted: at about one o'clock the Affembly were informed, that the King was in the Chambre des Conférences; on which Barrere, the Prefident, having reminded the Affembly and audience of the filence they ought to maintain, defired that he might be conducted to the bar.

An awful filence prevailed; every eye was fixed on the door at which he entered: The King appeared with a ferene air and undifturbed countenance. The fpectators betrayed great emotion.

After a fhort interval, Barrere addreffed him: " Lewis, the French Nation accufe you of having committed various crimes to re-eftablifh tyranny on the ruins of liberty; the National Convention has decreed
that

that you shall be tried—and the Members who compose it are to be your Judges. You will hear the accusation read, after which you will answer to the questions which shall be proposed."

To this the King made no reply.

The general Act of Accusation was then read, after which the President repeated the first article of accusation, and added, "Lewis, what have you to answer?" On which the King gave his answer, and the President proceeded to read the second article, and demanded the King's answer in the same words; and so on, until the whole of the articles were finished.

During this examination, some new questions occurred to the Committee, which were put in writing, and handed to the President, who put them in the same manner to the King, and received his answers.

The King's behaviour during the whole of his appearance in the Convention was calm,

calm, recollected, and that of a man resign-
ed to the necessity of circumstances, without the consciousness of guilt; his answers
were sensible, pertinent, and prompt. He
never lost his composure, except in one instance, when the President read the following strange accusation: "You distributed
money among the populace for the treacherous purpose of acquiring popularity,
and enslaving the nation."

The perversion of his very benevolence
into a crime, astonished the unfortunate Monarch, and deprived him for a moment of the
power of utterance—he shed tears—but a
consciousness of the purity of his intentions
rendered them tears of comfort. "I always took pleasure," said he, "in relieving
those in want, but never had any treacherous purpose."

Upon the whole, when it is considered
that the questions were deliberately drawn
up by a Select Committee, and afterwards
corrected

corrected and enlarged by the whole Convention, while the King's anſwers were given extempore, and without even a previous knowledge that he was to be examined in that manner, it places his underſtanding in a very advantageous point of view.

To keep the King ignorant to the laſt of any intention of examining him, and then hurry him unprepared to their bar, was ungenerous and ſhameful in the higheſt degree—it might have diſconcerted him in ſuch a manner as to have given ſcope to malice; his enemies would have imputed to conſcious guilt that diſorder in his anſwers and conduct, which ſurpriſe or indignation might naturally have produced:—and it is impoſſible not to ſuſpect that the ſecrecy was employed for that very purpoſe. If ſo, all thoſe enemies have been diſappointed; the malignity by which they attempted to obfcure his character, has only ferved to put it in a fairer light.

When the King had anfwered all the queftions, the original papers on which part of the accufation was founded were laid on the table. Valazé taking them up one by one, and reading the title, faid, as he prefented each to the King, " Loûis Capet, la reconnoiffez-vous ?" If the King anfwered that he knew it, Valazé faid, " Louis la reconnoit ;" and the Prefident repeated, " La piece eft reconnue." If the King difavowed it, they faid, " Louis ne la reconnoit pas—La piece n'eft pas reconnue."

The King difavowed many of them. When the whole had been inveftigated in this manner, the Prefident addreffing the King faid, " I have no other queftions to propofe—have you any thing more to add in your defence ?"- " I defire to have a copy of the accufation," replied the King, " and

2

ef

of the papers on which it is founded.——I alſo deſire to have a Counſel of my own nomination." Barrere informed him, that his two firſt requeſts were already decreed, and that the determination reſpecting the other would be made known to him in due time.

After which the King withdrew, and was conducted back to the Temple in the ſame carriage, and with the ſame attendants that he had when he came to the Aſſembly. The crowd in the ſtreets was greater than in the morning; the continued cries of " Vive la Republique !" accompanied the coach from the Aſſembly Hall to the Temple, and the cry "A la Guillotine!" was alſo heard more frequently than in the morning, but leſs ſo than was expected by thoſe who had taken ſo much pains to irritate the populace againſt him.

In the coach, the King aſked Chaumet, the Procureur Syndic, " if he thought the Convention would allow him to have Coun-

ſel."

fel." This man, by the account which he afterwards gave of what paffed, anfwered fhortly, " that his duty was to conduct him to and from the Affembly, and not to anfwer queftions."

When he arrived at the Temple, and was in his apartment, he fent a meffage, defiring to fpeak to the Mayor, who, being in his carriage and ready to drive away, immediately obeyed the fummons, and afcended to the King's chamber. " I hope," faid he to Chambon, " that you will not delay to let me know, whether I am allowed Counfel." The Mayor replied, " that he might rely upon being informed as foon as poffible ; adding, that he was perfuaded the Convention were too juft to refufe to him what the law allowed to all."

Every member of the Convention was not of the fame way of thinking with the Mayor: about thirty or forty Deputies of the faction called the Mountain were

againft

againſt granting that requeſt, and oppoſed it by the moſt indecent clamours; but finding their efforts vain, they next inſiſted that he ſhould be allowed only one perſon for Counſel. The great majority on the contrary were for allowing him three: the debate became ſo tumultuous, that the Preſident was obliged to put on his hat *: the Mountain was at laſt obliged to relinquiſh this ſhameful attempt; and it was decreed that the King ſhould have Counſel, without limiting the number, and that a meſſage ſhould inſtantly be ſent to inform him of this. One of thoſe who had oppoſed his having any Counſel, propoſed that two of the ſervants of the Aſſembly (huiſſiers) ſhould carry this meſſage; but the Convention ordered four of their members for that purpoſe.

After the Mayor left the Temple, the

* This is a ſignal to order, never given but in caſes of great confuſion, and is generally obeyed.

King

King immediately examined the *Constitution*, of which he had a copy, and said to the Commissioner, who was now alone with him, " Yes, I find that the law allows me Counsel; but may I not also be allowed the satisfaction of having my family with me?" The Commissioner answered, " that he did not know, but would go and consult the Committee." He went accordingly, and returned soon after; he informed the King that he could not see his family.—" That is hard," said the King.—" But my son, they will not deny me the comfort of his company at least—he is a child, Sir, of only seven years of age."

" The Committee have declared," replied the Commissioner, " that you shall have no communication with your family—Your son is of your family."

The Commissioner left the King, and went to the Queen's apartment, where all the Royal family were. The Queen immediately asked,

aſked, if they might not all wait on the King, who they knew was returned from the Convention. The Commiſſioner gave the ſame anſwer he had given to the King.— "At leaſt," ſaid the Queen, " let him have the company of this child; pray allow his ſon to go to him." The Commiſſioner replied, " that as the child could not be with both, it was beſt that the perſon who might be ſuppoſed to have the greateſt courage ſhould ſuffer the privation : beſides," he added, " a child of that age has more need of the care of a mother than of a father."

The following day the four Deputies informed the Convention of their having been with the King, and that he had named Target and Tronchet as his Counſel.

Tronchet accepted, declaring at the ſame time, that he was aware of the delicacy and danger of the office, which humanity to a *man*, over whoſe head the ſword of juſtice hung, impoſed on him—and for which, in all events, he would accept of no recompenſe.

Target

Target wrote a letter to the President of the Convention, excusing himself on account of his age and infirmities, and desiring that his letter might be sent to the King, that he might choose another.

This afforded some Members of the Assembly a fresh opportunity of displaying their disposition—they complained of the incidents which continually occurred to retard the final issue of the process. Offelin * said, that one Counsel might refuse after another, to the loss of much precious time, and therefore proposed that the Convention should name Counsel for the King, whom he must either accept, or find others within twenty-four hours.

This revolted the greater part of the Assembly; and when it was asked, how it could be imagined that the King could place confidence in those of their nomination, Tallien said with a rancour that well ac-

* This same Offelin was President of the Criminal Tribunal of the 17th of August!

corded

corded with his character, " Qu'il s'arrange, qu'il trouve des Conseils qui acceptent; c'est son affaire; la nôtre est de venger la Majesté nationale *."

Fermond and Rabaut de St. Etienne spoke against this savage precipitation; another proposed to adjourn: Thuriot, and Bentabole, the same who had accompanied Marat on his visit to Dumourier, opposed the adjournment. " Do tyrants ever adjourn their vengeance against the people ?" said Legendre, " and yet you talk of adjourning the justice of the people against a tyrant." This argument was well suited to the understandings and inclinations of the audience in the galleries, and met with their applause.

In the mean time, a deputation from the Council of the Commune of Paris came to communicate to the Convention a decree which they had passed regarding the mea-

* He must do the best he can, he must find those who will accept, that is his business ; it is ours to avenge the Majesty of the Nation.

sures

fures they thought neceffary to follow in the prefent circumstances. By this decree, the King was to have no communication with his family:—his valet de chambre was to be locked up with him, and to have no inter-courfe with any body elfe:—his Counfel were to be ftrictly examined (fcrupuleufe-ment examinés, fouillés jufqu'aux endroits les plus fecrets). After having thrown off the clothes in which they entered, they were to be dreffed in others provided for them in the Temple, and under the infpection of the Commiffioners who attended the King, and were not to be allowed to leave the Temple till after fentence was pronounced. It was alfo an article in this Decree, that the Counfel fhould take an oath never to mention any thing they heard while in the Temple."

Decrees have fometimes been propofed, and meafures have been adopted, by thefe men, of fuch a deteftable and atrocious na-ture, that we are almoft tempted to fufpect

that

that fome individual among them is bribed to fuggeft and perfuade them into mea- fures which muft render them and their caufe for ever odious and deteftable. What could the enemies of civil liberty wifh more, than that thofe who call themfelves her friends fhould act fo as to fhock common decency, and revolt all the feelings of humanity?

This abominable decree was with diffi- culty heard to the end; it excited the greateft marks of difguft; there was a cry from all parts of the Affembly to annul the decree, and cenfure thofe who made it. Robefpierre had the courage to face this ftorm; he de- clared that he was convinced that a very laudable fpirit had dictated the decree,— " which," added he, " is perhaps too mild for the occafion." This declaration pro- duced violent murmurs, and many voices were heard exclaiming—" *Hors de la tri- bune!*"

" I know," refumed he, " that there is a

party

party in this Affembly for faving the traitor; but I am furprifed that thofe who fhew fo much tendernefs and fympathy for an oppreffor, have none for the good people whom he oppreffed."

This gained the galleries in an inftant, and they refounded with applaufe.

Several Members however put the inquifitorial and fhameful Decree of the Commune in a juft light; and conjured the Affembly, in the name of decency, humanity, and juftice, to annul it; which was carried.

The Convention were afterwards informed, that feveral people had offered to be Counfel for the King; all of whom he had refufed except M. Malefherbes and M. Tronchet, who having been at the Temple and admitted into the King's prefence, on the 14th, found that he had not then received any of the papers he had demanded.

Monfieur de Lamoignon-Malefherbes is a man of an amiable and refpectable cha-

3
racter;

tacter; of distinguished sense, probity, and learning; of one of the chief families of what is called The Robe in France; he is grandson of the Chancellor Lamoignon, who was an intimate friend of Boileau, Racine, and other men of genius in the reign of Lewis the Fourteenth.

The present Monsieur de Malesherbes distinguished himself towards the end of the reign of Lewis XV. by some very eloquent and courageous remonstrances which he drew up when he was first President of the *Cour des Aides*, and for which he was banished.

In the beginning of the reign of Lewis XVI. he succeeded Monsieur de St. Florentin in the Ministry; but afterwards, for reasons which are variously stated, he desired and obtained leave to retire.

This respectable man is seventy-two years of age; his generous offer to be Counsel for the King gains him the applause of the public, and forms a contrast greatly in his

favour

favour with the cautious conduct of M. Target, which has been condemned by all parties. —— Even the fishwomen of Paris marked the difference, went in a body and hung garlands of flowers and laurel on the gate of Monfieur de Malefherbes, and afterwards proceeded to the houfe of Monfieur Target, in the intention to infult him in a manner peculiar to themfelves. Fortunately for him, he was advertifed of their intention, and made his efcape.

It is much to be wifhed that all the Members of the Convention had been endowed with equal fentiments of juftice with thefe Poiffardes. The difcrimination difplayed on this occafion is a proof that the loweft inhabitants of Paris are not devoid of fentiments of generofity ; and that if they were acquainted with the real character of the King, the fpirit of rancour which has been perfidioufly raifed againft him wou'd foon be turned againft his perfecutors.

It

It will not be improper here to infert an anecdote which does honour to the heart of this unfortunate Prince. Two Commiffioners of very oppofite difpofitions were with the King when the fhocking exhibition of the head of Madame de Lamballe was made under his windows, on the third of September. One of thofe men hearing the noife, and recognifing the head, had the brutality to invite the King to come to the window, and he would fee a very curious fight. The King was advancing towards the window, when the other ran and withheld him, faying, the fight was too fhocking for him to fupport.

The perfon to whom the King afterwards related thefe circumftances, afked the names of the two Commiffioners. The King freely told him the name of the latter, but refufed to mention that of the former—" becaufe," faid he, " it can do him no credit at any time; and might poffibly at
                                                            fome

some future period bring him to trouble." As the benevolence of the King's difpofition appeared through the whole of his reign, his enemies have endeavoured to conceal and mifreprefent every circumftance of this kind. But notwithftanding all the pains they have taken, fo many proofs of his candour, moderation and integrity were known, that thofe who wifhed his death were in conftant dread of a return of humanity and affection in the hearts of the people towards him; and therefore were at great pains to fill the tribunes with perfons hired to make an outcry againft him: and they were fo apprehenfive on this fubject as to fufpect thofe very agents of relenting.

When the King was indifpofed in the month of November, and the phyfician Lemonier ordered to vifit him, fome fymptoms of concern were manifefted by the people, which alarmed the King's enemies greatly. It was reported and believed for one day, that

that he was dead; I myfelf heard it infinuated in a pretty large company that he was murdered; one perfon exclaimed with indignation—"Les fcelerats l'ont empoifonné * !"

The King's appearance in the Convention, the dignified refignation of his manner, the admirable promptitude and candour of his anfwers, made fuch an evident impreffion on fome of the audience in the galleries, that a determined enemy of Royalty, who had his eye upon them, declared that he was afraid of hearing the cry of Vive le Roi! iffue from the tribunes; and added, that if the King had remained ten minutes longer in their fight, he was convinced it would have happened: for which reafon he was vehemently againft his being brought to the bar a fecond time.

The Commiffioners who do duty at the Temple were cenfured for drawing up their

* The villains have poifoned him !

reports fo as to excite compaffion, and were required to avoid this for the future. The thing was impoffible, unlefs they had been permitted to falfify; for a bare relation of the facts, in the coldeft language, muft have produced the effect they wifhed to prevent.

Terror has acted a principal part fince the beginning of this Revolution—Terror firft produced the emigrations, to which a great proportion of the miferies which France has fuffered are owing—Terror produced that fhameful paffivenefs in the inhabitants of Paris and Verfailles during the maffacres — Terror prevented fympathy from appearing in the faces of many who felt it in their hearts for the unfortunate monarch, during this procefs, and Terror at laft pronounced the fentence of his death.

Befides the means already mentioned, of inflaming the populace by pamphlets and hand-bills, men were hired to mix with the groups, in the Palais Royal, and on the

terrace

terrace of the Feuillans, to harangue on the neceffity of condemning the King without farther form of procefs : and fome of thefe men went the length of afferting, that if the Convention did not, the people would take that bufinefs on themfelves, and afterwards execute the fame juftice on all the Deputies who fhould vote for faving him.

All thofe inhuman manœuvres did not prevent its being ftrongly ftated by fome members in the Convention, that if the King's counfel were not allowed fufficient time to prepare his defence, the decree by which counfel was granted to him would be confidered as an infult, and the trial a mockery.——It was alfo boldly afferted by one member, that " if rancour and mean felfifh " views had not hardened the hearts of fome " prefent, fo plain and obvious a piece of " juftice never would have afforded a mo- " ment's debate."——" It has been faid," added another, " that there are Royalifts in the M m 2 " Convention.

" Convention. So there are; but they con-
" fift of thofe who puſh on the proceſs with
" royal fury and precipitation—men who
" are not for trying but butchering Lewis
" XVI, and thereby gratifying all the
" princes at war with the Republic, by
" raiſing a general indignation all over
" Europe, at the manifeſt cruelty and injuſ-
" tice of a Republican Aſſembly."

Theſe remonſtrances ſeem to have had
ſome effect; for it was decreed, that the King
fhould be allowed till the 26th of December
to prepare his defence.

It was alſo propoſed, that during this interval the King fhould have a free inter-
courſe with his family.——This was no ſooner
mentioned than it was aſſented to by the exclamations of a great majority of the Aſſembly. " You may decree this as much as
you pleaſe," cried Tallien; " but if the Municipality do not chooſe it, he will be allowed to ſee none of them."

Here

Here this man's malice carried him farther than his accomplices approved ; it was moved that he fhould be cenfured, and that the cenfure fhould be inferted in the verbal procefs : he attempted to avert this by a filly explanation, which proved ineffectual.

The Affembly feemed pretty generally difpofed to allow a free communication between the King and all his family, when Reubell afferted, that it would be highly improper to allow him any communication with the Queen and the Princefs Elizabeth, who were involved in the accufation, as there was reafon to believe they had fent their diamonds to their brothers, to help them to make war on the nation. On this defpicable pretext the King was allowed to have intercourfe with his children only, and they were ordered to be kept feparate from their mother and aunt till the end of the procefs.

It had been obferved, that very few of

the

the real Bourgeoifie of Paris could of late get
accefs to the tribunes, the places being pre-
occupied by a fet of hired vagabonds, generally the fame every day : fo that when the
other departments complain of being under
the controul of the fingle city of Paris, they
do not ftate the grievance in its full mag-
nitude. All the departments of France, including that of Paris, are, in reality, often
obliged to fubmit to the clamorous tyranny
of a fet of hired ruffians in the tribunes,
who ufurp the name and functions of the
Peuple Souverain, and, fecretly directed by a
few demagogues, govern this unhappy nation.

To remedy this, Manuel propofed, that
a certain number of tickets of admiffion
fhould be fent every day to the fections to
be diftributed among the real citizens.——
As this plan would have prevented certain
manœuvres of the Mountain, that faction
oppofed it with great violence ; the people 
in the galleries thundered againft it ; fome
of

of them called out, " A l'Abbaye Manuel, à l'Abbaye l'ariſtocrate Manuel !" Legendre, the butcher, propoſed, that it ſhould be decreed, that Manuel had loſt his ſenſes.——This ſally, the fineſſe of which will not be apparent to all the world, was thought exquiſite by the people in the tribunes. When they had done with their applauſe, Manuel returned his thanks to Legendre, for not having moved that it ſhould be decreed that he was an ox ; becauſe, if that had paſſed, Legendre might have thought he had a right to ſlaughter him.

Monſieur Deſeize was added to Meſſrs. de Maleſherbes and Tronchet, as a counſel for the King : the buſineſs they had to go through was too laborious for two perſons only, and the time allowed ſtill too ſhort.

From the report of one of the Commiſſioners we learn the following particulars, which, though minute, ſerve to illuſtrate the character of the King :——The Commiſſioners,

who

who were ordered on duty at the Temple,
having, according to custom, drawn lots for
their different posts, that of the King's apartment fell to a M. Cubieres, who, with another Commissioner, was introduced at eleven
at night, the King being then asleep. He rose
as usual at seven, and took a book, which
they afterwards found was a breviary;—
breakfast was brought at nine, but the King
refused to eat because it was the fast of Le
Quatre Tems.—He spent some time in prayer,
and afterwards asked Cubieres about the
health of the Queen and his sister.—He walked musing through the room; and then, raising his eyes to Heaven, "This day (said he)
my daughter is fourteen years of age." The
unhappy Prince repeated the same expression
after a pause, during which the tears flowed
from his eyes, and he was greatly agitated.

Monsieur de Malesherbes and the other
two counsel came, and he passed most of
that day and the next with them, and with
four

four deputies from the Convention, who came with papers relative to his trial.

One of the Commiſſioners ſaid to Maleſherbes, in a converſation apart, that he was ſurpriſed to obſerve that he gave the Moniteur and other Journals to Lewis, becauſe he would by it become acquainted with many things very diſagreeable, and particularly to what a degree the people were prejudiced againſt him. Monſ. Maleſherbes replied, that the King (for he perſiſted in calling him the King) was of a ſt rong character, and beheld his misfortunes with magnanimity.

The Commiſſioner hinted to M. de Maleſherbes, that, by the free admiſſion he had to the King, he might, if he were not an honeſt man, furniſh him with poiſon.

" If I ſhould," replied M. de Maleſherbes, " the King is too ſincere a chriſtian to make uſe of it."

The reſolution of the Convention to try the King and to be themſelves his judges, aſtoniſhed aftonifhed Europe, and was heard with forrow and indignation by the unfortunate natives of France, whom the violence of the late meafures, or the fears of affaffination, had driven from their country.

Some of them, diftinguifhed for their talents as well as for the offices they had held in their own country, were in England at this interefting period, and fhewed a ftrong defire of doing every thing in their power, in juftification of a prince of whofe innocence they all feemed fully convinced.

M. Louis de Narbonne, who had been Minifter of War when the hoftilities began between France and the Emperor, and from that circumftance was enabled to throw great light on the fubject, wrote to the Prefident of the Convention, offering to appear at the bar as one of the defenders of the King, provided a protection was fent to make it fafe for him to pafs and repafs through France. The Convention paffed

I

to

to the order of the day on this requeſt, without even allowing the reaſons which M. de Narbonne gave for its peculiar propriety to be read.

M. de Narbonne then drew up a declaration in juſtification of his Sovereign, which he tranſmitted to Meſſrs. Tronchet and Maleſherbes: from the laſt he received the following letter :

Paris, 31 Decembre 1792.

" J'ai reçu, Monſieur, votre lettre et la déclaration de vos ſentimens.

" Vous ne me mandez pas quel uſage vous voulez que j'en faſſe. Si c'eſt de la faire imprimer, ce ne peut pas être moi qui m'en charge, parce qu'étant le conſeil de celui qui fut mon Roi, je ne peux faire aucune démarche qui ne ſoit regardée comme faite par lui. Au reſte, votre déclaration ne peut avoir aucune influence ſur le jugement de la Convention Nationale, parce que à l'heure

l'heure où je vous écris, on procéde au jugement.

" Il est possible que le jugement qu'on
rendra, entraine une autre discussion en pré-
sence de la nation. Ce sera alors à vous de
voir si vous croyez devoir faire paraître
votre déclaration en faveur du plus malheureux et du plus vertueux des hommes.

" Quant à moi, si la cause se plaide devant
la nation, je suis très déterminé à la soutenir
aussi publiquement que je pourrai, quand
même on prononcerait que je ne suis plus le
défenseur légal de l'innocent.

Dans ce cas-là, Monsieur, je vous pré-
viens que je me servirai de plusieurs articles
de votre lettre sans prétendre me les appro-
prier, parce qu'il ne me serait pas possible
de rendre aussi bien que vous, plusieurs
grandes vérités, qu'il sera important de met-
tre sous les yeux de la nation.

" Mais la plus grande partie de votre dé-

7                                        claration

claration concerne des faits qui vous font
personnels, et que vous feul avez droit de
certifier.

(Signé)        MALESHERBES*.

" A Monfieur Louis de
Narbonne, ancien Miniftre
de la Guerre de France, à
Londres."

M. de

* I have received your letter, and the declaration of
your fentiments. You do not inform me what ufe
you wifh to be made of them. If you defire to have
them printed, I am not the perfon who can take upon
me to do it ; becaufe, being one of his counfel who was
my King, whatever I do will be confidered as done by
him. Befide, your declaration can have no influence
on the decifion of the National Convention, becaufe, at
the very time I am writing, they are proceeding to
judgment.

It is poffible that the fentence they will pronounce
may occafion another difcuffion in prefence of the whole
nation. You will then confider whether it will be proper for you to publifh your declaration in favour of the
moft unfortunate and moft virtuous of men. As for
my part, if the caufe fhall be brought before the nation,
I am refolved to fupport it as publicly as I can, even
although they fhould decide that I am no longer the legal defender of the innocent.

In

M. de Narbonne wrote the following anſwer to M. Maleſherbes :

" En m'annonçant, Monſieur, que vous avez reçu la déclaration que j'ai eu l'honneur de vous addreſſer, vous ſemblez déſirer que je vous indique l'uſage que je ſouhaite qui en ſoit faite. Permettez-moi de m'en rapporter ſur cela à votre courageuſe vertu, et ſoyez ſûr que j'apprendrai avec reconnoiſſance tout ce qui ſera fait par vous. Au moment du jugement de celui que je choiſirois avec orgueil et avec tranſport pour mon roi, je fis propoſer aux miniſtres Francois, actuellement en Angleterre, de ſe rendre ſur le champ à Paris, pour nous ranger autour de nôtre malheureux monarque. Ils

In that caſe, I ſhall avail myſelf of ſeveral articles in your letter, without alteration, becauſe it is not in my power to expreſs ſo well as you have done, certain great truths, which it will be of importance to lay before the nation.

But the greateſt part of your declaration conſiſts of facts perſonal to yourſelf, and which you alone have the right to certify.

(Signed)                    MALESHERBES.

crurent

crurent voir dans cette démarche, des incon-
veniens pour fa caufe ; ils en trouvèrent
également à écrire une lettre fignée de nous
tous, pour demander un fauf-conduit qui
nous mit à même de reclamer toute notre
refponfabilité. Je fus réduit à faire feul
cette démarche, et ma lettre ne fut pas
même lue par l'Affemblée. Il ne m'eft donc
refté de moyen d'acquitter cette dette de ma
confcience, que par la déclaration à laquelle
vous daignez donner quelque éloge.

" Ah ! c'eft vous, Monfieur, et vos re-
fpectables collegues, qui les méritez toutes.

" Un de mes amis, Monfieur d'Arblay*,
retiré avec moi à la campagne, a cru que la
dépofition qu'il vous a envoyée, pourroit
être de quelque utilité dans une difcuffion ;
il fe joint à moi pour vous exprimer les
mêmes fentimens.

" J'ai l'honneur, &c. &c.
(Signé)      L. de NARBONNE†."

* This is the fame gallant officer of whom mention is
made vol. i. p. 233.
† In informing me that you have received the declaration

M. de Narbonne afterwards received the letter which follows :

Malefherbes, 29 Janvier, 1793.

" Votre lettre du 10 Janvier m'eſt ar-

ration which I had the honour to fend to you, you feem to defire that I fhould acquaint you with the uſe I wiſh to be made of it. Allow me to leave it entirely to your intrepid virtue, and be perfuaded that I fhall gratefully approve of what you think moſt proper.

At the moment of the trial of him, whom with pride and tranfport I would chooſe for my King, I fent a pro-poſal to the French Miniſters, who are at preſent in England, that we fhould immediately fet out for Paris, and take our ftand by the fide of our unfortunate King. They thought fuch a meaſure would be prejudicial to his cauſe, and thought it would be equally fo, to write a letter figned by us all, demanding a fafe-conduct, which fhould enable us to challenge the refponfibility of our refpective offices at the bar of the Convention. I was obliged to adopt this meaſure alone, but my letter was not fo much as read in the Affembly; and no other means remained for me by which I could fatisfy my confcience, but the declaration on which you are pleafed to beſtow fome commendation. It is to you and your refpectable colleagues that every praife is due. M. d'Arblay, one of my friends, who lives with me in the country, thinks that the depofition which he fends may be of fervice ; he joins me in expreffing the fame fenti-ments.

I have the honour to be, &c.

rivée,

rivée, Monſieur, à la campagne où je ſuis retiré depuis l'evenement.

" Vous ſavez ſûrement que la déclaration de vos ſentimens que vous m'avez envoyée manuſcrite a été imprimée. Je ne ſais pas ſur quelle copie a été faite cette impreſſion : je n'y ai eu aucune part. Le ſeul uſage que j'ai fait de votre lettre, et de la déclaration qui y était jointe, a été de les lire à celui que cela intéreſſait. Il en fut touché, et même attendri : il me recommanda de ne les pas publier par la crainte de vous compromettre ; car il a eu, ſur cela, les attentions les plus ſcrupuleuſes juſqu'au dernier ſoupir. L'original fut remis par lui à un de mes collegues, qui deſira de l'avoir pour le relire à tête repoſée ; et il m'a aſſuré qu'il n'eſt pas ſorti de ſes mains.

" J'ai l'honneur, Monſieur, de vous aſſurer de tout mon attachement.

(Signé) " MALESHERBES*."

* Your letter of the 10th of January I received in the country, where I have been ever ſince the *event*.

Le Comte de Lally-Tolendal had as early
as the fifth of November addreſſed a letter to
the Convention, requeſting to be permitted
to plead the cauſe of the King at their bar,
on which they alſo paſſed to the order of the
day : and hearing afterwards that M. Target
had declined to affiſt Monſieur de Maleſherbes in that honourable taſk, he repeated
his requeſt to the Convention ; but before
this ſecond application arrived, the aſſo-
ciates of Monſieur de Maleſherbes were already appointed.

Monſieur de Lally, however, while he had
the expectation that his offer would be ac-

You know undoubtedly that the declaration which
you ſent me in manuſcript has been printed.  I am ignorant from what copy this has been done ; I had no
hand in it.  The only uſe I made of your letter, and of
the declaration which came with it, was to read them to
the perſon whom they moſt concerned.  He was very
much affected ; he deſired me not to publiſh them, leſt
it ſhould bring you to trouble ; for on that head he obſerved the moſt ſcrupulous attention until his laſt moment.  The original was delivered by him to one of my
colleagues, who wiſhed to read it in more tranquillity.
He aſſured me that it never was out of his poſſeſſion.

 I have the honour, &c.

cepted,

cepted, had prepared a very eloquent defence of the King in the form of an addrefs to the Convention, which he publifhed during the procefs.

M. Cazales, who had been a Member of the Conftituent Affembly, was at that time in London. This gentleman wrote a letter to Lewis XVI. requefting, in cafe he fhould fo far acknowledge the jurifdiction of the Convention as to make a defence before their tribunal, that he would choofe him for his advocate. M. Cazales urges fome particular reafons for this requeft, that feem equally juft and generous.

He addreffed the Prefident of the Convention, that he might be allowed a fafe-conduct to enable him to perform the honourable tafk which he had folicited, and was in hopes of obtaining leave to execute; adding, that he did not make this requeft in the expectation of having his name effaced from the lift of emigrants, for he gloried in parti-

cipating

cipating their political opinions and their misfortunes.

M. Cazales enclofed both thefe letters in one to Petion, the Mayor of Paris ; begging him, after he had read them, to deliver the one to the King and the other to the Prefident of the Convention, and requefting an anfwer as foon as poffible from Petion.

This propofal of M. Cazales was treated with the fame neglect with the others. The Convention paffed to the order of the day when it was laid before them.

It will, no doubt, be thought extraordinary that the Convention fhould have made the fmalleft difficulty in admitting any body as the defender of the King who was agreeable to him ; but what is much more extraordinary, and muft be confidered as a piece of ftriking injuftice, was, to intercept papers intended for his juftification from reaching him, or thofe who were charged with his defence. Yet this injuftice, ftriking as it feems,

was

was certainly exercifed towards this unfortunate Prince.

M. Bertrand de Moleville, late Minifter of the Marine, was obliged to conceal himfelf, and afterwards to fly to England, in confequence of a decree of accufation iffued on the 16th of Auguft againft all the late Minifters *.

Being at London when the King's procefs began, and in poffeffion of facts which he thought might be of ufe for his juftification, he tranfmitted them with the proofs to the Minifter of Juftice, requiring that they might be delivered to the King.

Afterwards, under cover to the fame Minifter, he addreffed a packet of papers to M.

* This decree was inftantly agreed to, on reading in the Affembly the note mentioned in Vol. I. page 278. M. de Bertrand was not acquainted either with M. Barnave or M. Lameth; he knew nothing of the note, which befides was in itfelf of no importance. Yet it is evident, from what has fince happened, that he has had a juft notion of the difpofition of thofe he had to deal with, and acted very wifely in taking refuge in England.

de Made Malefherbes, infcribed *Pieces pour la Juf-tification de Louis XVI.* and he wrote at the fame time to M. de Malefherbes, informing him of the two parcels which had been fent.

Nothing can be conceived more facred than this depofit in the hands of a Minifter of Juftice.

One of the abufes complained of in the ancient government was, that the papers fent to prifoners neceffary for their defence, were fometimes intercepted, and not deli-vered to them in time; the Conftituent Affembly therefore had decreed, that accufed perfons fhould freely receive all papers or memorials for their defence within the fpace of twenty-four hours.

M. de Bertrand muft have been greatly furprifed and fhocked when he received the following letter from M. de Malefherbes :

Paris, le 31 Octobre, 1792.

" Le Miniftre de la Juftice a reçu un pa-quet

quet de M. de Bertrand pour être remis à Louis XVI. et contenant des pieces pour sa juſtification.

" Le Miniſtre n'ayant point de communication avec le priſonnier, a envoyé ce paquet à la Convention Nationale.

" Le même Miniſtre a reçu une lettre depuis du même M. Bertrand, adreſſée à moi, et il y avoit ſur l'adreſſe, Pieces pour la Juſtification de Louis XVI. Ces mots ont fait penſer au Miniſtre qu'il étoit auſſi obligé de renvoyér ce paquet devant la Convention Nationale. C'eſt ce que ce Miniſtre m'a dit quand j'ai été le réclamer.

" J'ai ſu que ces deux paquets avoient été renvoyés par la Convention à un comité ; j'ai été à ce comité pour réclamer au nom de celui dont je ſuis le défenſeur, le paquet qui eſt pour lui, et en mon nom celui qui eſt pour moi. J'ai vu que les paquets avoient été ouverts : il y avoit des pieces imprimées, et dans un des paquets, qui n'eſt pas le mien,

N n 4        des

des pieces manufcrites qu'on ne m'a pas laiffé lire, et qu'on m'a dit être des actes.

" On m'a remis fans difficulté les imprimés que j'avois déjà : pour les manufcrits, on n'a pas voulu me les remettre fans avoir un ordre de la Convention Nationale.

" Quelqu'un du comité a été à la Convention, les pieces à la main, pour demander l'ordre. Il eft revenu, et m'a dit que fur fa demande on a paffé à l'ordre du jour. Mais il n'a point rapporté les pieces, et m'a dit qu'il les avoit laiffées fur le bureau. Il ne m'a pas parû qu'il ait fait conftater, par aucun acte, que ces pieces qui étoient dans fon depôt en étoient forties.

" J'ai demandé à ces M. M. comment je pourrois me pourvoir pour avoir ces pieces. Tout le monde s'eft regardé, et perfonne ne m'a rien répondu.

" Voila où nous en fommes. Je n'ai pas crû devoir infifter fur cet objet auprès de la Convention,

Convention, pendant qu'elle eſt occupée à délibérer ſur le jugement de Louis.

(Signé) " MALESHERBES *."

* The Miniſter of Juſtice received a packet from M. de Bertrand, to be delivered to Lewis XVI. containing papers for his juſtification.

The Miniſter having no communication with the priſoner, ſent the packet to the Convention.

The ſame Miniſter has ſince received a letter from M. de Bertrand addreſſed to me, with a parcel entitled *Papers for the Juſtification of Lewis XVI.* Theſe words made the Miniſter think that it was his duty to deliver this packet alſo to the Convention. This is what the Miniſter told me when I waited on him to demand the papers.

Being informed that thoſe two packets had been tranſmitted by the Convention to a Committee, I attended that Committee to demand in the name of him whoſe Counſel I am, that which is for him, and in my own name the other which is addreſſed to me. I perceived that both packets had been opened. Some of the contents were in print; and in that packet which was not addreſſed to me, there were papers in manuſcript, which I was not permitted to read, and which they told me were acts.

They gave me without difficulty the papers which were in print, and which I had already: as for the manuſcripts, they did not chooſe to give me them without an order from the Convention.

A Member of the Committee having gone to the Convention

The language of this letter is very guarded; the writer has not allowed the fentiments he muft have felt at fuch conduct to appear; but a simple detail of the facts is fufficiently expreffive.

M. de Bertrand, in a denunciation tranfmitted from London to the Convention, did not think the fame caution neceffary; he appeals in terms of juft indignation to the reflection of the Convention on fuch a flagrant breach of their own decrees, and

vention with the papers to obtain the order, returned and informed me, that on this requeft they had paffed to the order of the day; but he did not bring back the papers, telling me he had left them on the table of the Convention. It does not appear that he has afcertained by any act that thofe papers which were in his poffeffion were taken from him.

I requefted of the Members of the Committee to inform me by what means I could recover thofe papers. They all looked at each other, but none of them made any anfwer.

This is the prefent ftate of things. I thought it would not be prudent to infift on this, while the Convention were deliberating on the fentence to be pronounced on Lewis.

deviation from every rule of common equity.

The Minifter of Juftice informed the Convention, on the 14th of January 1793, that he had received this denunciation of M. Bertrand; that he underftood it was alfo publifhed in the Courier de l'Europe, and the minute placed in the hands of the Lord Mayor of London.

One member obferved, that Bertrand having emigrated, was dead in law——that a dead perfon could not be fuppofed to write or fpeak. Another faid, that if the Convention fhould beftow attention on what appeared in newfpapers, they muft neglect the bufinefs of their country : and the Minifter of Juftice declared, that he did not think it became him, as Minifter of the Republic, to correfpond with a man who was not only an emigrant, but under a decree of accufation : and Valazé, who was of the Committee, faid they were teafed with the num-

4

ber of papers fent to them ; and that as for the manufcripts which Bertrand mentions, he knew nothing of them, if they were not in a packet which the Committee had not thought it worth while to break open.

On this candid and fatisfactory ftate of the matter, the Convention paffed to the order of the day; by which means the King's Counfel were precluded from the knowledge of certain facts, which M. de Bertrand thought material in the King's defence ; which feems alfo to have been the opinion of thofe who fo bafely intercepted them.

The day preceding that on which the King was to appear with his Counfel before the Convention, Santerre informed them, that the King, as he believed, might be conducted in fafety to and from the Affembly, provided he returned while there was day-light ; but if he was detained till it was dark, he could not anfwer for what

might-

might happen; so great was the fury of the people against him.

When those who express a fear that the populace will destroy the King, are the very persons who have been active in exciting the public against him——it may naturally be thought that the fear is affected, on purpose to prevent any attempt to rescue him, rather than to prevent his being destroyed.

The hypocrisy that has been displayed, and the artifices that have been used to impose upon the people, to inflame their minds against the King, and stifle every sentiment of humanity and remorse, are odious and wicked in the extreme.

When the Deputies went on the morning of the 26th of December to the Convention, all those who were suspected to favour the King were insulted by the crowds, who beset the passages into the Assembly-hall, as Rolandists, Brissotins and Royalists: most of the Deputies were there

6                                                    by

by eight; and notwithſtanding that a decree had paſſed the evening before to clear the galleries, and not to admit any until a certain hour that morning, the galleries were found full of people, who had remained there all night. It was pretended that the guards could not poſſibly put the decree in execution.

Manuel moved, that the galleries ſhould be cleared of thoſe who had ſhewn ſuch contempt to the decree; and that another ſet of citizens ſhould be admitted. This propoſal met with loud murmurs and hooting, from thoſe who were in poſſeſſion of the tribunes, ſupported by all the faction of the Mountain, who exclaimed for the order of the day. Others ſupported the motion of Manuel. The Preſident divided the Aſſembly, whether they ſhould maintain their own decree, or yield to thoſe who openly deſpiſed it: it was carried to paſs to the order of the day.

Here

Here the influence of terror is evident.

Some time previous to the King's arrival, one of the Commiffioners who had been on duty at the Temple prefented a parcel of keys, which the King had given to Clery, his valet.

The Commiffioner obferved, that one of thefe keys opened the iron cheft lately found full of papers in the Palace, and alfo opened other cabinets belonging to the King; and that of courfe he muft be acquainted with the keys and papers contained in the iron cheft.

We fee men every day who are led into the commiffion of crimes by the influence of their paffions, although they have the fame idea of virtue and vice with thofe who live a more virtuous life ; but the conduct of many actors in this Revolution, particularly of late, tempts us to believe that they have different ideas of the plaineft cafes of right and wrong, from what have been generally entertained by mankind.

When

When the Council of the Municipality met on the 25th of December, to decide on the manner in which the King should be conducted to the Convention, Chaumet, the Procureur Syndic, said, that as the King could be considered in no other light than as a condemned criminal soon to be executed, it would be dishonourable for the Magistrates of the people to accompany him to the Convention; and that he ought therefore to be conducted by the military only.

This was declaring that the trial was a mere farce, and that it was already determined to put the King to death, whatever proofs might be brought of his innocence, and whatever might be urged in his defence. There is great reason to think that this was really the case; but it is most extraordinary that it should be mentioned as a thing quite reasonable and proper, and it is still more extraordinary that it was rejected by only a very small majority, who at last decreed, that the King should be accompanied

nied by the Mayor, the Procureur-Syndic, and thirty Municipal Officers.

On the 26th of December, his Majefty, with whom his Counfel had been from an early hour, left the Temple a little before nine in the Mayor's coach, and was conducted as formerly to the gate of the Capucins, rue St. Honoré, where the National Guards formed a line, through which he walked to the Chambre des Conferences, where he again met his Counfel.

General Berruyer, Commander in Chief of all the military of the department of Paris, with all the Field Officers then in the capital, who were not otherwife on duty, accompanied the King on horfeback from the Temple to the Affembly Hall. Berruyer informed the Prefident, that the King was arrived. The Prefident defired he might be conducted to the bar; which was done in the following order : Berruyer and Santerre walked firft, the Mayor of Paris and the Procureur after them, and the King with Meffrs. Malefherbes, Tronchet and Seze followed. The Prefident faid, "Lewis, the Convention has decreed, that you fhould be ultimately heard this day."

His Majefty anfwered, "Monfieur de Seze, one of my Counfel, will read my defence."

M. de Seze then read the defence, which entirely refutes fome of the charges, fhews the conftitutional objections to others, and with equal candour and ingenuity gives a favourable interpretation to all.

During the defence, M. de Seze was obliged to ftop two or three times: at thofe intervals the King was obferved to fpeak to one or other of his Counfel, which he did with a fmiling countenance.

When the defence was finifhed, he arofe, and, holding a paper in his hand, pronounced in a calm manner, and with a firm voice, what follows:—" Citizens, you have
heard

heard my defence; I now speak to you perhaps for the last time, and declare that my Counsel have asserted nothing to you but the truth; my conscience reproaches me with nothing; I never was afraid of having my conduct investigated; but I observed with great uneasiness, that I was accused of giving orders for shedding the blood of the people on the 10th of August. The proofs I have given through my whole life of a contrary disposition, I hoped would have saved me from such an imputation, which I now solemnly declare is entirely groundless." The President ordered the keys to be shewn to the King, and asked if he knew them. The King answered, " that he remembered to have given a parcel of keys to Clery; but it was so long since he had made use of them, that he did not know whether these were the same."

The President having asked, " Whether he wished to say any thing farther," and

being

being anfwered in the negative, the King withdrew into the Chamber of Conferences. Obferving that M. de Seze was greatly heated, he expreffed anxiety about his health, and enquired whether he could not find means to change his linen.

On the way from the Temple to the Affembly, fome perfon in the carriage with the King made mention of fome of the Roman hiftorians, which gave him occafion to fay, that he preferred Tacitus to Livy : he accufed the latter of having compofed fpeeches for the Generals, which certainly had never been pronounced. On his return from the Affembly, he preferved the fame ferenity. The Procureur had his hat on, which had not been the cafe when he was in the carriage with the King the firft time he went to and from the Convention. The King took notice of this piece of rudenefs, by faying to him, " You had forgot your hat the laft time you attended me ; but you have

been

been more careful of your health on this occasion."

Observing that the Procureur bowed and waved his hand with a look of familiarity to some persons in the streets, the King said, "I suppose these are citizens of your section?" The Procureur answered, " No, they do not belong to my section; but they were members of the General Council of the 10th of August, *whom I always see with pleasure.*"

The Mayor held his snuff-box in his hand : the Secretary of the Municipality looking at a portrait of M. Chambon's wife on the lid, made the usual observation, that the original was handsomer than the portrait.—The King also desired to see it ; which having done, he said, that Monf. Chambon was happy in possessing a woman more beautiful than such a portrait.

The King arrived at the Temple in safety, though the cries of the rabble were more noisy and frequent than on the former day.

He

He had no fooner withdrawn from the Affembly, than Manuel propofed that the King's defence fhould be printed, and fent to the eighty-four departments, and that all difcuffion concerning it fhould be adjourned for three days.

The mention of adjournment excited the moft noify murmurs from fome of the members, and all the people in the galleries. Duhem, deputy from the department of the North, diftinguifhed himfelf on this occafion. —He cried, that Lewis had been heard— —that there was no pretext for farther delay——and infifted that the Convention fhould inftantly proceed, by the nominal appeal, to pronounce judgment.—The murmurs were converted into applaufe. Lanjuinais began to fpeak :——" The time is paffed," faid he, " when bloody-minded men could force the Affembly, by threats, to pronounce degrading decrees; do they expect that we fhall difhonour ourfelves by pronouncing judgment, with-

out

out having had time to weigh the defence of the accufed?" He was interrupted by clamours. Some called out to fend him to the Abbaye, on the pretence of his having infinuated a reflexion againft the heroes of the 10th of Auguft : it was with infinite difficulty that he was allowed to explain. After which, Legendre and others recommenced their outcries for pronouncing judgment before they fhould feparate. " Do you intend to act as a judge, or as a *butcher ?*" faid Kerfaint ?

This farcafm was applauded by many of the Deputies, but hooted by the tribunes.

Raffron, of the department of Paris, always a very zealous, and often a very clamorous Member, attempted to fpeak ; a deaf perfon would have thought, from the violence of his geftures, and his gaping, that he was bellowing very loud : the man

was

was fo hoarfe with a cold, that he could not be heard, which increafed the anger of his heart, and the contortions of his countenance, but entirely fuppreffed his voice.——He was advifed, by thofe who were afraid that the violence of his efforts would throw him into convulfions, to put his opinion in writing——which he did; and it was read to the Affembly by the Prefident. The import of it was, that they ought directly to pafs fentence on the King, of whofe guilt, this temperate judge declared, no calm and candid man could have any doubt.

Raffron's opinion was loudly approved of by the galleries, but did not convince the majority of the deputies, fome of whom ventured to exprefs a defire of ftill more time to deliberate on the defence they had juft heard——The people exclaimed with horror at the idea. Some deputies moved, that they fhould be called to order, which
rendered

rendered them more diforderly than ever.
It was propofed to adjourn—This made
Duhem outrageous : he rufhed into the middle of the hall, followed by a number of the
members of the faction of the Mountain,
crying " La Mort du Tyran !"—and feeming to appeal to the galleries—and even to
threaten Fermond the Prefident.

Had Lewis XVI. really been the
bloody tyrant thefe men affected to call him,
ftill this behaviour in his judges, on his trial,
would have been indecent and odious ; but
to fhew fuch an unrelenting fpirit, and fuch
fury againft a Prince of fo mild a character
—one *who has borne his faculties fo meek*—is
not to be accounted for by any of the motives which ufually influence men, whether
virtuous or vicious.   Some members of this
National Convention feem as deaf to the
voice of expediency and felf-intereft as of
humanity and juftice.   Inftead of any ra-

4                                  tional

tional principle, they appear to be urged on by brutal and furious instinct to the death of the King, like blood-hounds, who never quit the scent till they have drunk the blood of their prey.

During this disgraceful scene, Fermond calmly kept his seat, allowing the fury of those men to exhaust itself: at length, perceiving that Petion was inclined to speak, he invited him to ascend the tribune, conceiving, from the strength of his former popularity, that he had a better chance of being heard than any other member who did not belong to the faction of the Mountain: it was with great difficulty, however, that he was allowed to speak.——He endeavoured to convince them of the indecency of proceeding to judgment immediately, and before the members had time to deliberate on the defence which they had just heard.

When it appeared that the majority of the

the Convention were not to be driven into the fhameful meafure of giving judgment directly, the point was given up; and it was decreed that every Member had a right to pronounce his opinion on the whole caufe from the tribune, before the day for the nominal appeal was fixed.

Whoever has attended to the conduct and fpirit of the Jacobins may have remarked, that however popular any perfon has been among them—however greatly he may have diftinguifhed himfelf by promoting their meafures with zeal and ability—if he chances to be feized with a qualm of confcience at laft, and hefitates to act with them in a fingle inftance, all his paft merit is forgotten, and he is execrated by the fo-ciety as a determined enemy.

The night after the King's defence was made, a Member of the Jacobins gave an ac-count in that fociety of what had paffed at the Convention—particularly that Manuel had propofed

propofed to adjourn the difcuffion for no lefs a period than three days; and that Petion had fpoken againft pronouncing judgment without feparating. This was heard with horror and indignation : it was immediately decreed, that Manuel fhould be expelled from the fociety. Petion with difficulty efcaped the fame fate, which, however, was poftponed only for a fhort time.

For feveral days after the defence, the time of the Convention was moftly taken up in hearing the opinions of the members: all of them prefaced their difcourfes, by declaring a conviction of the King's guilt; perhaps they thought this neceffary to fecure them the liberty of proceeding. They differed however with refpect to the penalty he had incurred; many being of opinion that juftice and policy forbade the pains of death : all the Rolandifts, Briffotins and Girondifts were of this number.

ber. Danton's and Robespierre's party argued for immediate death ; and became so impatient at the delay, from hearing so many discourses, that they repealed the decree that had passed a few days before ; and instead of hearing every member from the tribune, they resolved that the discourses should be printed, and laid on the table to be read by those who chose, and the 14th of January was appointed for pronouncing ultimately. It was not till the 15th, however, that the first appeal was made, owing to the long and warm discussions which took place in the Convention before it was determined in what terms, and in what order the questions should be stated on which the Convention was to decide: at last, it was decreed that the following questions should be put to all the members, and decided by the nominal appeal :

1. Is Lewis Capet, late King of France, guilty of a conspiracy against liberty, and

of

of attempts against the general safety of the State ? Yes, or No.

2. Shall the judgment to be pronounced on Lewis, be submitted to the ratification of the people in the Primary Assemblies ? Yes, or No.

3. What punishment has he incurred?

These questions were artfully and wickedly arranged in this order, to render the King's condemnation more certain.

Several deputies who thought the appeal to the Primary Assemblies a wrong measure in itself, gave their votes against it, in the belief that the King would not be condemned to death—but had the question respecting the punishment been brought on in the second place, they would have seen that the appeal to the people was the only means of saving the life of the King, and would then have voted for that measure, although in general they did not approve of it.

2                                                        This

This accounts for the length and violence of the debates, on a question apparently of fo little importance as the order in which the propofitions were to be voted :—for fome of thofe who wifhed to fave the life of the King faw this in the light above ftated, and ftrove to have the queftions otherwife arranged :—neither party, however, avowed the real reafon of their zeal, and the malice of the King's enemies prevailed.

On the firft queftion, the Affembly voted almoft unanimoufly in the affirmative.—But many of the deputies declared, that they gave this opinion as citizens and legiflators, but not as judges; becaufe they neither thought themfelves qualified for that office, nor authorifed by their Conftituents to affume it.

Moriffon, of the department of Vendée, refufed to vote: he faid, " he would give his reafons if the Convention exacted it," which was not done: a very few others declined voting; among whom was Noel,

of

of the department of Vosges, who said, "that his son having been killed on the frontiers, fighting against the enemy, he considered the King as the primary cause of his son's death, and felt so much prejudice against him, that he was unqualified for being his judge."

. Offelin, who had been one of the Judges belonging to the Tribunal appointed in August, gave his vote in the affirmative, and at the same time stated, "that one of the accusations against the King is, that he continued to pay his guards after they were reduced, although many of them had emigrated; that his Counsel, conscious of the force of this accusation, had taken great pains to destroy it, and had asserted that the King had not paid the guards after the 1st of January 1792; but that he himself, as one of the Administrators of the Commune of Paris, had had business to transact with M. Laporte, and that Madame Laporte had made a deduction

duction from the revenues of the Civil Lift of 1,200,000 livres in the month of July 1792, for the payment of the guards, then well known to have emigrated."

What ftrefs ought to be laid on fuch evidence fo given, I leave to lawyers to decide; but common juftice might have dictated to a man, who thus volunteered himfelf as a *witnefs*, that he ought not to vote as a *judge*.

When the name of M. Egalité was called, it was imagined that he alfo would have declined voting ; and when he pronounced *" Oui,"* a murmur of furprife and indignation was heard.

The fecond queftion was undoubtedly intended as a means of faving the life of the King, and would in all probability have had that effect, if it had not been brought forward until the fentence of death was carried.

The meafure of referring the King's fate

to the people themfelves, which from its nature was highly popular, had been rendered the reverfe by the unwearied exertions of thofe who feared that, if carried, it would fave his life.

In giving their votes on this fecond queftion in the affirmative, feveral of the Deputies faid, they were aware of the danger to which they expofed themfelves; but being convinced that their conftituents had elected them as legiflators, and not as judges; and as it was repugnant to their confciences to unite the characters of jury and accufers, they would run every rifk rather than do it.——One Member faid, " As I give my vote for referring this matter to the Primary Affemblies of the people, I expect the worft, and I glory in being of the number of thofe who brave the danger." Another, " that in pronouncing the fame vote, he devoted himfelf to the daggers of affaffins."

The

'The fpeech that Manuel made on giving his vote was remarkable.—" I fee here a Legiflative Affembly, but not an affembly of judges ; for judges do not murmur at the opinions of their brethren, though different from their own : they do not openly abufe and calumniate each other; they are cold as the law of which they are the organs.   If the Convention had been a tribunal of law, a near relation of the King, who has not been reftrained either by a fenfe of fhame or by his confcience, would not have been permitted to vote on this occafion."

The Prefident called Manuel to order, telling him to avoid perfonalities. Manuel then voted for the appeal.   Raffron, Panis, Legendre and Marat, who are all of the Department of Paris, and feem of congenial difpofitions, voted againft it.

It was midnight before the Appeal was ended:—there were 424 againft, 283 for the reference ; 10 refufed to vote.   The Affembly adjourned till the 16th, and when it met, incidental bufinefs prevented the appel nominal from being begun till the evening. Many of the members particularifed their reafons for voting as they did. The ceremony lafted through the whole night. The refult was a majority for death. Three hundred and nineteen voted for imprifonment till the end of the war, and then banifhment. Had all who voted for death with reftriction, that the fentence fhould not be executed till the peace, or till the Conftitution was framed and accepted, been fubftracted from the majority, it would have been diminifhed to a furplus of only five or fix votes.

On this occafion, M. Egalité voted for death without reftriction. A murmur of horror was heard. One deputy ftarted from his feat, ftruck his hands together, and exclaimed, " *Ah le fcélérat!*" others repeated the fame expreffion. The terms in which he delivered his vote are remarkable: " Unique-

"Uniquement occupé de mon devoir, convaincu que tous ceux qui ont attenté ou attenteront par la fuite à la fouveraineté du peuple, méritent la mort, je vote pour la mort*."

Previous to the fcrutiny, and after every member had voted, the Prefident informed the Convention that he had received a letter

---

* Influenced by no confideration but that of performing my duty, convinced that all who have confpired, or fhall hereafter confpire againft the fovereignty of the people, deferve death, I vote for death.

I have it from good authority, that an acquaintance of M. Egalité underftanding that he was not to vote on the favourable fide, advifed him to declare, that on account of the ill treatment which he imagined he had formerly received from the King, there would be an impropriety in his voting—that this would be confidered as a good reafon for declining, and would preclude the indignation which muft be the confequence of his voting againft the King. Egalité promifed either to follow this plan or to ftay from the Convention on the day of the appel nominal ; but having the day before that took place been waited on by Robefpierre, Marat, and others of that party, they urged reafons which made him act as he did.

from

from the Spanish Minister, and one from the King's Counsel. There was a cry from the Mountain for the order of the day. Garan-Coulon said, that the King's Counsel should be heard, but the Spanish Minister's letter should not be read. " How !" exclaimed Danton, " the Spanish Court have not acknowledged our Republic, and they attempt to influence our deliberations ! If all the members were of my opinion, we should declare war against Spain for this interference alone."

Genfonnet proposed that the King's Counsel should be heard after the result of the scrutiny was known, but that in the mean time the Convention should refuse to hear the letter of the Spanish Minister, and pass to the order of the day. It was unanimously agreed not to hear the letter, and Robespierre declaimed also against hearing the Counsel. In this he failed.

Duchastel,

Duchaftel, Deputy from the department of Deux-Sèvres, having been indifpofed, had not been in the Aſſembly when his name was called the preceding night. He now was fupported into the hall, and as the fcrutiny was not yet clofed, demanded to give his vote. It was fufpected that he came to give his vote on the merciful fide; and thofe who had during the whole pro-cefs thirfted for the King's blood, and were now doubtful how the fcrutiny ftood, op-pofed his voting. Valazé, one of the fecre-taries, declaring that the fcrutiny was *not* clofed, Duchaftel gave his voice for banifh-ment. A fhameful attempt was next made, on a frivolous pretext, to erafe his vote—this was not permitted. The Prefident an-nounced the iſſue of the fcrutiny as above mentioned, and the King's Counfel were ad-mitted to the bar.

Defeze faid, that the law and a decree of

the

the Convention having entrusted them with the defence of Lewis, they came with sorrowful hearts to perform their last duty to their client; he then read what follows from a paper signed by the King: " I owe to my honour, I owe to my family, not to acknowledge the juftice of a fentence that declares me guilty of a crime with which I cannot reproach myfelf. I therefore appeal to the Nation at large from the fentence of its reprefentatives; and I empower my Counfel by thefe prefents, and exprefsly charge them on their fidelity, to make this appeal known to the National Affembly, and to require that it fhall be inferted into the minutes of their fittings.

(Signed) Louis."

Each of the Counfel made a fhort addrefs to the Convention : Defeze conjured them in the name of humanity and juftice, to revife, or leave to the ratification of the People,

ple, a sentence carried by a majority of only five votes, and against which three hundred and nineteen of the Assembly had declared their opinions.

Tronchet represented that many of those who voted for death, had declared that they founded their opinion on the penal code—yet the penal code requires two thirds of the voices to condemn an accused person. A decree of the Convention, passed only that morning, had pronounced that the majority of a single voice was sufficient. On that decree being objected to, they had simply passed to the order of the day; but in a matter of such immense importance, the appel nominal was necessary: he therefore demanded the repeal of that decree.

M. de Malesherbes said, that he had formerly had occasion to reflect with great attention on the important question of how the votes ought to be taken in criminal cases;

eafes ; but that not being in the habit of
fpeaking extempore, he begged in the moft
earneft and affecting manner, that he might
be allowed till the next day to arrange the
ideas which he wifhed to fubmit to their
confideration.

Robefpierre and others argued on the other
fide ; and the Convention rejected the appeal
made in the name of the King, paffed to the
order of the day on the requifition of Malefherbes, and adjourned till next day the debate
on the delay of the execution of the fentence,
which was difcuffed at length accordingly.

Two remarkable incidents occurred during
this debate, which fhew what an excefs of
wanton barbarity and perfevering rancour
fome men are capable of upon the moft folemn and affecting occafions. Tallien, with
diabolical irony, argued for the King's immediate execution, on what he called motives of humanity. " He knows," faid the
wretch,

wretch, " that he is condemned, and that a respite is demanded—to keep him in suspense is prolonging his agony. Let us, in tenderness for his sufferings, decree his immediate execution, and put him out of anguish."

This shocked even Danton, who expressed disapprobation of it.

The other incident occurred when Thomas Paine, who had formerly given his opinion against the death of the King, ascended the tribune: as he was not in the habit of pronouncing French, one of the secretaries read his discourse translated from the original English. His reasoning against the execution of the sentence probably was thought very persuasive, since those who had heard the discourses of Buzot, Condorcet and Brissot to the same purport without interruption, broke out into murmurs while Paine's opinion was reading ; and Marat at length losing all patience, exclaimed that Paine was a Quaker, and insinuated, that

his

his mind being contracted by the narrow principles of his religion, was incapable of the *liberality* requisite for condemning men to death. This shrewd argument not being thought convincing, the Secretary continued to read, " That the execution of the sentence, instead of an act of justice, would appear to all the world, and particularly to their allies the American States, an act of vengeance ; and that if he were sufficiently master of the French language, he would, in the name of his brethren of America, present a petition at their bar against the execution of the sentence."

Marat and his associates cried, that these could not possibly be the sentiments of Thomas Paine, and that the Assembly were imposed on by a false translation.

On comparing it with the original, however, it was found just.

They proceeded to the fourth appel nominal, which was terminated at midnight on Saturday the 19th of January 1793.

The

The voters were reſtricted to pronounce a ſimple yes or no, without any reaſoning; 310 voted for a reſpite of the ſentence, 380 againſt it.

It may be thought, from the reſult of this queſtion, that the reference to the Primary Aſſemblies would have been equally rejected, at whatever time that propoſal had been voted; but it ſhould be remembered, that it was ſtill leſs obnoxious to vote for referring the ſentence entirely to the people, than to vote for a reſpite of a ſentence actually pronounced.

The Executive Council were ordered to notify this to the King the day following, and that the execution was to take place within twenty-four hours of the notification. It was decreed at the ſame time, that he ſhould be allowed free communication with his family, and to have any eccleſiaſtic he pleaſed to attend him.

The Executive Council, of which Garat the Miniſter of Juſtice was Preſident, met

on

on the morning of the 20th. He, with two other Members of the Council, and the Secretary, set out for the Temple, where they arrived at two.

Being introduced into the King's apartment, Garat, who was greatly agitated, said with a faltering voice—" Lewis, the Executive Council is ordered to notify to you the decree which the National Convention passed last night."

The Secretary began to read the decree. In the preamble, the King is charged with having *conspired against the general safety of the Nation*—He was shocked at the idea, and repeated the expression with emotion. The Secretary, who had paused, resumed, and the King heard the rest, including the sentence, with calmness.

When the Secretary had finished, the King took a paper from his pocket, the contents of which he informed them of, and desired the Minister of Justice to present it to the Executive Council.

Garat

Garat informed him, that the Council could not decide on the fubjects of his demands, but that he would immediately carry them to the Convention, who had already agreed to fome of them.

He went accordingly, and read to the Affembly the paper which the King had given him.

It contained a requeft of a refpite of three days, that he might prepare himfelf for appearing in the prefence of God : and for that purpofe, that he might be freely vifited by a perfon, whofe name he would mention to the Commiffioners.

That he might be freed from their infpection during the interval allowed him to live.

That he might have free communication with his family.

That the National Convention would permit his family to withdraw from France to any other country they chofe. Finally, he recommended to the generofity of the nation

5                                    a number

a number of old fervants, many of whom had nothing to live on but the penſions he had allowed them.

When the Miniſter of Juſtice returned to the Temple, he informed the King, that the Convention acquieſced in moſt of his demands; he gave a favourable interpretation to the general anſwer which had been given to that reſpecting the lot of his family, but added, that *the delay was refuſed.*

" Allons," ſaid the King, " il faut ſe ſoumettre."

There is ſomething infinitely harſh and revolting to humanity in the refuſal of this laſt requeſt; which there is every reaſon to believe, from the character and conduct of the King, proceeded from the pious motive which he aſſigned—and not, as his enemies have ſuggeſted, from a weak deſire of prolonging a wretched exiſtence.

Should it be the fate of any of thoſe men who rejected this requeſt of the unfortunate Monarch,

Monarch, ever to be in similar circumstances, as they will have more need of it
than he had, I sincerely hope that they will
be allowed more than three days to prepare
themselves for eternity.

When the Minister of Justice had retired,
the King gave to one of the Commissioners
a letter addressed to Mr. Edgeworth, who
was the person he wished to attend him in
his last moments.

Mr. Edgeworth's father was originally a
Protestant clergyman of a good family in
Ireland, who was converted to the Roman
Catholic religion, and had established himself in France, where he bred his son as an ec-
clesiastic, in the faith which he himself preferred.——The son recommended himself so
much by his good conduct and excellent
character, that he was chosen by the Princess Elizabeth as her confessor; by which
means he became known to, and highly
esteemed by, the King; of which he gave the

ftrongeft proof, by fending for him on this awful occafion.

The King's letter was carried to Mr. Edgeworth by three foldiers, fent by the Council of the Commune. The contents of the letter were requefting his attendance; but if he found himfelf, from apprehenfion of the confequence, or any other caufe, averfe to come, entreating him to find another prieft who had not the fame reluctance.

Mr. Edgeworth informed the foldiers, that he would attend them directly to the Temple. His mother and fifter were then at a fmall diftance from Paris; he defired Madame d'Argouge, a relation with whom he lived when in town, not to inform them of what had happened, becaufe he faw that lady herfelf greatly alarmed, and feared that fhe might communicate her apprehenfions to them.

Mr. Edgeworth was conducted firft before the Council in the Temple, and then to the

the King. On his being introduced, he instantly shewed such marks of respect and sensibility as affected the unfortunate Prince so much, that he burst into tears, and was for some moments unable to speak: at length he said—" Excuse me, Mr. Edgeworth, I have not been accustomed of late to the company of men like you."

After passing some time with his confessor, the King thought he had acquired sufficient fortitude to bear an interview with his family. The Queen, Princess Elizabeth, with the Prince and Princess Royal, were conducted to his apartment. They continued near three hours together—No tragic poet has imagined a scene more affecting than what was realized at this interview—The actors, so lately placed in the most brilliant situation that the world can give—hurled from the summit of human splendor to the depth of human misery. A sister, children, and a wife, in a prison, taking their last leave of a

Q q 2                          brother,

brother, father, and hufband, rendered more dear than ever by his paft fufferings, their common calamity, and the dreadful fate awaiting him the following day.

The King, though affected at different times beyond the power of expreffion, retained his recollection to the laft. When they were to feparate, the Princefs Elizabeth mentioned their hopes of feeing him again in the morning. He allowed her to expect it. The Queen could liften to no words of comfort. No confideration could prevent her from pouring forth her indignation in the moft violent expreffions againft the enemies of her hufband. In the bitternefs of her foul fhe beat her breaft and tore her hair; and her fcreams were heard at intervals, all that night of agony and horror.

After his family had withdrawn, the King remained for fome time with his eyes fixed on the ground without fpeaking; then with a proa profound figh he pronounced—" Ce moment étoit terrible."

I have it from the beft authority, that after his family were withdrawn, the mifery of his own fate did not engrofs his mind fo entirely as to exclude all folicitude for the fate of others; he enquired in a moft affectionate manner of Mr. Edgeworth for feveral whom he confidered as his friends, and particularly for the ecclefiaftics, who had been perfecuted with the greateft cruelty; and exprefled fatisfaction at hearing that many of them had efcaped to England, where they were received with kindnefs and hofpitality.

Mr. Edgeworth prevailed on him to go to bed for four hours.

He rofe at five; and exprefling an inclination to hear mafs, Mr. Edgeworth informed the Council who were fitting in the Temple of the King's requeft. Some difficulties were made, which Mr. Edgeworth removed, faying that the ufual ornaments and

all

all that was requisite for the ceremony could be procured from a neighbouring church.

Mr. Edgeworth shewing great solicitude that the King should be gratified, one of the Commissioners said, he had heard of people who had been poisoned taking the sacrament.

To this horrid insinuation Mr. Edgeworth made no other reply, than by calmly reminding him that the Committee were to procure the host.

What was necessary was provided. Mr. Edgeworth said mass, and administered the sacrament to the King; and then mentioned that his family expected to see him before he left the Temple. The King, fearing that he had not sufficient firmness for a second interview, wished to spare them the agony of such a scene, and therefore declined it.

At half an hour after eight Santerre came

7

and

and informed him that he had received orders to conduct him to the place of execution. After paffing three minutes in private with his Confeffor, he came to the outer room where Santerre had remained, and addreffing him, faid, "Marchons, je fuis prêt." In defcending to the court, he begged the Commiffioners to recommend certain perfons who were in his fervice to the Commune; after which, not imagining that Mr. Edgeworth intended to accompany him any further, he was bidding him adieu. But the other faid, his attendance was not over. "What," faid the King, "do you intend to adhere to me ftill?" "Yes," replied the Confeffor, "to the laft."

The King walked through the Court with a firm ftep, and entered the Mayor's coach, followed by Mr. Edgeworth, a Municipal Officer, and two Officers of the National Guards.

Qq 4 The.

The King recited the prayers for persons in the agonies of death during the conveyance from the Temple to the Place de la Révolution, formerly the Place de Louis XV.

When the carriage ftopped at the fcaffold, the King faid—" Nous voici donc arrivé." He pulled off his coat, unbuttoned the neck of his fhirt, afcended the fcaffold with fteadinefs, and furveyed for a few moments the immenfe multitude; then approaching the edge, as there was a good deal of noife, he made a motion with his hand for fïlence, which inftantly took place *—then fpeaking

* It has been faid that the ferenity which the King fhewed at his death, did not proceed wholly from the fupport he derived from religion, but was partly owing to the hope he entertained to the laft, even when on the fcaffold, that his life would be faved by the people, and that his Confeffor encouraged him in this hope.

Nothing can be more improbable than this ftory. Had the King entertained any fuch hope, it muft ftill have been intermingled with fear; and fuch a ftate of mind, inftead of calmnefs, was more likely to produce agitaion.

The

With a raised voice, he said—" Francais, je meurs innocent. Je pardonne à tous mes ennemis, et je souhaite que la France———"

Santerre, who was on horseback near the scaffold, made a signal for the drums to beat, and for the executioners to perform their office. The King's voice was drowned in the noise of the drums.

Three executioners then approached to feize him : at the fight of a cord, with which one of them attempted to tie his arms, the King for the firft time shewed figns of indignation, and as if he was going to refift. Mr. Edgeworth put him in mind that the Saviour of Mankind had allowed his arms to

The whole of his behaviour shews a manly and chriftian refignation to a fate which he thought inevitable, and proves that his hopes were removed from earth to heaven.

The character of Mr. Edgeworth precludes him from the fufpicion of having encouraged a hope which would have difturbed that turn of mind which it was his duty to promote and cherifh in the King.

be

be tied: he no fooner pronounced this than the King became paffive as a lamb. The executioners laid hold of him, and placed him on the guillotine. The Confeffor then kneeling with his face near to that of the King, pronounced aloud—" Enfant de Saint Louis, montez au ciel."—The blow was given—Mr. Edgeworth's face was fprinkled with the King's blood. The executioner walked round the fcaffold, holding up the head to be feen by the people. A few, who had probably been hired for the purpofe, cried—" Vive la Nation! Vive la Republique!"

Thus did the French Nation, who had endured the cruelties of Lewis the Eleventh, the treachery of Charles the Ninth, and the tyranny of Lewis the Fourteenth, condemn and execute for the pretended crimes of cruelty, treachery, and tyranny, the mildeft, moft juft, and leaft

tyrannical

tyrannical Prince that ever fat on their throne.

Let us confider the conduct of the Convention with regard to the King, and decide whether it can be reconciled to good fenfe, juftice, or humanity.

When the Deputies firft met and formed a National Convention, they knew that a moft extraordinary event had happened; that the palace of their King had been attacked; that many citizens had been killed, and almoft all his guards flaughtered; that the King himfelf with all his family had been thrown into prifon, where they ftill remained; and that their duty, as the reprefentatives of the nation, was to inveftigate the caufes of this extraordinary event, and to punifh the guilty.

The Convention were informed by thofe *who had planned and directed* the attack on the palace, " That the citizens had been wantonly fired on by the guards, in confequence

of

of orders from the King; that the King was betraying the country to an invading army, with the leaders of which he was in correspondence; and that unless he had been attacked and imprisoned, the nation would have been enslaved."

Having heard this accusation, it was natural to have imagined that the Convention would, in the next place, have wished to know the King's account of these transactions, that they might be the better able to judge which account was the most probable, and the best supported by known and incontrovertible facts.

One fact they must have known, namely, that when the King had reason to believe that his palace was to be attacked, he sent for the Mayor of Paris and other Civil Officers to be near his person, and to be witnesses of his conduct.

From this it was to be presumed, that the King wished to avoid force, and if he should be be driven to the neceffity of ufing it, that it fhould be under the direction of the Civil Magiftrate.

The Convention might have recollected, that although one of the many evils which are inherent in a *defpotic* government, be, that there is no door to freedom but through infurrection; yet the moderate and equitable character of Lewis XVI. had early inclined him to fuch alterations in the old fyftem, as would gradually have united the prerogatives of limited monarchy with the rights of free men.

Such confiderations, with a moderate fhare of candour and gratitude, one would imagine, would have made them fufpend their belief in the full extent of the crimes imputed to the King; and at all events have prevented their giving a decifion injurious to him, till he was heard, and till as many of their brother Deputies as were expected had arrived.  Inftead of this, they thought proper, on the

very

very firſt day of their meeting, when not above half of their number had arrived, without hearing the King, to pronounce the ſevereſt ſentence againſt him which they had a right by the Conſtitution to have done, even if all of which he was accuſed had been clearly proved *.

They next proceed with more deliberation, to determine whether the King may not ſtill be tried for his life.

The inviolability with which the Conſtitution had inveſted the monarch, was, in the minds of many of the Deputies, an inſurmountable objection to this meaſure.

It might have been imagined, that if the terms in which this inviolability was expreſſed by the Conſtitution had been obſcure and ſomewhat dubious, ſtill it would have been becoming in the legiſlators of a great nation to have explained them in the moſt

* Abolition of Royalty.

favourable

favourable fenfe for their unfortunate monarch: there was no room, however, for their exercifing their generofity in this manner; for the terms are as clear as language can make them.

This had no effect on a majority of the Deputies, who declared, that they confidered the inviolability as a mere chimera, which ought not to be regarded.

The reafoning by which they fupported this propofition will appear extraordinary. " The Conftitution," fay they, " could only render the King inviolable while he was King, but it can have no fuch effect now that Royalty is abolifhed ; and therefore we may now with propriety try him as a private citizen."

According to the military law and cuftom of fome countries, an officer of the army may be condemned to lofe his commiffion, and to ferve in the ranks for certain crimes, for which a common foldier would be con-

demned

demned to undergo a corporal punifhment;
—but nothing fo unjuft was ever thought of,
as firft to make the officer fuffer the punifhment appointed by the military-code for his
crime as an officer, and afterwards, on the
pretence of his being a common foldier, to
inflict a fecond punifhment for the fame
crime.

Other Deputies reafon in this manner:

The inviolability is very good in ordinary cafes, but it is of no ufe in the prefent.
The people are fovereign, independent of
the Conftitution, and cannot be bound by
any law made by the Conftitution.—Louis
XVI. n'étoit Roi que par la Conftitution;
La Nation étoit Souverain fans Conftitution
et fans Roi *.

Thus that metaphyfical monarch, le Peuple Souverain, is conjured up, on convenient occafions, to anfwer for every kind of

* Rap. de Mailhe, 7 Nov. 1792.

injuftice

injuftice and cruelty:—he was at one time declared to be the author of the maffacres of the prifoners, on purpofe to fcreen the real murderers; and in this inftance he is brought forward to annihilate the moft folemn and facred of all obligations.

The Committee who formed the Decree of Accufation againft the King, feem to have been very much perplexed, on account of the force and precifion in which his inviolability is declared by the Conftitution. Mailhe, who prefented it in their name to the Convention, after repeating this embarraffing article, fays, with fome degree of paffion, " Cela veut-il dire que le Roi, tant qu'il feroit affez adroit pour éluder les cas de la décheance, pourroit impunément s'abandonner aux paffions les plus féroces, et feroit-il quitte pour la perte d'un fceptre qui lui étoit odieux, parce qu'il n'étoit pas de fer ?"

Without taking notice of the falfe and

childifh exaggerations which his queftion infinuates, Mailhe may be anfwered, that if
the King had the addrefs to elude all the
cafes to which the Conftitution has affixed
the pain of forfeiture of the crown, he certainly ought not to forfeit it——and if Mailhe
himfelf were on his trial for murder or robbery, and it clearly appeared, that the accufation was falfe, or, to ufe Mailhe's expreffion, that he had had the addrefs to elude
thofe crimes, I confefs I fhould be for ac-
quitting him; for whatever may be the opinion and practice in France, I adhere to the
old notion, that a man, who has the addrefs
to be innocent, ought not to be punifhed as
guilty.

Nothing can be more unworthy, than for
the legiflators of a nation to attempt to explain away the obvious meaning of a propofition fo clearly expreffed, as that relating
to the King's inviolability is by the French
Conftitution; and the arguments they have

ufed

ufed are as fophiftical as the attempt is unbecoming. For my own part, I do not
think it extravagant to queftion, whether
Lewis XVI would have accepted of the Conftitution, had the inviolability been explained to him *then*, in the manner in which it is
*now* explained. I am convinced he would
not, if he had thought that Danton, Robefpierre, Legendre, and Marat were, in any
prefumable cafe, to be his judges.

But had all objections founded on the
inviolability of the King's perfon been
removed, were it clear that he might have
been tried and dealt with as a private citizen, for crimes laid to his charge as a King;
ftill the Convention, as it was compofed,
could not, with any colour of impartiality,
be confidered as a proper tribunal for his
trial: to have rendered it fuch, it would have
been neceffary to remove all thofe who had
in print, or from the tribune, declared themfelves convinced of his guilt, or in any way

R r 2                    manifefted

manifested a desire that he should be executed. What possibility is there, for example, that the King's innocence should be proved to Saint-Just, Deputy for the department of l'Aisne, who, in the discourse he read to the Convention, says, " Le procés doit être fait au Roi, non point pour le crime de son administration, mais pour le crime d'avoir été Roi: on ne peut point regner innocemment. Tout roi n'est qu'un rebelle et un usurpateur." And Robespierre, in the Society of Jacobins, where there were several who had been members of the Legislative Assembly, and were then of the Convention, said, " that if the King were absolved, *they* must of course be considered and punished as rebels." Were such men impartial judges ?

And if the objections to particular Deputies were entirely removed, one solid one remains against the whole Assembly, namely, that being the King's accusers, they

were

were difqualified from being his jury or judges.

When we next come to confider the nature of the proofs in fupport of the accufation, and the manner in which they were obtained, the force of the objections againft them is obvious and ftriking. The papers found in the King's cabinet on the 10th of Auguft, and thofe afterwards difcovered in the iron cheft in the wall of the Tuileries, are not fair and legal evidence——becaufe papers may have been introduced and mixed with the others by the King's enemies; becaufe papers may have been loft or removed which would have explained and accounted for what appears criminal in others; becaufe a perfon's having criminal papers in his cuftody, is no proof that he approves of, or is even acquainted with their contents; and ftill lefs of his intending to adopt the opinions, or follow the plans or counfels of the writers.

Let

Let us farther fuppofe, that all the papers prefented to the Convention are the genuine papers found in the King's clofet, without any having been added or fubftracted ; ftill they do not conftitute a proof of his having formed any fcheme of deftroying the Conftitution, or betraying the country to its enemies.

Briffot in his writings, Louvet and Barbaroux in their fpeeches in the Convention, affert, that they, and their affociates, brought about the Revolution of the 10th of Auguft, with a view to eftablifh a Republic. They were fo precife and minute on this important point, as even to particularife the place. —It was at Charenton, as they declared, that the meafure of attacking the King in his palace was determined on ; it was at firft agreed to be on the 29th of July, but afterwards poftponed to the 10th of Auguft. Danton, Robefpierre, and Chabot, infift that this honour belongs to them. Petion, who

had

had been sent for by the King, who was actually in the palace as a Civil Magistrate, and in the character of a mediator, early that morning, was afterwards very much hurt, because Robespierre insinuated that he had had very little share in the insurrection of the 10th of August. "Les hommes," says he, in his letter to Robespierre, "qui se sont attribué la gloire de cette journée, sont les hommes à qui elle appartient le moins; elle est due aux braves fédérés, *et à leur directoire secret qui concertait depuis long temps le plan de l'insurrection.*" And in his letter to the Society of Jacobins he claims his own right to part of the glory: "Je n'ai pas peu contribué," says Petion, "à amener la journée du 10 Août." After this, how could any men of common sense, and common candour, hear with patience the King accused of being the aggressor on that occasion? Yet this was done in the act of accusation, and repeated by many of the members in their speeches during the procès.

Finally,

Finally, let it be supposed, that the person of the King was not rendered inviolable by the Constitution; that the Convention was the proper tribunal by which he ought to have been tried; that the papers were unexceptionable evidence; and that the proof against him was convincing: after all this has been admitted, still it is clear that it was most inexpedient and unwise in the National Convention to decree his execution, because it would exasperate many of the Princes of Europe; and if it pleased any, it would afford even them a pretext for making war with France; thus creating new enemies to their infant Republic, and strengthening the hands of the old.

Because the great object of punishment is to prevent, and not to avenge crimes; and in a Republic the same case could never again occur.

Because a living and dethroned King would have been less interesting to the pub-

5

lic,

lic, and therefore lefs formidable to the prefent government of France, than a young
Prince, whofe character calumny could not
touch, and whofe father had been beheaded.

A French lady, diftinguifhed for wit,
having remarked the ingenuity of a footman
belonging to a man of high quality, who
was as ugly and ftupid as his fervant was
the reverfe, faid, "Il faut avouer que la
Nature n'eft pas Ariftocrate."——If Nature
has been partial to democracy, it muft be
confeffed, however, that the Democrates of
France have been moft ungrateful to Nature,
by violating all her laws, and wounding all
her feelings.

The records of mankind exhibit no example of crimes deliberately committed,
attended with fo many circumftances of
wanton unrelenting cruelty, and fo evidently
pernicious to the caufe of the perpetrators.

*F I N I S.*

# EXPLANATION of the MAP.

THE march of the Duke of Brunſwick from Luxembourg to Longwy and Verdun, and from Verdun, by Grand Pré, to the Camp of La Lune, is indicated by a line of a green colour.

The march of General Dumourier from Sedan to Grand Pré and St. Menehould is marked by a red line.

The march of General Dillon from Mouzon to Biefme, red.

The march of General Kellermann from Metz, by Bar le Duc, St. Dizier, and Vitry, red.

The fields where engagements took place, are indicated by ſwords croſſed.

The rivers are pale green.

The roads yellow.

The Duke of Brunſwick's Camp at La Lune is coloured yellow.

Thoſe of Dumourier and Kellermann near St. Menehould, red.

Dillon's Camp at the Côte de Biefme, red.

The Heſſian Camp near Dombaſle, green.

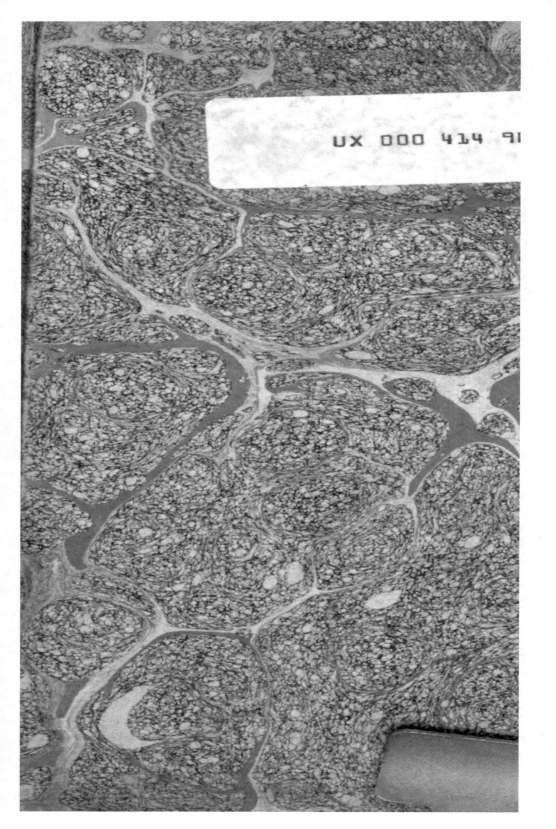

CPSIA information can be obtained
at www.ICGtesting.com
Printed in the USA
BVHW082339260819
556819BV00005B/723/P